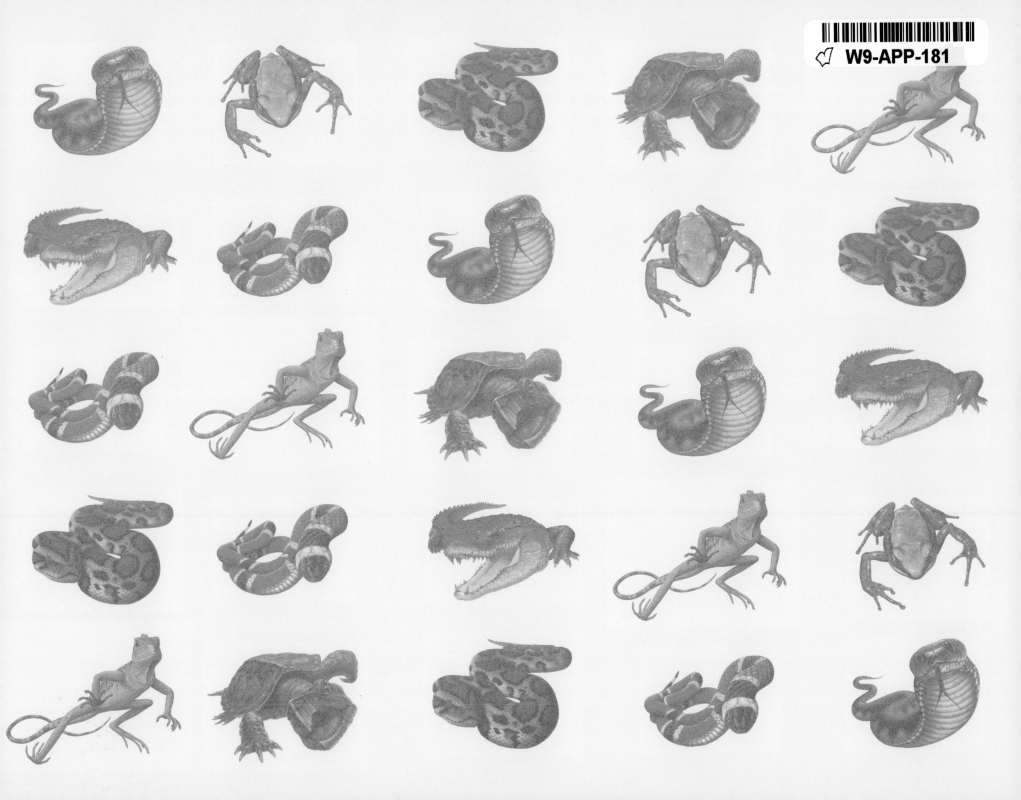

# SNAKES
## AND REPTILES

# SNAKES
## AND REPTILES
### THE SCARIEST COLD-BLOODED CREATURES ON EARTH

General Editor: Susan Barraclough

BACKPACKBOOKS
o
NEW YORK

Backpack Books
122 Fifth Avenue
New York, NY 10011

ISBN-13 978-1-4351-0774-8
ISBN-10 1-4351-0774-8

Library of Congress Cataloging-in-Publication Data available upon request.

Printed and bound in China

1   3   5   7   9   10   8   6   4   2

Editorial and design by
Amber Books Ltd
74–77 White Lion Street
London
N1 9PF
United Kingdom
www.amberbooks.co.uk

Project Editor: Sarah Uttridge
Designer: Andrew Easton at Ummagumma Design

All illustrations © IMP AB

# Contents

| | |
|---|---|
| Introduction | 6 |

**Snakes** 8

| | |
|---|---|
| Death Adder | 10 |
| Cottonmouth Snake | 12 |
| Bush Viper | 14 |
| Puff Adder | 16 |
| Rhinoceros Viper | 18 |
| Boa Constrictor | 20 |
| Mangrove Snake | 22 |
| Fer-De-Lance | 24 |
| Jumping Viper | 26 |
| Eyelash Viper | 28 |
| Desert Horned Viper | 30 |
| Green Tree Python | 32 |
| Golden Tree Snake | 34 |
| Emerald Tree Boa | 36 |
| Rattlesnake | 38 |
| African Egg-Eating Snake | 40 |
| Green Mamba | 42 |
| Black Mamba | 44 |
| Boomslang | 46 |
| Long-Nosed Snake | 48 |
| Saw-Scaled Viper | 50 |
| Rainbow Boa | 52 |
| Anaconda | 54 |
| Ringhals | 56 |
| Bushmaster | 58 |
| Coral Snake | 60 |
| Carpet Python | 62 |
| Asian Cobra | 64 |
| Blackneck Cobra | 66 |
| Tiger Snake | 68 |
| King Cobra | 70 |
| Fierce Snake | 72 |
| Taipan | 74 |
| Mulga | 76 |
| Red-Bellied Black Snake | 78 |
| Brown Snake | 80 |
| Asian Python | 82 |
| Reticulated Python | 84 |
| Massassauga | 86 |
| African Twig Snake | 88 |
| Asian Pit Viper | 90 |
| Asp Viper | 92 |
| European Adder | 94 |

**Lizards** 96

| | |
|---|---|
| Marine Iguana | 98 |
| Green Anole | 100 |
| Basilisk Lizard | 102 |
| Ground Chameleon | 104 |
| Jackson's Chameleon | 106 |
| Panther Chameleon | 108 |
| Frilled Lizard | 110 |
| Sungazer Lizard | 112 |
| Flying Lizard | 114 |
| Mexican Beaded Lizard | 116 |
| Gila Monster | 118 |
| Green Iguana | 120 |
| Thorny Devil | 122 |
| Regal Horned Lizard | 124 |
| Bearded Dragon | 126 |
| Chuckwalla | 128 |
| Tuatara | 130 |
| Shingleback Skink | 132 |
| Leaf-tailed Gecko | 134 |
| Savannah Monitor | 136 |
| Gigantic Lace Lizard | 138 |
| Komodo Dragon | 140 |
| Nile Monitor | 142 |
| Salvador's monitor | 144 |

**Turtles, Crocodiles, & Alligators** 146

| | |
|---|---|
| American Alligator | 148 |
| Matamata | 150 |
| Snapping Turtle | 152 |
| Nile Crocodile | 154 |
| Saltwater Crocodile | 156 |
| Gharial | 158 |
| Alligator Snapping Turtle | 160 |
| Stinkpot Turtle | 162 |

**Amphibians** 164

| | |
|---|---|
| Axolotl | 166 |
| Giant Salamander | 168 |
| Cane Toad | 170 |
| Ornate Horned Frog | 172 |
| Poison-Dart Frog | 174 |
| Mantella Frog | 176 |
| Budgett's Frog | 178 |
| Horned Toad | 180 |
| Pipa Toad | 182 |
| Paradoxical Frog | 184 |
| African Bullfrog | 186 |
| Crested Newt | 188 |
| Glossary | 190 |
| Index | 191 |

# Introduction

**American Alligator**

**Marine Iguana**

**Death Adder**

Welcome to the slithery, scaly, cold-blooded world of reptiles. These creatures have been around since the age of dinosaurs and can be found all over the globe. They can be tiny or huge, ferocious or meek. Snakes and lizards are reptiles, and so are turtles, crocodiles, and alligators. Amphibians are similar to reptiles but spend part of their lives in water. Frogs, toads, salamanders, and newts are all amphibians. Snakes are first-class hunters, they strike with lightning speed. The emerald tree boa, puff adder, and other snakes blend in with their surroundings, so they can ambush unsuspecting victims. Many snakes, such as the fer-de-lance, inject toxic venom that quickly leaves their victims dead. Some snakes are monstrously large, including the anaconda. It coils around its victims and squeezes them to death.

Lizards are proof of nature's dizzying variety. The thorny devil, covered in spikes, is one of

**Basilisk Lizard**

**Poison Dart Frog**

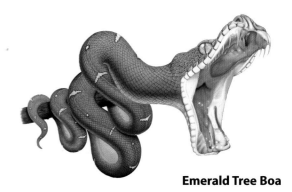

**Emerald Tree Boa**

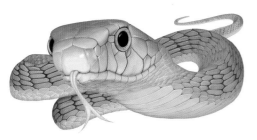

**Green Mamba**

**Alligator Snapping Turtle**

**African Twig Snake**

many small lizards. The much larger Komodo dragon can take down a deer. Some lizards glide through the air, while others swim in the sea.

Some reptiles are extremely rugged and ready for battle. The alligator snapping turtle is protected top and bottom by a strong, bony shell. Few animals win against alligators and crocodiles, with their powerful tails, thick skins, and tooth-filled jaws. The massive saltwater crocodile has been known to eat people.

Amphibians are good at finding a meal—and not becoming one. Many frogs have huge mouths and insatiable appetites. Predators lose their appetite if they try to eat the nasty-tasting crested newt. Some amphibians, such as the poison-dart frog, have beautiful colors. Others, such as the giant salamander, are downright ugly. Along with reptiles, these creatures show some of the amazing diversity in the animal kingdom.

**Mangrove Snake**

**Stinkpot Turtle**

# Snakes

*Snakes are deadly hunters that claim their victims in a variety of ways. Their forked tongues "taste" the air for their next meal, and snakes that hunt at night sense the body heat of nearby prey.*

Many snakes trick their victims. The death adder lures prey with its wiggling, worm-like tail, and the African twig snake looks like a tree branch. Some snakes become airborne to get their prey. The jumping snake leaps from the ground, and the golden tree snake glides from tree to tree. Many snakes are dangerous to people, injecting a deadly venom with their long fangs. The venom of the fer-de-lance destroys tissues in the body, while the Mulga's venom paralyzes all the body's muscles. Not all snakes kill with venom.

The huge and powerful anaconda is a constrictor snake. It coils around its victims and squeezes until they suffocate. Some snakes send a clear message to stay away. The rattlesnake makes noise by shaking loose shells at the tip of its tail. The deadly king cobra expands its ribs to spread a fearsome "hood." Many snakes have an eyecatching appearance. The rhino viper has scales on its head that resemble horns, while the coral snake is covered in bands of bright colors. No matter how they look, snakes are expert killers.

# DEATH ADDER

**Latin name:** *Acanthophis species*

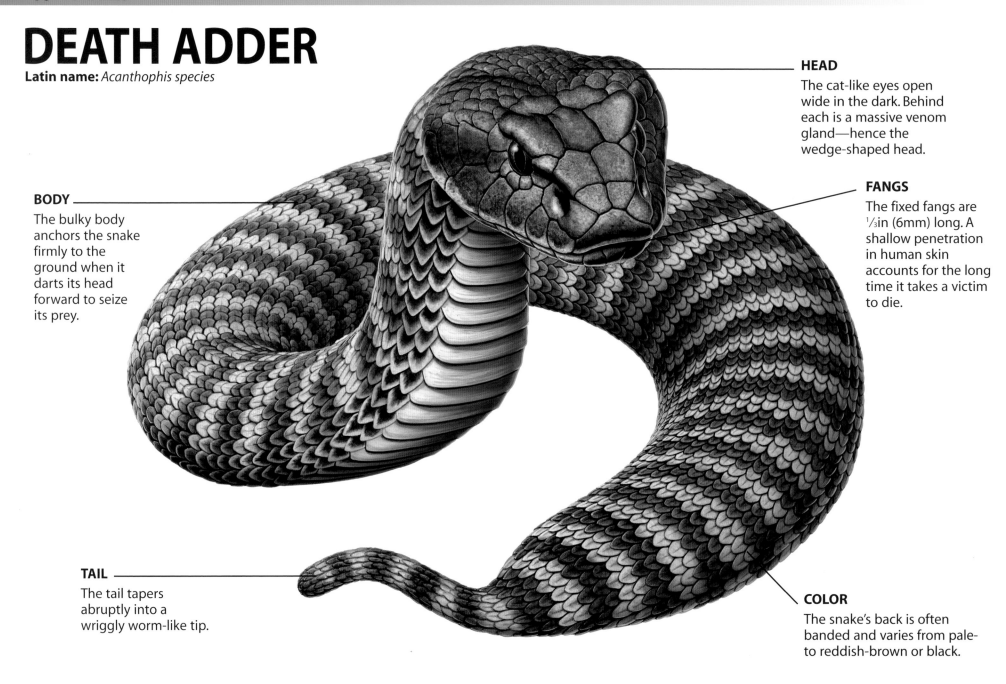

**HEAD**

The cat-like eyes open wide in the dark. Behind each is a massive venom gland—hence the wedge-shaped head.

**FANGS**

The fixed fangs are ⅓in (6mm) long. A shallow penetration in human skin accounts for the long time it takes a victim to die.

**BODY**

The bulky body anchors the snake firmly to the ground when it darts its head forward to seize its prey.

**TAIL**

The tail tapers abruptly into a wriggly worm-like tip.

**COLOR**

The snake's back is often banded and varies from pale- to reddish-brown or black.

The death adder ambushes prey with a combination of cunning and venomous fangs. At dusk in the Australian bush, it lies on the ground in camouflaged coils and waggles its tail like a worm. The death adder clearly doesn't believe in over-exerting itself. After a day lazing about in a pile of leaves it is in no hurry to move, it just stays where it is. But now it's alert, and waggling its tail slowly and surely to entice the curious mouse.

SIZE

## KEY DATA

| | | |
|---|---|---|
| LENGTH | Up to 3ft (1m) | |
| PREY | Lizards, frogs, birds, mice | Experts disagree on how many different species of death adder there are, but all species are similar. The snake is found throughout Australia, except for the extreme southeastern part of the continent. It also lives in the forests of southern New Guinea. |
| ATTACK | Single strike | |
| VENOM | Contains a cocktail of deadly nerve toxins | |
| LIFESPAN | Unknown | |

**2** The lure wriggles faster and faster, enticing the marsupial closer and closer until—wham!—quick as a whip, the snake seizes the animal.

**1** It's night in the forest, and a hopping mouse (a small marsupial) detects movement in a heap of dead leaves. Curious, it investigates.

## Did You Know?

● The death adder's viper-like appearance and habits convinced early naturalists that it actually was a viper. It was some time before it became clear that there are no vipers in Australia or New Guinea.

● This snake can inject 1–1½ grain (60–70mg) of venom at a time—less than ½ grain (20mg) is enough to kill a man. The venom can act slowly. Symptoms such as breathing failure often don't appear until after 24 or even 48 hours.

● As the death adder's fangs wear out or break off, new ones replace them. The snake often swallows the old fangs. They pass through its body without causing any damage.

● In experiments, scientists have repeatedly jumped up and down near a resting death adder without provoking any response from it.

● The non-venomous New Guinea boa (*Candoia aspera*) mimics the death adder, to scare off predators.

# COTTONMOUTH SNAKE

**Latin name:** *Agkistrodon piscivorus*

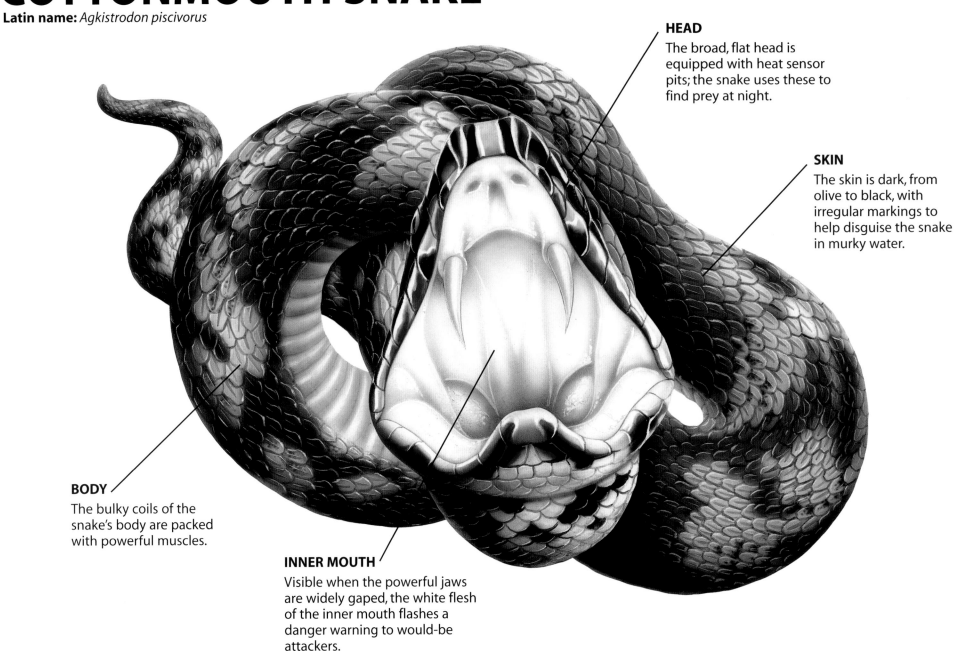

**HEAD**
The broad, flat head is equipped with heat sensor pits; the snake uses these to find prey at night.

**SKIN**
The skin is dark, from olive to black, with irregular markings to help disguise the snake in murky water.

**BODY**
The bulky coils of the snake's body are packed with powerful muscles.

**INNER MOUTH**
Visible when the powerful jaws are widely gaped, the white flesh of the inner mouth flashes a danger warning to would-be attackers.

There is something about the cottonmouth that instils panic. Maybe it is the way it glides unseen through murky water and then strikes, its fangs bared and its white mouth gaping wide. As dark and sinister as its swampland habitat, this fierce hunter haunts the sluggish waters of southeastern USA. A swimming cottonmouth seems too slow to be a threat, but don't be misled: it has quickfire reflexes and tough jaws. After the snake plunges its fangs into a victim, it hangs on until its venom starts to work.

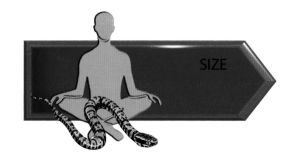

SIZE

## KEY DATA

| LENGTH | Up to 6ft 3in (1.9m) | |
|---|---|---|
| PREY | Fish, frogs, tadpoles, reptiles, birds, and small mammals | Also called the water moccasin, the cottonmouth lives in all kinds of waterways—including bayous, swamps, streams, and lakes—along the Atlantic coast and Gulf of Mexico, from southern Virginia down to the Florida Keys, and west to Texas, Oklahoma, and Illinois. |
| WEAPONS | Hinged front fangs that inject blood- and tissue-destroying venom | |
| LIFESPAN | Unknown | |

**2** A cottonmouth clamps its jaws on the man's wrist. At once, powerful muscles begin to pump venom deep into the man's flesh.

## Did You Know?

● A cottonmouth's strike reflex is so strong that even specimens killed on the road have been known to give a powerful bite to unwary handlers.

● On some small islands in the Gulf of Mexico, cottonmouth snakes gather in vast numbers beneath the nesting sites of seabirds to feast on dropped fish and fallen fledglings.

● The cottonmouth often ranges far from water, foraging in woods, fields, and farmland. It sometimes visits yards, searching outhouses for mice and rats, and entering ponds in pursuit of frogs and goldfish.

● The baby cottonmouth has a bright sulfur-yellow tip to its tail, which it waves in order to lure prey within striking distance.

● The cottonmouth may hunt at night but it isn't shy of being seen during the day. The snake regularly basks in the sun on the branches and fallen trunks of waterside trees.

**1** Two vacationers are navigating their canoe along a Florida bayou. As one paddles, the other trails his hand in the water, unaware of the dark form heading toward him.

**3** The man jerks his hand out of the water in a frantic bid to shake off the snake. At best, the venom will cause massive tissue damage around the bite—at worst, it will kill him.

# BUSH VIPER

**Latin name:** *Atheris species*

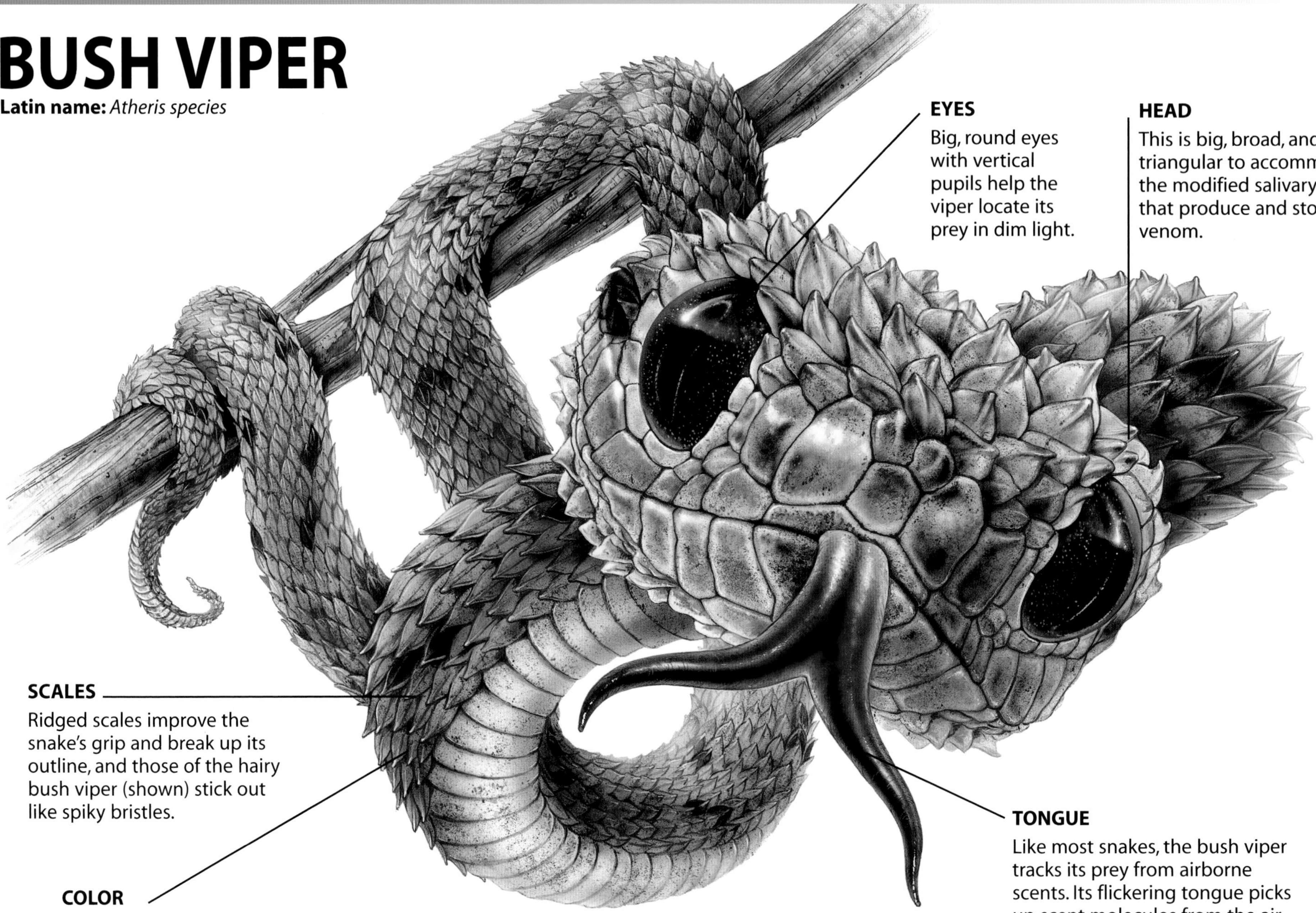

**EYES**

Big, round eyes with vertical pupils help the viper locate its prey in dim light.

**HEAD**

This is big, broad, and often triangular to accommodate the modified salivary glands that produce and store the venom.

**SCALES**

Ridged scales improve the snake's grip and break up its outline, and those of the hairy bush viper (shown) stick out like spiky bristles.

**TONGUE**

Like most snakes, the bush viper tracks its prey from airborne scents. Its flickering tongue picks up scent molecules from the air and transfers them to the Jacobson's organ: a pit in the roof of its mouth lined with sensitive receptor cells.

**COLOR**

Bush vipers come in an amazing variety of shades, from green and brown to yellow and black, but they all rely on color and disruptive skin patterns to avoid detection.

You'd better think twice before you walk under trees where this scaly predator hangs out, for despite its rough scales and gripping tail, you never know when it might come tumbling from its perch. Bush vipers tend to live in isolated populations far removed from human settlements, and as they spend most of their time in the trees they rarely tangle with people—but they have been known to…

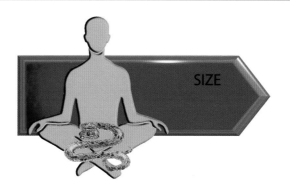

SIZE

## KEY DATA

| | | |
|---|---|---|
| LENGTH | Up to 29in (75cm) long; females usually larger than males | |
| PREY | Amphibians, lizards, and rodents; occasionally snails, slugs, birds, and other snakes | |
| WEAPONS | Venom-primed fangs | |
| LIFESPAN | Unknown | |

Bush vipers are found throughout equatorial Africa, from Guinea in the west to Mozambique in the east. They live in a range of habitats: from evergreen, mountain, and tropical rainforests to swamps and high grasslands. Of the nine species, only *Atheris superciliaris* and *Atheris hindii* are land-dwelling; the others spend most of their time aloft in the branches.

**1** A bush viper is preoccupied with catching a small lizard perched at the end of a branch, coiling itself in readiness for a strike.

**2** But even snakes can make mistakes, and as the viper lunges forward it loses its grip. Plunging from the trees, it hurtles toward a passing farmer, who is oblivious to the unfolding drama.

**3** The bush viper drops right on to the startled man below, who shouts in alarm—prompting the snake to strike painfully at his shoulder.

## Did You Know?

● Along the west coast of Africa, plantation workers risk being bitten by the green bush viper, *Atheris squamigera*, which often lurks among the coffee bushes.

● Some bush vipers have pale tips to their tails. They are thought to wiggle them like maggots to entice their prey.

● Protruding scales above the eyes give the horned bush viper, *Atheris ceratophora*, a devilish appearance.

● Bush vipers were once more widely distributed than they are today, as their numbers are declining. Forest species are particularly at risk, for much of their habitat is being cleared by loggers or for new houses.

● Compared with other species of snake, vipers have the longest fangs.

# PUFF ADDER

**Latin name:** *Bitis arietans*

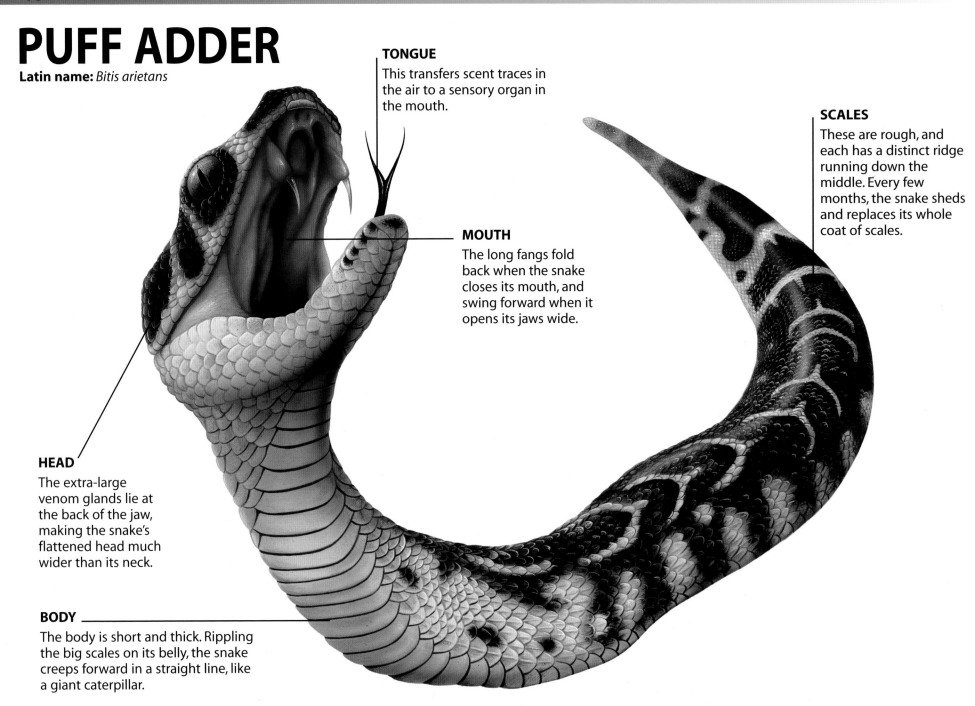

**TONGUE**
This transfers scent traces in the air to a sensory organ in the mouth.

**SCALES**
These are rough, and each has a distinct ridge running down the middle. Every few months, the snake sheds and replaces its whole coat of scales.

**MOUTH**
The long fangs fold back when the snake closes its mouth, and swing forward when it opens its jaws wide.

**HEAD**
The extra-large venom glands lie at the back of the jaw, making the snake's flattened head much wider than its neck.

**BODY**
The body is short and thick. Rippling the big scales on its belly, the snake creeps forward in a straight line, like a giant caterpillar.

Thanks to its camouflage and lethal venom—injected by ¾in-long (2cm) fangs—the bloated and sluggish puff adder is one of the most dangerous snakes in all Africa, killing many people every year. Lying in ambush, concealed by its camouflage, the puff adder constantly tastes the air with its forked tongue. When a victim strays by, the snake prepares to strike, opening its jaws wide and unfolding its long fangs.

SIZE

## KEY DATA

| LENGTH | 2½–5ft (0.7–1.5m) |
| --- | --- |
| WEIGHT | 3lb 4oz–4lb 8oz (1.5–2kg) |
| PREY | Rats, lizards, birds, frogs, and other small animals |
| VENOM | Causes internal bleeding and organ failure, or death if not treated promptly |
| TYPICAL ATTACK | Single bite with hinged, hollow fangs |
| LIFESPAN | Up to 15 years in the wild; longer in captivity |

The puff adder is found throughout most of Africa and in parts of the Arabian peninsula. It lives in nearly all lowland areas, up to about 6560ft (2000m), except for the hottest, driest parts of deserts and the deep interiors of dense rainforests. Typical puff adder terrain is grassy savannah.

When the puff adder goes for the kill, its fangs swing forward so it can thrust them deep into its prey. Its jawbones have very flexible joints, allowing the mouth to open wide and engulf prey in one.

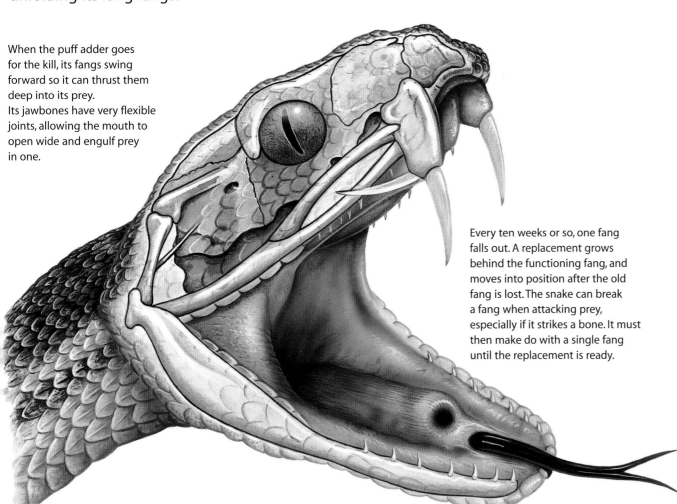

Every ten weeks or so, one fang falls out. A replacement grows behind the functioning fang, and moves into position after the old fang is lost. The snake can break a fang when attacking prey, especially if it strikes a bone. It must then make do with a single fang until the replacement is ready.

## Did You Know?

● A lurid African folk tale has it that baby puff adders eat their way out of their mother.

● The female gives birth to fully formed young that can hunt within days. Usually, she bears 20 to 30, but the record is an amazing 154.

● Rival male puff adders compete for the same female by rearing up, intertwining, and hissing at each other until one backs down.

● If the puff adder breaks both its fangs at the same time, it doesn't starve. Like all reptiles, it can go for several weeks without food.

# RHINOCEROS VIPER

**Latin name:** *Bitis nasicornis*

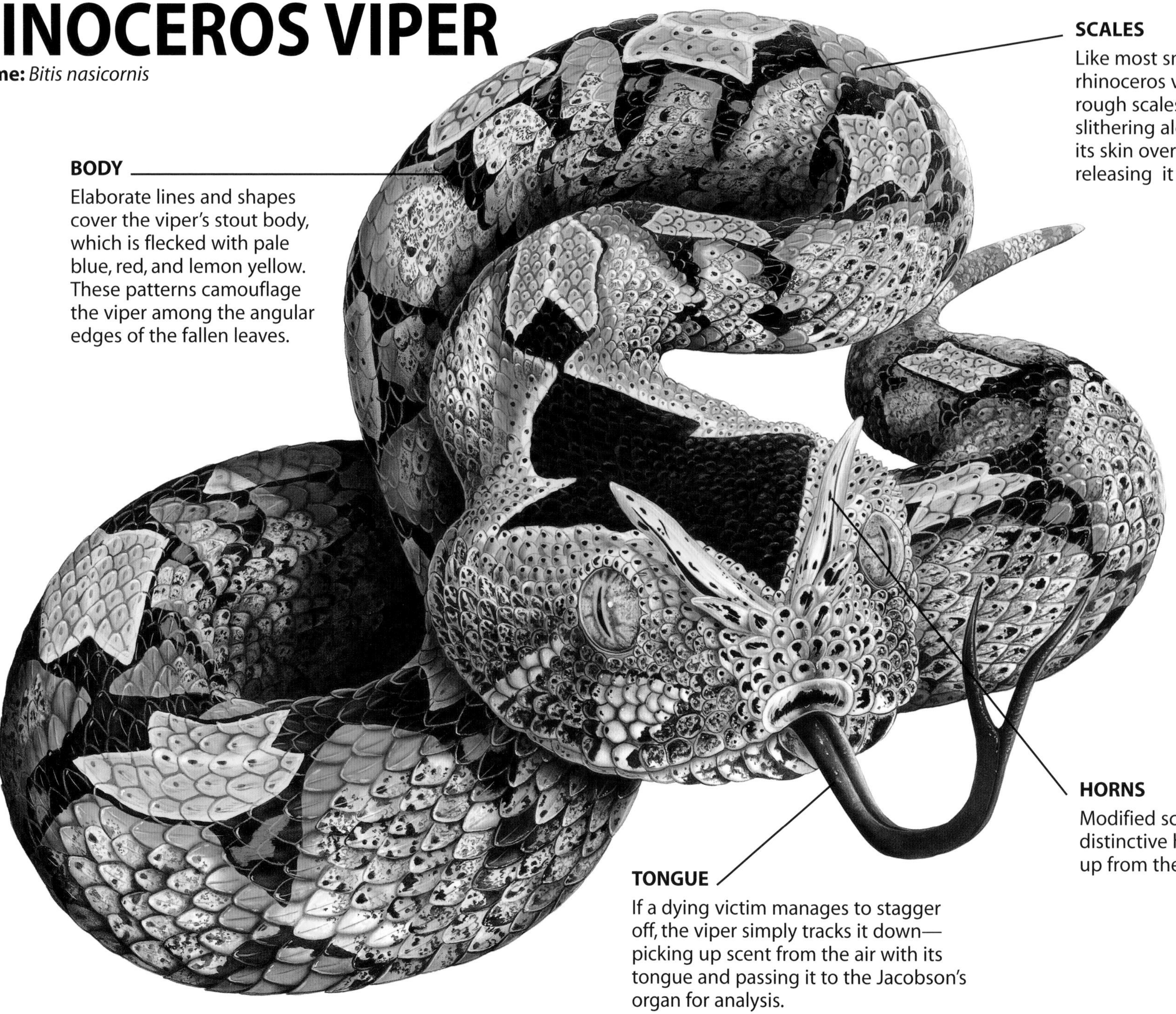

**SCALES**

Like most snakes, the rhinoceros viper uses its rough scales for grip, slithering along by stretching its skin over its ribs and then releasing it again.

**BODY**

Elaborate lines and shapes cover the viper's stout body, which is flecked with pale blue, red, and lemon yellow. These patterns camouflage the viper among the angular edges of the fallen leaves.

**HORNS**

Modified scales form distinctive horns that stick up from the viper's head.

**TONGUE**

If a dying victim manages to stagger off, the viper simply tracks it down— picking up scent from the air with its tongue and passing it to the Jacobson's organ for analysis.

A tiny dose of this snake's powerful, blood-destroying venom means a drawn-out death. Attacking the circulatory system, it causes internal bleeding, tissue decay, and organ failure. It might look fat and sleepy, but the rhinoceros viper can attack an enemy at whipcrack speed. Coiled as tight as a spring, it shoots forward to strike a target up to half its body length away—much farther than you might expect.

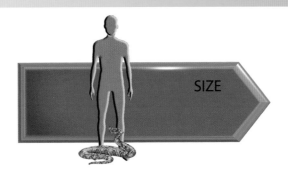

SIZE

## KEY DATA

| LENGTH | Up to 6ft (1.8m) (female) |
| PREY | Small mammals, birds, lizards, toads, and fish |
| WEAPONS | Long, venomous fangs |
| LIFESTYLE | Nocturnal |
| LIFESPAN | Up to 15 years |

The rhinoceros viper lives in the lush, tropical rainforests of Central and West Africa, from western Sudan and Kenya, through Chad and Nigeria, to Guinea and Senegal. The viper prefers damp terrain close to streams, rivers, lakes, and swamps, and although it can climb, it spends most of its time on the ground.

**1** On a trip to the jungle a tourist spots an intriguingly colored snake coiled among the leaf litter. The lethargic-looking creature barely seems to register his presence, so standing at what seems to be a safe distance, he goads it with a long stick.

**2** Big mistake! Finally irritated beyond endurance, the viper launches an attack. Hurling the front of its body forward, it easily bridges the gap, and the tormentor barely has time to blink as the snake buries its venomous fangs in his flesh.

## Did You Know?

● The rhinoceros viper can attack from any direction, catapulting its wide head forward, backward, or sideways with startling speed.

● After a strike, the rhinoceros viper immediately recoils. It does this to avoid breaking its fangs in a struggle, but just in case, it has up to six replacement pairs growing—each in a different stage of development.

● The rhinoceros viper is also known as the river jack, because of its preference for damp, forested areas close to rivers and lakes.

● Many vipers have nose horns like those of the rhinoceros viper, but the function of these peculiar appendages remains a mystery.

● The rhinoceros viper can control the movement of its hinged fangs, and doesn't always flip them down when it opens its mouth. When it does attack, it is occasionally known to deliver 'dry' or venomless bites.

# BOA CONSTRICTOR

**Latin name:** *Boa constrictor*

**CAMOUFLAGE**

The boa is camouflaged from predators and prey. In rainforests, it has bold, bright markings that melt into a dappled background. In sandy, open areas it has much paler markings.

**EYES**

These are small, but the vertical pupils open wide at night to gather as much light as they can.

**TONGUE**

This collects scent molecules from the air and passes them to a sensory organ in the roof of the mouth for analysis.

Relentlessly tightening its powerful coils, the mighty boa constrictor squeezes the last breath out of its victims, listening for their final heartbeat before engulfing them in its cavernous jaws. It may look sluggish, but once the boa constrictor has a target in its sights it moves with whipcrack speed, grabbing the creature with its jaws and throwing coils around the animal. For the victim, there's no escape.

SIZE

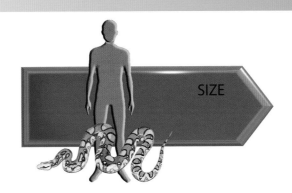

## KEY DATA

| | | |
|---|---|---|
| LENGTH | Usually 6ft 6in–12ft 6in (2–4m); rarely 19ft (6m) | |
| WEIGHT | Up to 33lb (15kg) in the wild; up to 66lb (30kg) in captivity | The boa constrictor lives in Central and South America, from northwestern Mexico through the Amazon Basin to northern Argentina, in a variety of habitats ranging from rainforest to dry scrub. It is also found in the Lesser Antilles (Leeward and Windward islands) in the Caribbean. |
| PREY | Mainly mice, rats, lizards, and birds | |
| LIFESPAN | Unknown in the wild; up to 40 years in captivity | |

**1** Each time its prey breathes out, the boa tightens its grip, until it suffocates the animal—in this case a capybara, a big rodent. The boa then starts to work its jaws over the lifeless creature's head.

**2** The boa moves each side of its lower jaw forward independently, getting a grip with its sharp, backward-pointing teeth, then moves its upper jaw forward to engulf a little more of its prey. It's a slow process, but then there's no hurry. The boa's jaws flex and move apart, and its skin stretches like elastic to allow the fat rodent to pass down its throat.

**3** The boa "walks" its prey into its stomach with muscular contractions. Its ribs splay out to make room for the huge mouthful, which makes the snake look like it has swallowed a vast football. It will take the boa about a week to digest the capybara. When swallowing such big animals, the boa often loses some of its teeth, but new ones soon grow.

## Did You Know?

● Scientists classify the boa constrictor as a primitive snake, since it still has aspects of its lizard ancestry. For example, while most snakes have only one lung, the boa has two.

● Another clue to the boa's lizard ancestry is the two tiny, claw-like spurs on its pelvis, which were once hindlegs. They are larger in the male snake, and it may be that he uses them to stimulate the female to mate.

● The boa constrictor can swim well and often lives alongside rivers and lakes, and in marshes.

● In areas with cold or dry spells, the boa constrictor may lie dormant in a burrow or tree hollow for weeks.

● A male boa constrictor called Popeye died at Philadelphia Zoo in 1977 aged 40 years, the greatest age recorded for any snake.

# MANGROVE SNAKE

**Latin name:** *Boiga dendrophila*

**BODY**

This heavy snake's body is slightly compressed from side to side so it can wriggle through narrow gaps between tree branches.

**FANGS**

This killer is one of a group of rear-fanged snakes: a pair of grooved fangs sprout from the back of the upper jaw, which forces the snake to gape wide to deliver its venom.

**COLORING**

Its vivid coloring makes the mangrove snake unmistakable; the glossy blue-black background color is marked with 40 to 50 narrow, bright yellow bands. This yellow also covers the entire underside of the snake.

on't be deceived by this creature's beguiling beauty. Its glittering black and yellow scales may invite a closer look, but its bite brings nothing but pain and suffering. The mangrove snake likes to bask in the sunshine by lying on branches that overhang open waterways. Despite its garish coloring, busy fisherfolk do not always spot the bad-tempered serpent lurking above them.

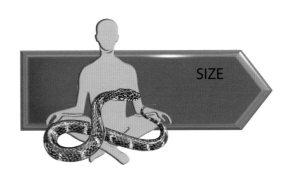

SIZE

## KEY DATA

| | | |
|---|---|---|
| LENGTH | Up to 8ft (2.5m) |  |
| PREY | Small mammals, birds, frogs, and reptiles | |
| WEAPONS | Venom-primed fangs | |
| TOXICITY | Dangerous to children | The mangrove snake ranges through southeastern Asia, including Malaysia, Indonesia, and the Philippines, living mainly in mangrove swamps, or lowland rainforests near pools and rivers. |
| LIFESPAN | Unknown | |

**1** A mangrove snake is lolling on a bare branch above the waters of a mangrove creek, soaking up the tropical sunshine beaming on to its exposed perch. But the splash of paddles nearby gives it a rude awakening. The snake fixes a wary eye on an approaching boat that has a fisherman and his son on board.

**2** Intent on navigating their craft between the trees, the two do not notice the reptile. The boy grabs the snake's branch to steady his craft, and tips the beast into the boat.

**3** The lad grabs the snake's tail and tries to fling the animal overboard. But the angry serpent whips round and clamps its jaws over the child's arm, pumping venom deep into his tender flesh.

### Did You Know?

● Although aggressive in the wild, the mangrove snake is easily tamed by experts. It is one of the species often kept by snake charmers who perform throughout southern Asia. While a snake charmer plays his flute and sways from side to side, the snake rises eerily out of its basket, seemingly enchanted by the hypnotic sound of the music.

● The female mangrove snake lays several clutches per year, carefully placing the large eggs in treeholes, away from predators.

● Because of its beautiful skin pattern, the mangrove snake is a popular pet. But owners must take extra care, not only to avoid its bite but also to provide ideal conditions. The reptile needs to be kept in a large sealed home with plenty of branches and a humid atmosphere. The creature cannot share its home with other species of snake, or they'll soon end up in its belly.

# FER-DE-LANCE

**Latin name:** *Bothrops asper, B. insularis & others*

**BODY**

A powerfully muscled body enables the snake to strike with force and speed.

**MARKINGS**

A fer-de-lance is neatly patterned with darker "triangles" against a lighter background. This breaks up its outline and provides effective camouflage against leaf litter and tangled vegetation.

**HEAD**

The snake's large venom glands lie behind its eyes, broadening the back of its head and making it distinctly triangular or lance-like in shape.

In the tropics of America, those who live and work in the countryside fear the fer-de-lance above all other snakes, for one foot wrong could provoke a lightning injection of its lethally destructive venom. The deadliest fer-de-lance of all, the golden lancehead, lives only on the island of Quemada Grande in Brazil, where it rules supreme. Its venom is notoriously toxic, and it thrives in such high numbers that chilling tales are told of its victims.

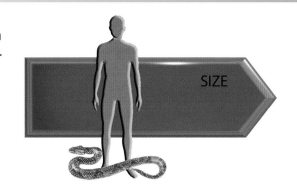

SIZE

## KEY DATA

| | | |
|---|---|---|
| LENGTH | Up to 7½ ft (2.4m) | The most common species of fer-de-lance, *Bothrops asper* (also known as *barba amarilla* or yellowbeard), ranges through much of Central and South America from southern Mexico to central Brazil, where it has colonized many rural areas. Other close relatives with a more restricted range include *B. andianus*, *B. insularis* (the golden lancehead) and *B. lanceolatus*. |
| PREY | Small mammals, birds, lizards, and frogs | |
| WEAPONS | Potent venom containing both anticoagulant and flesh-destroying chemicals | |
| LIFESPAN | Up to 20 years | |

**1** A fisherman ventures on to the island to pick bananas, but as he wanders through the forest a golden lancehead strikes his ankle. Panicking, the man stumbles back to his boat, suffering several more bites from lanceheads coiled along the track.

**2** Racked with pain as the terrible venom eats away at his flesh, the fisherman casts off. As he drifts out to sea he cuts the bite wounds and tries to suck out the venom, but soon collapses into unconsciousness. He bleeds to death long before anyone spots his boat, and is found sprawled in a pool of his own blood.

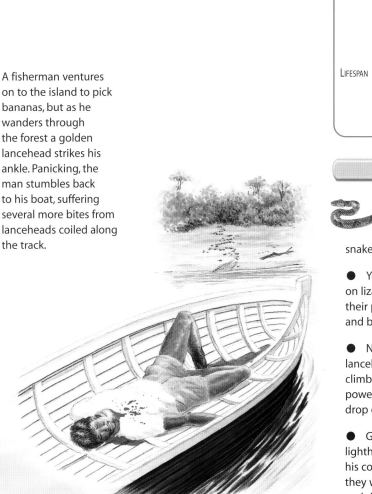

## Did You Know?

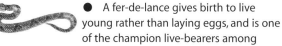

● A fer-de-lance gives birth to live young rather than laying eggs, and is one of the champion live-bearers among snakes—producing litters of up to 70 babies at a time.

● Young fer-de-lance snakes often feed predominantly on lizards and tree frogs, but as adults, they prefer to use their pit-organs to hunt down "warm-blooded" mammals and birds.

● No mammals live on Quemada Grande, so golden lanceheads feed almost exclusively on small birds, climbing into the trees to wait in ambush. They need a powerful venom, otherwise their prey would fly away and drop dead in the sea.

● Golden lanceheads are said to have killed the last lighthouse keeper on Quemada Grande after gliding into his cottage one night. When the keeper and his family fled, they were bitten by more snakes hanging in the trees— and their bodies were found scattered across the island.

# JUMPING VIPER

**Latin name:** *Bothrops nummifer*

**BODY**

The coarse scales are often mottled so that, at rest, the viper blends with the shadows cast by trees in the forests.

**HEAD**

The wedge-shaped head is unpatterned except for a single thick, dark band on each side, which runs back from the eye.

**HEAT PITS**

The pits, located on either side of the head between the nostril and the eye, constantly monitor the air for the body heat of nearby animals.

**COLOR**

The snake's thickset body may be gray, brown, or beige. Triangular blotches along the its spine break up the snake's outline.

f ever you wander through the forests of Central America, beware this jack-in-the-box of a snake. It catapults itself into the air to deliver a miserably painful bite. Being so perfectly camouflaged, it often just waits in a pile of leaves for rodents to blunder into it. But the fearless jumping viper also moves out of the forests into clearings in search of food, which may include domestic pets! Despite its relatively small size, it becomes very aggressive when disturbed.

SIZE

## KEY DATA

| | | |
|---|---|---|
| LENGTH | Up to 2ft (60cm) | |
| PREY | Rodents, lizards, and frogs | |
| WEAPONS | Venom-primed fangs | |
| TYPICAL ATTACK | Jumps to make single bite | |
| LIFESPAN | Unknown | |

The jumping viper is found in the rainforests and plantations of Central America, from southeastern Mexico down to Panama, but particularly in western Guatemala and El Salvador. In some places it is endangered because of the destruction of its forest habitat by loggers and farmers.

**1** A poor farmer moves his small stock of cattle through some dry forest in Central America, looking for fresh grazing. As his beasts trample heavily through the grass, they disturb a jumping viper. Wary of the sharp, plodding hooves, the snake coils itself up instantly into an S-shape ready to launch an attack.

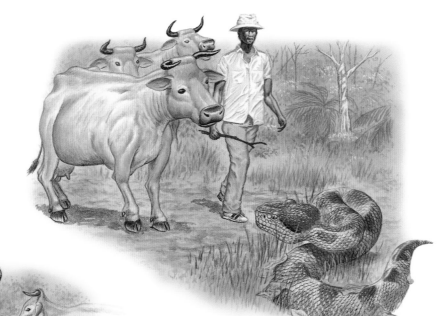

**2** As the farmer coaxes one of his cattle along with a stick, the snake springs up and bites the cow high on its foreleg. The startled farmer swings his stick angrily at the snake—he can't afford to lose such a valuable animal or pay a vet for treatment. If he is quick, he may prevent the viper from delivering a lethal dose of venom.

## Did You Know?

● Other "jumping" snakes around the world include African horned vipers and the Asian saw-scaled viper. The golden tree snake of southeastern Asia goes one step farther, gliding from tree to tree!

● The jumping viper is a species of pit viper. These snakes are named after the pits at the front of their head. Experts used to think that these were ears or nostrils. In some parts of Latin America, pit vipers are still called *cuatro narices*, meaning "four nostrils." The pits are actually used to detect the heat of prey.

● In experiments to discover how important heat pits are, one blind rattlesnake was found to have a success rate of 98 percent when striking at prey. When its nasal pits were covered up, the snake's success rate fell to only 27 percent.

● Some pit vipers' sensitive heat pits can detect the tiniest changes in temperature.

# EYELASH VIPER

**Latin name:** *Bothrops schlegelii*

**EYES**

The vertically slit pupils open wide in the dark. Snakes can see movement and color but not detail.

**EYELASHES**

A distinctive patch of bristly, spiny scales over each eye gives the viper a forbidding "frown."

**PITS**

A pit in front of each eye detects the body heat of warm-blooded prey.

**TONGUE**

The snake flicks its forked tongue in and out repeatedly to "taste" the air for the scent of prey.

S caly "eyelashes" give this colorful viper a menacing appearance even by venomous snake standards. What's more, this appearance is no bluff—for the eyelash viper can kill with a single swift and deadly bite. Eyelash viper venom is nasty stuff. It's *haemotoxic*: it kills blood vessels and red blood cells. The outcome for a farmer bitten far from medical aid is bleak: bleeding from the eyes, mouth, and kidneys—and a painful death.

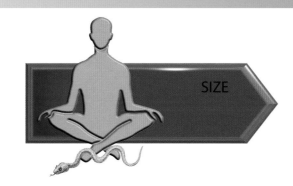

SIZE

### KEY DATA

| | | |
|---|---|---|
| LENGTH | To 29in (75cm); usually 18–24in (45–60cm) | The eyelash viper lurks in shrubs, vines, palms, and other trees, usually along riverbanks, throughout the American tropics. It ranges from southern Mexico south through Central America—where it is known locally as the bocaracá—into Colombia, Ecuador, and western Venezuela in northern South America. |
| PREY | Small mammals, small birds, lizards, and frogs | |
| WEAPONS | Venom-primed fangs | |
| ATTACK | Single stabbing bite | |
| LIFESPAN | About 10 years in the wild | |

**1** In the forests of Costa Rica, a farmer treads a shady path. Watching the uneven ground, he fails to spot the eyelash viper resting on a low branch overhead. His head brushes against the reptile.

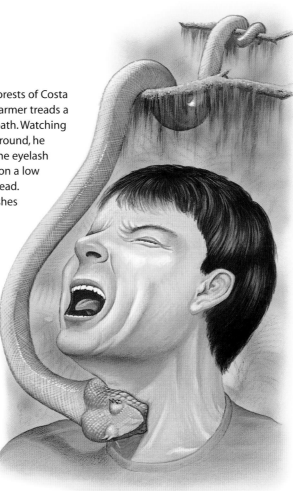

**2** The disturbed snake whips round and plunges its fangs into the intruder. It hasn't eaten recently, so its venom glands are full—and the man is doomed.

### Did You Know?

● The female eyelash viper gives birth to 12 or more live young—each of which may be a different color.

● Some experts think the purpose of the snake's "eyelashes" may be to protect its eyes as it slithers through foliage or swings from branches.

● The caterpillar of the *Hemerplanes triptolemus* moth defends itself by mimicking the appearance of the eyelash viper.

● A viper's fangs are hinged. Each fang has a series of replacement or "embryo" fangs growing behind it. When the next fang in line is fully grown, the first fang loosens and is left in the snake's next victim.

● The eyelash viper is known to kill up to six people every year in Costa Rica alone.

● The eyelash viper is a popular pet with enthusiasts and breeds readily in captivity.

# DESERT HORNED VIPER
**Latin name:** *Cerastes cerastes*

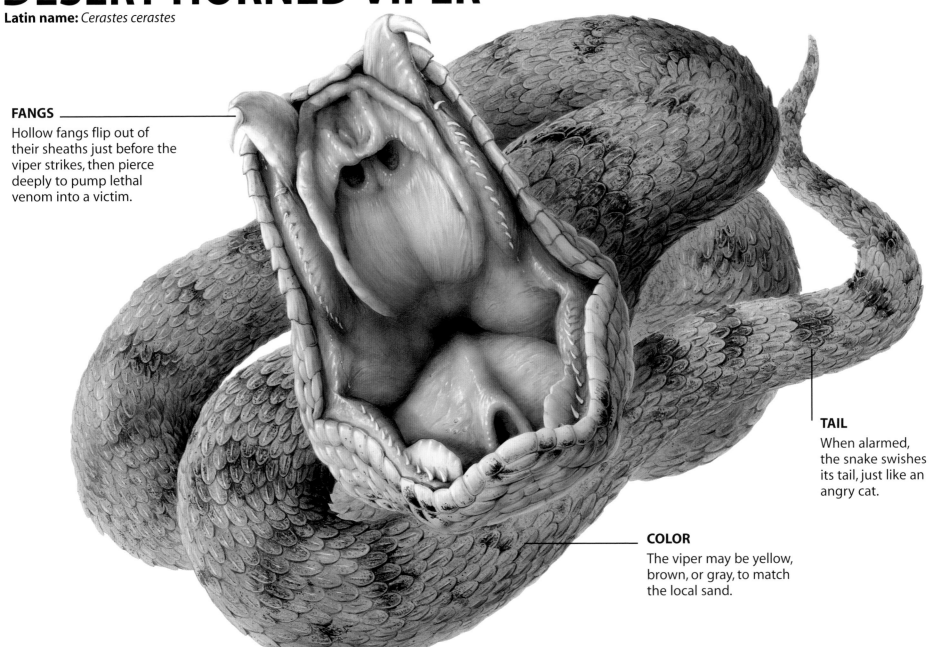

**FANGS**
Hollow fangs flip out of their sheaths just before the viper strikes, then pierce deeply to pump lethal venom into a victim.

**TAIL**
When alarmed, the snake swishes its tail, just like an angry cat.

**COLOR**
The viper may be yellow, brown, or gray, to match the local sand.

t's bad enough when venomous snakes slither across the ground, but it's even worse when they start delving under the surface—striking out at those going about their business above. While it's possible to protect yourself from venomous creatures you can see, you're unlikely to spot a desert horned viper buried in the sand. If you do find one, it's usually because it has just sunk its fangs into your foot…

SIZE

**1** It's a moonlit night, and a Bedouin boy sets off boldly across the desert sand. Unfortunately, he disturbs a horned viper which, believing him to be a threat, slips rapidly from sight.

**2** Poised for action, the snake waits silently beneath the sand, feeling for vibrations. The Bedouin boy comes closer and steps right on the snake, which rears up instantly and stabs its fangs deep into his foot. Yelling in pain and shock, the boy drags himself away, but although badly affected by the venom, he'll probably recover.

## KEY DATA

| | | |
|---|---|---|
| LENGTH | 24–29in (60–75cm) | |
| PREY | Small mammals and lizards | |
| WEAPONS | Long fangs dripping with fast-acting venom |  The desert horned viper lives beside the deserts of North Africa, from Mauritania and Morocco, across the Sahara to Egypt. It is also found in Jordan, Iraq, Saudi Arabia, and Kuwait. |
| TACTICS | Ambush predator | |
| LIFESPAN | Up to 17 years in captivity | |

## Did You Know?

● If the desert horned viper feels threatened, it rubs its rough scales together to produce a loud rasping, hoping to frighten its enemies away.

● North African snake charmers often use a desert horned viper in their act because of its menacing appearance. But if these snakes are in short supply, they may substitute the hornless species, *Cerastes vipera*, jabbing porcupine quills into its head to resemble horns. Not surprisingly, the unfortunate snake soon dies.

● The desert horned viper usually hunts at night, when the temperature drops and small prey animals leave their daytime shelters to find food.

● While the desert horned viper is historically associated with queen Cleopatra, the Levant viper, *Vipera lebetina mauritanica*, appears in Bible stories as an embodiment of the devil. Its venom, which is strong enough to fell the hardiest camel, was believed to be the Evil One's perspiration.

# GREEN TREE PYTHON

**Latin name:** *Chondropython viridis*

## PITS

Special pits in front of the eyes contain heat-sensors that enable the snake to locate prey at night.

## EYES

This nocturnal killer's vertical pupils narrow in the brightness of day, but open fully after dark when it sets off to hunt.

## SCALES

Enlarged belly scales help the snake to grip tree-trunks and branches when climbing.

## TAIL

The prehensile tail bends tightly round branches to take the snake's dangling weight.

## BODY

The muscular snake can cross big gaps with ease, pushing its head out rigid until it can reach the next support branch.

L ike a deadly vine, the green tree python hangs from a branch high in the forest canopy. Its verdant scales perfectly matching the hue of the foliage. The green tree python is an ambush expert. A gripping tail and total muscle control enable the predator to dangle unmoving for long periods awaiting prey. The killer is easy to overlook among the tangle of vegetation, until it's too late.

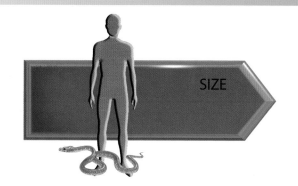

SIZE

## KEY DATA

| | | |
|---|---|---|
| LENGTH | Up to 6½ft (2m), but more usually 3-4ft (1–1.3m) | The green tree python inhabits the dense rainforests of New Guinea and the surrounding islands, and the Cape York peninsula of Australia. As soon as it hatches, the python climbs high into the jungle canopy. Males never leave the trees; only females descend to the forest floor, to lay their eggs and incubate them for two months until they hatch. |
| PREY | Frogs, lizards, birds, and small mammals | |
| WEAPONS | Powerful jaws and long fangs | |
| LIFESPAN | Unknown | |

### Did You Know?

● Sometimes a green tree python appears that has a blue coloring. This occurs when the snake's scales lack yellow pigments. In normal specimens, the yellow and blue pigments in the skin combine to produce the green appearance.

● Adults may be pea green, but not so the young. Juvenile green tree pythons are usually bright yellow, or sometimes orange or brick-red. No other python species has a juvenile form so distinctly different in color from the adult.

● Young green tree pythons are believed to use their tiny tails as worm-like lures, wiggling them as a ploy to attract inquisitive prey.

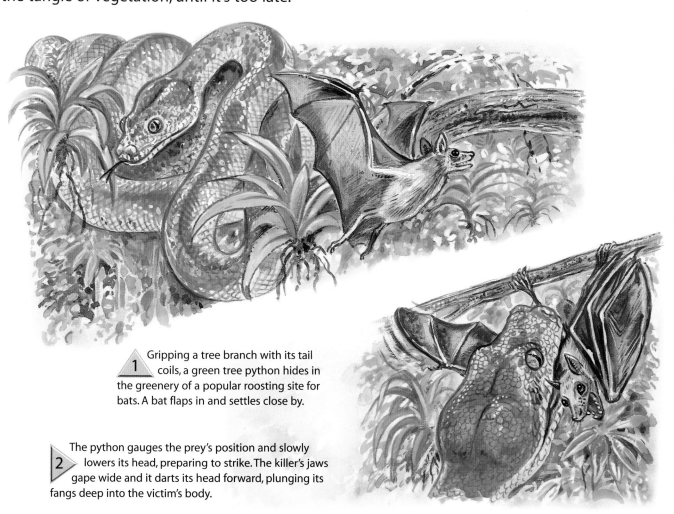

**1** Gripping a tree branch with its tail coils, a green tree python hides in the greenery of a popular roosting site for bats. A bat flaps in and settles close by.

**2** The python gauges the prey's position and slowly lowers its head, preparing to strike. The killer's jaws gape wide and it darts its head forward, plunging its fangs deep into the victim's body.

# GOLDEN TREE SNAKE

**Latin name:** *Chrysopelea ornata*

**SCALES**

Although the scales on the snake's underbelly have rigid sides, the central sections fold upward. This helps the snake create the concave shape required for jumping.

**EYES**

The snake has large eyes and keen vision —vital for a daytime predator that hunts fast-moving animals.

**SKIN**

Intricate patterns of dark and pale tones mark the skin. They help camouflage the snake in the sun-dappled foliage.

**NOSTRILS**

Sensitive nostrils test the air for the scent of prey.

T ales of leaping snakes were once thought to be conjured up by the feverish minds of early explorers, but this handsome tree snake makes such great, gliding jumps it almost seems to fly. Golden tree snakes climb tree-trunks with the greatest of ease, and pursue their prey by simply leaping the yawning gaps between one branch and another. But perhaps their most remarkable trick is to glide down from on high like living parachutes.

SIZE

## KEY DATA

| | |
|---|---|
| LENGTH | Up to 4ft (1.3m), usually 3ft (1m) |
| WEIGHT | |
| PREY DIET | Lizards, frogs, birds, and small mammals such as bats |
| BREEDING | |
| HABITAT | Forests, woodlands, and plantations, although it avoids dense areas of trees |
| LIFESPAN | |
| LIFESPAN | Unknown |

The golden tree snake is found across a wide area of southern Asia, stretching from eastern India, through Burma (Myanmar) and southern China, over much of southeastern Asia. The snake is also found in Sri Lanka and the Philippines.

**1** After climbing the trunk of a forest tree, a golden tree snake wriggles on to a comfortable branch and basks in the sun. Despite its relaxed pose, it keeps its eyes open for movement, and its looping coils are ready for action. Later, it's roused by an urge to find food. The ground lies more than 164ft (50m) below, but this doesn't deter it from launching into the abyss.

**2** Spreading its ribs, the snake flattens its body and pulls in its underside, forming a half-cylinder shape like a split bamboo cane. This traps a cushion of air beneath its body. It turns what would otherwise be a swift drop into a graceful glide.

**3** By writhing its body and using its tail for balance, the snake controls the speed and direction of its fall. Reaching a suitable site, it lands among the foliage with a thud. It turns back into its usual cylindrical shape a split second later.

## Did You Know?

● Golden tree snakes often live close to humans, and have been known to strike viciously if handled. Fortunately, although bites from their small fangs cause local bruising, their venom is not strong enough to have a serious effect on humans.

● The golden tree snake is also called the ornate tree snake because of its beautifully patterned skin.

● The female lays 6 to 12 soft, leathery-shelled eggs in a safely concealed site in a tree. These take between 10 and 13 weeks to hatch into young, each measuring about 8in (20cm) long. Initially, these baby snakes are colored and patterned differently from their parents.

● Golden tree snakes have various natural enemies, including humans, who sometimes believe them to be dangerous. Other predators include larger, fiercer, or more poisonous tree-dwelling snakes, such as the mangrove snake (*Boiga dendrophila*).

# EMERALD TREE BOA

**Latin name:** *Corallus canina*

**EYES**
By day, the pupils narrow to cat-like slits, but when the boa hunts at night they open wide to help it see in the gloom.

**BODY**
The bulky body is flattened from side to side, enabling the boa to squirm along branches and up tree trunks.

**TEETH**
Slender and sharp, these slip easily through fur and feathers to pierce flesh. They also curve backward to prevent the boa's prey escaping.

**HEAT SENSORS**
Pits between the lip scales contain heat-sensitive organs that detect the warmth of a victim's body in the dark.

**TAIL**
Muscular and mobile, the tail winds firmly around branches to support the snake head-down above the forest floor.

**COLOR**
The boa's bright green scales match the glowing, evergreen leaves, while the white bars on its back mimic the dappled sunlight.

**HEAD**
When the boa is coiled over a branch, its wide head usually sits neatly in the center of its coils.

Suspended from a branch in the steamy Amazon rainforest, this boa is a living trap for any animal that strays within range. And if it gets bored of sitting around, it chases its prey through the trees. Many forest creatures end their lives in the terrible embrace of the emerald tree boa's gleaming green coils, and with its needle teeth and speedy reflexes, it can even pluck birds from the air as they fly home to roost.

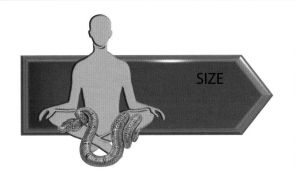

SIZE

## KEY DATA

| | |
|---|---|
| LENGTH | 3ft–6 ft 6in (90cm–2m) |
| PREY | Mammals, birds, and lizards |
| WEAPONS | Sharp fangs and muscular, constricting coils |
| BREEDING | Bears 10 to 20 live young |
| LIFESPAN | Up to 17 years in captivity |

The emerald tree boa lives in South America, where it lurks in the foliage of wet, lowland rainforests around the Amazon basin. Its range extends from southern Venezuela and Colombia, down through eastern Ecuador, Peru, and Bolivia, and right across northern Brazil to Guyana, Surinam, and French Guiana.

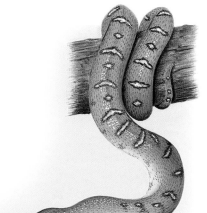

**1** Dangling from a branch like a vine, its long body secured by its tightly coiled tail, an emerald tree boa watches intently as a macaw flies into range.

**2** The boa judges its moment to perfection, then drops its jaw and strikes—sinking its slender teeth straight through the bird's feathers. Trapped and bleeding, the macaw can only flutter feebly.

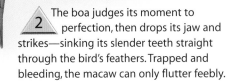

**3** The boa goes in for the kill, looping its coils around the hapless bird and slowly piling on the pressure. As it squeezes harder, life ebbs slowly from its breathless prey until, finally, the snake can begin to swallow its meal headfirst.

## Did You Know?

● The heat sensors in the emerald tree boa's lips can detect minute changes of temperature, making the snake incredibly sensitive to the approach of warm-bodied victims.

● Usually, the emerald boa hangs head-down to consume its prey, as it can swallow more easily like this.

● Although an adult emerald tree boa is bright green, its young are often orange or brick-red. This may be a protective device that mimics the color of venomous tree vipers.

● Like other boas, this species has two spurs at the base of its tail: the remains of hindlegs that disappeared during the process of evolution.

● Carlos Linneus gave the emerald boa its Latin name, *Corallus canina*, in 1758. Corallus probably refers to the coral-shaped patterns he saw on some forms. *Canina* means "of dogs," due to the shape of the boa's wide head and its long, dog-like teeth.

# RATTLESNAKE

**Latin name:** *Crotalus atrox*

**RATTLE**

This is a series of horny shells that fit loosely inside one another. They rattle when the snake vibrates its tail—which it does faster than the human eye can follow when it is disturbed.

**HEAT SENSORS**

Two pits, one in front of each eye, detect the glow of body heat.

**EYES**

Each eye has a vertically slit pupil that opens wide in the dark to let in faint light.

**MARKINGS**

The snake has a distinctive diamond pattern on its back. This helps to camouflage it while it rests or waits in ambush.

When walking in the American West it's vital to tread cautiously, especially if you hear a sinister rattle. Ignoring this snake's trademark warning is a mistake so serious it's rarely repeated. Many predators out west relish eating snakes, but few go one-to-one with a western diamondback rattler. This big snake isn't afraid to fight its ground—hardly surprising, considering its weaponry.

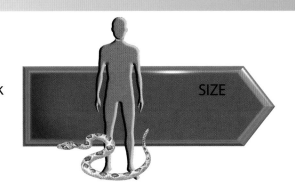

SIZE

## KEY DATA

| | |
|---|---|
| LENGTH | 29in–6ft 6in (75cm–2.1m) |
| WEIGHT | Up to 12lb (5kg ) |
| WEAPONS | Fangs, venom, stealth |
| PREY | Small mammals, birds and lizards |
| LIFESPAN | 30 years in captivity |

The western diamondback shakes its rattle from central southern California to the Gulf of Mexico in Texas and northeastern Mexico, and on several small islands in the Gulf of California. It lives mainly in dry areas, especially scrubby ones with rocky outcrops. It is most common in lowlands but is found in mountain ranges up to about 2000m (6560ft).

**1** A coyote scouting for food disturbs a fully grown western diamondback basking in the sun. The coyote's interested—it hasn't eaten since it left its den at dawn and the snake would make the perfect late breakfast.

**2** The rattler rears up as the coyote approaches, and rattles its tail angrily. The coyote decides the annoying rattle is the part to deal with first.

**3** The rattler instantly strikes with its long fangs, pumping a full dose of venom deep into the coyote's flesh. The coyote howls in pain and staggers away to die in agony, leaving the snake to resume sunbathing.

## Did You Know?

● People used to think that rattlers used their rattle to "talk" to each other and "charm" prey, which then walked straight into their open mouth. It's now thought the rattle evolved to ward off bison, which once roamed North America in vast, trampling herds.

● In late fall the western diamondback gathers by the dozen in "dens," to hibernate in a warm huddle. These dens are often close to houses but go unnoticed.

● Often, when the snake emerges from hibernation the first (and last) thing it sees is the barrel of a gun. Each spring, people shoot thousands of western diamondbacks, and even more are caught and killed in front of crowds at rattler "round-ups."

● One reason this rattler is so dangerous is the sheer amount of venom it can inject—as much as a thimbleful if the snake hasn't bitten anything (or anyone) recently.

# AFRICAN EGG-EATING SNAKE
**Latin name:** *Dasypeltis species*

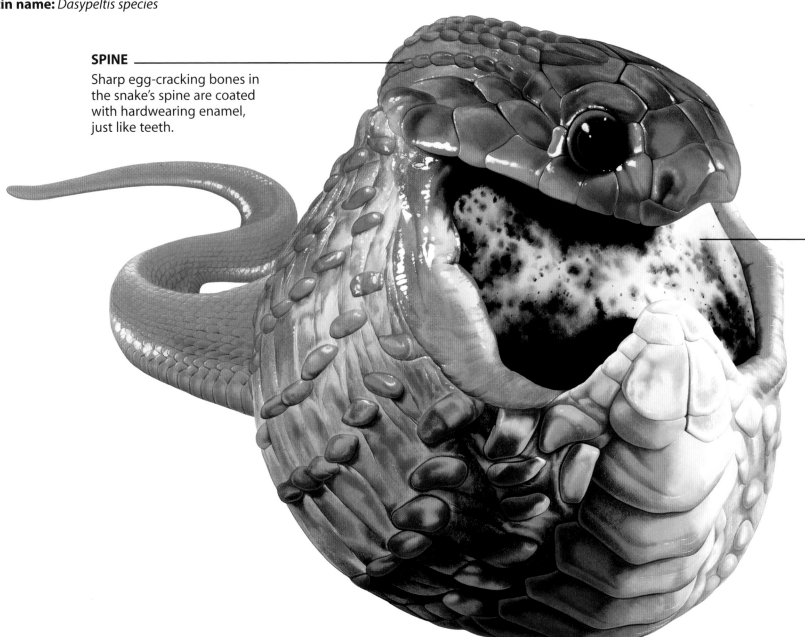

**SPINE**
Sharp egg-cracking bones in the snake's spine are coated with hardwearing enamel, just like teeth.

**TONGUE**
This is the snake's most important sense organ and can lead the reptile to a freshly laid egg from far away.

A s it slithers into the trees late at night, this sneaky thief is after only one thing—a nice fresh bird's egg, which it can gulp down before you can say "omelette." "Tasting" the air with its tongue, the egg-eating snake zeroes in on its target—a well-stocked bird's nest. The egg-eating snake stretches its jaws to the limit as it swallows an egg, then uses its inbuilt food processor to get at the contents.

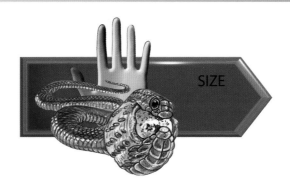

SIZE

## KEY DATA

| | | |
|---|---|---|
| Length | Up to 28in (70cm) | |
| Diet | Birds' eggs | |
| Defenses | Mimics the saw-scaled viper and other venomous snakes | |
| Breeding | Lays 6–25 eggs | |
| Lifespan | Unknown | |

The six species of African egg-eating snake live in forests and scrublands throughout most of southern, eastern, and western Africa, but are absent from the arid northern Saharan areas. Anywhere with large numbers of nesting birds can support this snake.

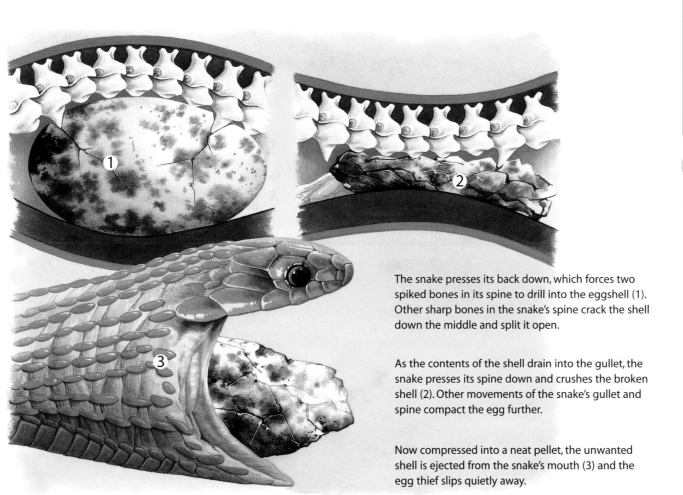

The snake presses its back down, which forces two spiked bones in its spine to drill into the eggshell (1). Other sharp bones in the snake's spine crack the shell down the middle and split it open.

As the contents of the shell drain into the gullet, the snake presses its spine down and crushes the broken shell (2). Other movements of the snake's gullet and spine compact the egg further.

Now compressed into a neat pellet, the unwanted shell is ejected from the snake's mouth (3) and the egg thief slips quietly away.

## Did You Know?

● Although the egg-eating snake is widespread throughout most of Africa, it is quite uncommon. This is because eggs are a seasonal food, so there are never enough of them at any one time to support a lot of egg-eaters living close together.

● There is also an Indian egg-eating snake, but it is so rare that little is known about its lifestyle, habitat, or self-defense measures.

● The African egg-eating snake only mimics a deadly snake, such as the saw-scaled viper, if it lives in the same neighborhood. The ruse works best if its enemies have already had a few scary near misses after tackling the truly venomous reptile.

● The African egg-eating snake only consumes new-laid eggs and rejects all others. Its acute sense of smell can easily recognize the difference between a fresh egg and one that is slightly addled or contains a developing chick.

# GREEN MAMBA

**Latin name:** *Dendroaspis angusticeps & D. viridis*

**HEAD**

This is coffin-shaped—appropriate for a ruthless killer—because of the bulges behind the eyes, where the snake's large venom glands are sited.

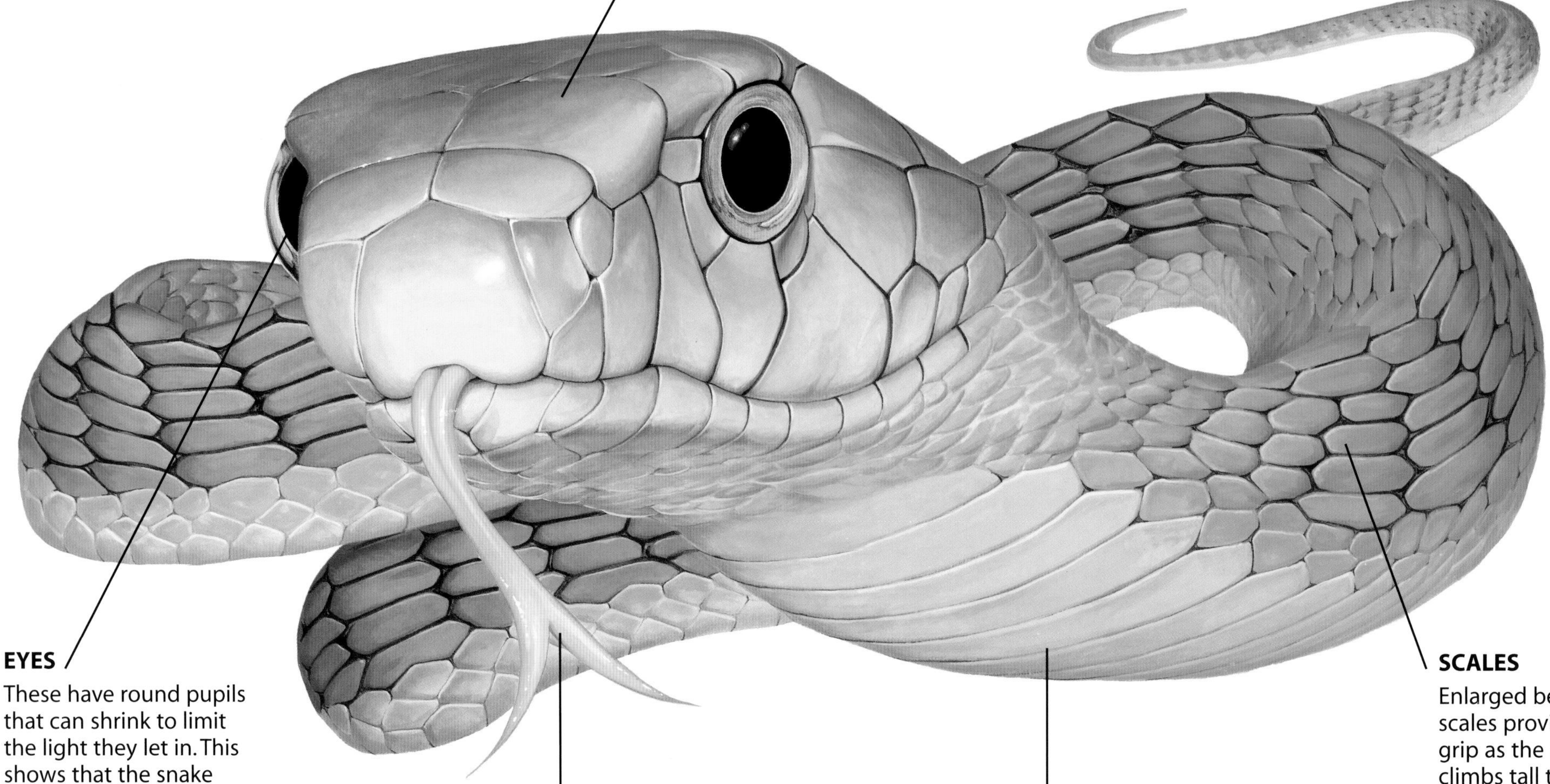

**EYES**

These have round pupils that can shrink to limit the light they let in. This shows that the snake hunts in daylight.

**TONGUE**

The super-sensitive tongue collects tiny scent particles in the air; this enables the hunter to home in on victims hidden in thick vegetation.

**BODY**

The slim body is ideal for chasing prey through trees and shrubs. The green coloring helps to hide the snake among dense foliage.

**SCALES**

Enlarged belly scales provide good grip as the snake climbs tall tree trunks and glides along branches.

This swift, slim African snake spends most of its time high up in the trees. It glides silently along the slender branches as it mercilessly tracks small animals before dispatching them with venom-laden fangs. The green mamba poses its deadliest threat when it slithers into a hut and sets up home inside the thatched roof. The snake sleeps at night with its head hanging down; seeing its outline in the dark, people can make a fatal mistake.

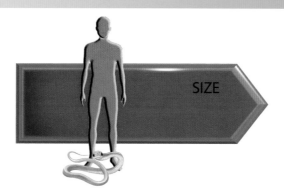

SIZE

## KEY DATA

| | | |
|---|---|---|
| LENGTH | Up to 8ft (2.5m) | |
| PREY | Mainly lizards, birds, and rodents; possibly bats too | The two species of green mamba inhabit humid rainforests in parts of sub-Saharan Africa. The eastern green mamba (*D. angusticeps*) lives in East Africa, from Kenya south to South Africa, and the western green mamba (*D. viridis*) lives in West Africa. |
| WEAPONS | Venom-primed fangs | |
| VENOM | Neurotoxic—often fatal | |
| LIFESPAN | Up to 15 years in captivity | |

**1** It's night, and a green mamba is dozing, with its head dangling through the thatched porch of an unlit hut. The owner returns home and sees what looks like loose thatch—and he reaches out to pull it.

**2** The snake reacts instantly to being grasped by the throat, sinking its fangs into the man's hand. The victim reels away from the attack, clutching his now throbbing limb. He needs a doctor—and fast!

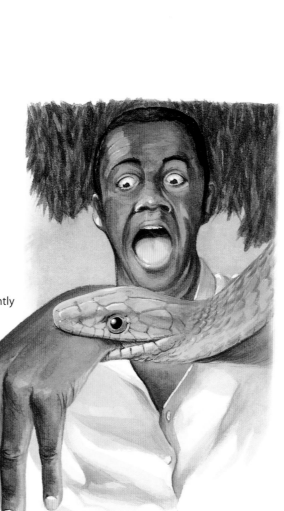

## Did You Know?

● In the breeding season, male green mambas take part in ritual combat "dances" to compete for the right to mate with a female. Two or three male snakes entwine their bodies and then threaten each other with their heads raised.

● Snakes need to shed, or slough, their old, worn skin periodically, to reveal new skin underneath. This is more difficult for tree-living reptiles such as the green mamba, which do not have easy access to jagged rocks and stones that they can rub against. The green mamba gets round this problem by snagging its old skin on a twig and then slowly easing itself out of its unwanted wrapping.

● Green mambas are often found on farm plantations that grow citrus fruits, cashew nuts, coconuts, and mangoes. The snakes are attracted to the plantations by the abundance of prey animals such as rats and birds, which are, in turn, drawn by the plentiful supply of fruit and nuts.

# BLACK MAMBA

**Latin name:** *Dendroaspis polylepis*

**EYES**

The glassy, lidless eyes have round pupils that shrink to limit the light they let in. This shows the snake is a daytime hunter.

**JAWS**

The black mamba's jawbones are only loosely connected, so it can stretch them apart to swallow victims that are much bigger than its own head.

**BODY**

The long, slender body is well suited to chasing prey, unlike the shorter, fatter body of an ambush killer.

**NECK**

When alarmed the snake spreads its neck to make itself look more menacing.

**COLOR**

Dark coloring helps conceal the snake when it is hiding in crevices.

**BELLY SCALES**

Enlarged belly scales help the snake to grip the ground when moving along.

As the biggest venomous snake in Africa, the black mamba's scary reputation is fully justified: if you get too close it will chase you at a phenomenal speed. The black mamba hunts by day over open ground, sliding into a rock crevice or a termite mound to digest its dinner. Usually it avoids people, but if disturbed it performs a terrifying threat display, before lashing out with its lethal fangs.

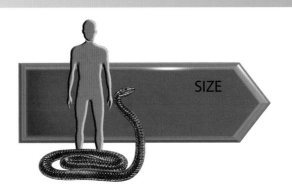

SIZE

## KEY DATA

| | | |
|---|---|---|
| LENGTH | Up to 14ft (4.3m) | |
| PREY | Small mammals and birds | |
| WEAPONS | Venom-laden fangs | |
| TYPICAL ATTACK | Chases a victim at high speed | |
| LIFESPAN | Unknown | |

The black mamba lives in eastern and southern Africa, from Sudan in the north to central South Africa and from Zaïre to Mozambique. The snake inhabits grassy savannahs, clearings, scrub, and open woodlands. At night and after eating a big meal, the mamba takes refuge in dark, secluded places such as caves, rocky crevices, and termite mounds.

**1** Coiled behind a termite mound, a black mamba shelters from the tropical sun, warily watching a group of village youngsters playing football nearby. A mistimed kick sends the ball rolling toward the mound, where it comes to rest at the base.

## Did You Know?

● The black mamba is the fastest of all snakes. The quickest recorded was measured at 10–12mph (16–19km/h) over a short distance. A fit person who gets a head start may be able to outrun a mamba over open ground. But in long grass the snake moves far more quickly than a human.

● Enraged by a man who teased it, a black mamba once chased its tormentor for some distance at a speed of over 7mph (11km/h).

● Despite its deadly bite, the black mamba kills relatively few people each year. This is because it is quite shy and prefers to keep away from places where people live. It is also relatively rare and usually moves away when people approach.

● At more than 12ft 6in (4m) long, the black mamba is one of the largest of all the world's venomous snakes. It is related to the hooded Asian cobra and the banded krait—two of the deadliest snakes in the world.

**2** Shouting excitedly, one player runs over to the mound to retrieve the ball. At that moment the disturbed snake slithers from its hiding place to investigate. Seeing the youth, the killer snake rears up, towering over the terrified teenager. Shrieking, the player turns and runs for his life.

# BOOMSLANG

**Latin name:** *Dispholidus typus*

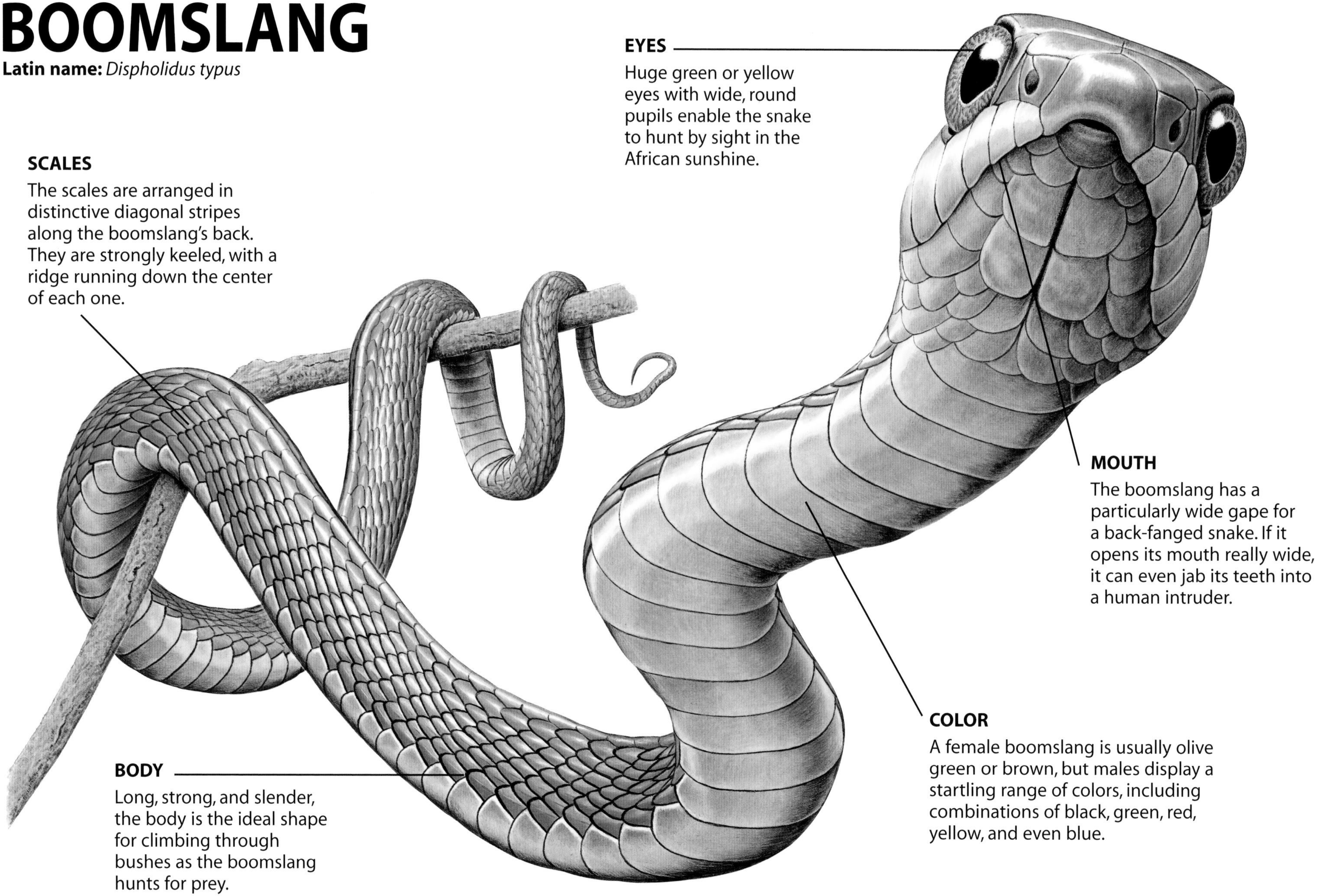

**EYES**

Huge green or yellow eyes with wide, round pupils enable the snake to hunt by sight in the African sunshine.

**SCALES**

The scales are arranged in distinctive diagonal stripes along the boomslang's back. They are strongly keeled, with a ridge running down the center of each one.

**MOUTH**

The boomslang has a particularly wide gape for a back-fanged snake. If it opens its mouth really wide, it can even jab its teeth into a human intruder.

**COLOR**

A female boomslang is usually olive green or brown, but males display a startling range of colors, including combinations of black, green, red, yellow, and even blue.

**BODY**

Long, strong, and slender, the body is the ideal shape for climbing through bushes as the boomslang hunts for prey.

This saucer-eyed tree-snake is feared through much of Africa as a potential killer, for despite its backset fangs, it can still manage to inject a fatal dose of powerful, blood-destroying venom. By day, the boomslang often hangs almost motionless in trees or bushes, waiting patiently for potential victims. Fixing a target with its big, round eyes, it judges the moment to perfection, then launches a sudden, lightning strike.

SIZE

## KEY DATA

| | |
|---|---|
| LENGTH | Up to 6ft 6in (2m) |
| LIFESTYLE | Tree-living predator |
| PREY | Lizards, small mammals, birds, and frogs |
| WEAPONS | Long, grooved fangs at the back of the mouth |
| VENOM | Potent haemotoxins that destroy blood cells |
| TOXICITY | Can be fatal within 24 hours |
| BREEDING | Lays 10–25 eggs |
| LIFESPAN | Unknown |

The boomslang is found through much of Africa south of the Sahara, from Senegal in the west, across to Eritrea in the east, and south to Cape Province. It lives in various habitats, from open forest to scrubland and savannah, but is absent from the thick rainforest of the Congo Basin, mountain grasslands, and the driest areas.

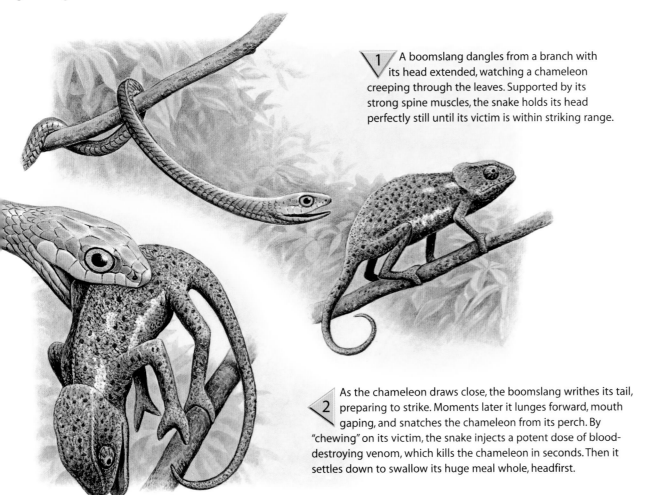

1 A boomslang dangles from a branch with its head extended, watching a chameleon creeping through the leaves. Supported by its strong spine muscles, the snake holds its head perfectly still until its victim is within striking range.

2 As the chameleon draws close, the boomslang writhes its tail, preparing to strike. Moments later it lunges forward, mouth gaping, and snatches the chameleon from its perch. By "chewing" on its victim, the snake injects a potent dose of blood-destroying venom, which kills the chameleon in seconds. Then it settles down to swallow its huge meal whole, headfirst.

## Did You Know?

● The boomslang usually tries to avoid people, but if it does run into trouble, its first instinct is to bluff its way out of danger. Inflating its neck in a threatening display, it stretches the scales apart to reveal the brightly colored skin beneath, hopefully scaring intruders away.

● Although many back-fanged snakes have simple, pointed teeth, the boomslang and a few others have longer fangs with grooves along their length. The venom flows down these grooves when the snake bites.

● Adult boomslangs come in many colors, but juveniles are all the same: with brown heads, white chins, and bodies speckled with brown or gray.

# LONG-NOSED SNAKE

**Latin name:** *Dryophis species*

**TAIL**

The snake grips a branch by coiling its long tail.

**EYES**

The slot-pupilled eyes have special quick-focusing lenses.

**SNOUT**

By looking along the grooves on each side of its snout, the tree snake gets an unimpeded view of its prey.

**COLOR**

Green scales provide excellent camouflage as the snake hangs motionless among the leaves.

**BODY**

Long and slim, the snake's body is flattened from side to side for horizontal strength.

By peering down the grooves on its long snout with its slitted eyes, this absurdly slender but deadly predator targets its unlucky victims with lethal, split-second precision. Tree-living lizards are this snake's favorite prey. The unfortunate lizards often fail to spot the slim, green serpent lurking among the leaves, but it most certainly notices them.

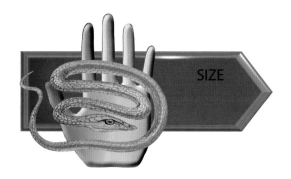

SIZE

## KEY DATA

| | |
|---|---|
| LENGTH | Up to 6ft (1.8m) |
| PREY | Mainly lizards; also birds, bats, and tree-climbing frogs |
| WEAPONS | Back fangs primed with a venom that attacks both blood and flesh |
| BREEDING | Bears up to 24 live young |

Eight species of long-nosed snake live in tropical Asia, where they spend their time in trees and bushes in areas of open forest. Their range extends from India and Sri Lanka, through southern China and Indo-China to the larger islands of southeastern Asia such as Java and Sumatra.

**1** A lizard forages busily up in the trees, searching for insects and other small creatures to snap up. Unfortunately, it's far too preoccupied to notice the long-nosed tree snake dangling motionless within a cluster of leaves, its sensitive long tongue flicking in and out to catch the scent of prey. Soon, the lizard wanders along a branch directly within range of the stealthy serpent.

### Did You Know?

● Although the venom of the long-nosed snake isn't dangerous to humans, a painful swelling may form around a wound, and the area often feels numb.

● When the long-nosed snake feels threatened, it may try to scare off an enemy by flattening its head, gaping its mouth and inflating its body—spreading its scales apart to reveal the bright blue skin beneath.

● The long-nosed snake rarely descends to the ground, and obtains all the water it requires by sipping drops of dew and rain from leaves, and by drinking from the small pools that form in the angles of branches.

● When an object is viewed from different angles its position appears to alter slightly—a phenomenon known as parallax. So when the tree snake is judging the distance of its prey, it may slowly sway its head from side-to-side to check the exact range before launching its attack.

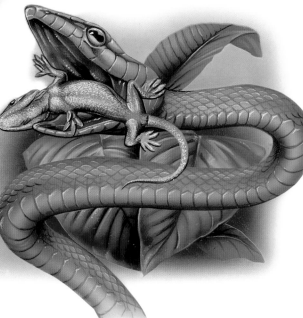

**2** The tree snake stares intently at its victim, peering down its nose and adjusting its eye-lenses to bring the lizard into focus. Thanks to its stereoscopic vision, the snake can judge range perfectly, and darting forward, it snatches the lizard from the branch. Then, it tosses its prey to the back of its mouth and chews, terminating the lizard's struggles with a dose of venom.

# SAW-SCALED VIPER

**Latin name:** *Echis carinatus*

**HEAD**
The head is broad. Some inviduals have a cross pattern on the crown.

**TONGUE**
As in most snakes, the tongue picks up scents from the air and passes them to sensory organs.

**FANGS**
Long, curved fangs stab a victim's skin to inject venom. They're folded back against the palate when not in use.

**PATTERN**
The back is patterned for camouflage, and some individuals have a wavy white line (this snake is also called the "carpet viper").

**SCALES**
Ridged scales on five rows on the flanks make the rasping noise.

**COLORATION**
This viper varies in base color from one individual to another—it can be buff, brown, sandy, or greenish.

Our fear of snakes is deep-rooted and ancient. And in most cases this dread is unfounded, but the saw-scaled viper is deservedly labeled public enemy number one. It's a killer on a simply massive scale. In India they call this snake the "phoorsa," a name that conjures up the crackling, fizzing sound made as it rubs its scaly coils together. It's a terrifying noise, especially for those whose daily work sends them into its domain.

SIZE

## KEY DATA

| | |
|---|---|
| LENGTH | Up to 3ft (90cm) |
| YOUNG | 4–16 per year |
| HOSTILE TACTICS | Scale-rasping, followed by multiple rapid strikes |
| VENOM | Cytotoxic (cell-killing) |
| LIFESPAN | Up to 2 years |

This snake occurs in drier parts of northern Africa and southern Asia—from the Sahara, across the Middle East, to Pakistan, India, and Burma (Myanmar). Experts disagree on how many species exist across this range.

**1** In many lands people rely on firewood for their cooking fuel, so someone has to collect it. In India a man walks into a patch of scrub with his barrow, and disturbs a saw-scaled viper. The angered snake rubs its coils noisily together.

**2** Since his boyhood the farmer has learnt to dread this awful sound, and he reacts at once. So, luckily for him, the snake's first strike just misses his leg. This time, the man will escape to tell his family.

## Did You Know?

● The African egg-eating snake (*Dasypeltis scabra*) is harmless to humans. As its name suggests, it steals birds' eggs, cracking them with its tiny teeth. Its only defense against enemies is to rub its scales noisily together. It makes a sound exactly like a saw-scaled viper, so most predators steer well clear of it.

● This snake's venom is especially nasty in the way its effects can develop gradually. At first there is local swelling, pain, and bleeding gums—but internal bleeding may erupt as much as two weeks later. In one case in 1971, a 10-year-old Indian boy was bitten on the foot. He was treated and sent home—and four months later, he died.

● A report in 1964 estimated that each year in India up to 300,000 people are bitten by snakes, nearly 10 percent dying from the bite. As well as the saw-scaled viper, India's killer snakes include the cobra and king cobra, krait, and Russell's viper.

# RAINBOW BOA

**Latin name:** *Epicrates cenchria*

**SKIN**
The colored scales have a thin coating of transparent skin. Light reflects off both skin layers, and the two reflections clash with each other to produce "interference" color. This is what creates the dazzling rainbow effect.

**BODY**
The snake uses the powerful muscles of its long body to suffocate prey to death.

**TAIL**
The tail is prehensile—capable of grasping—and helps the snake climb through bushes and trees, as high as the jungle canopy.

**EYES**
The pupils open wide to gather light at night, closing to narrow slits by day.

**TONGUE**
The tongue picks up scent traces and passes them to a special sense organ in the mouth, where they are analyzed.

Although it gleams with magical color by day, the rainbow boa is really a creature of the night: a hunter that stalks its prey through the steamy forests of the American tropics. Small mammals are quick on their feet, but by lying in wait on the forest floor the rainbow boa can often catch them off-guard. Tree-living animals such as small monkeys are particularly out of their element on the forest floor.

SIZE

## KEY DATA

| | | | |
|---|---|---|---|
| LENGTH | 35in–6ft 6in (90cm–2m) | | |
| WEIGHT | Up to 11lb (4.5kg) | | |
| PREY | Small mammals and birds | | |
| SENSORS | Heat-sensitive facial pits | | The rainbow boa is common and widespread through Central and South America, from Costa Rica south to Argentina, and from the Pacific to the Atlantic coasts. |
| WEAPONS | Long fangs and constricting coils | | |
| TYPICAL ATTACK | Fast strike from ambush during hours of darkness | | |
| BREEDING | Up to 30 live young | | |
| LIFESPAN | Up to 20 years in captivity | | |

1 Coiled in the shadows among the dense vegetation of a forest clearing, a hungry rainbow boa watches patiently and intently as a foraging squirrel monkey drops to the ground. Eventually the little monkey wanders into the snake's range.

2 With lightning speed the snake uncoils and strikes. Its long fangs punch through the victim's fur and flesh. Rapidly the snake entwines the gasping mammal in its coils. Squeezing tight, the predator gradually suffocates the life from the monkey, then prepares to swallow the meal whole—headfirst.

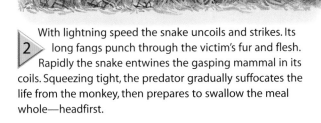

## Did You Know?

● Snake fanciers often keep rainbow boas as pets, even though the snakes can be a little nervous and inclined to bite their owners.

● There are at least nine races of rainbow boa in the wild, each created by local populations breeding in isolation. And some entirely new varieties have been produced from captive-bred pets.

● Although they work only at quite close range, the heat sensors on a rainbow boa's lips can detect minute heat increases in temperature.

● The rainbow boa can survive several days without eating at all.

# ANACONDA
**Latin name:** *Eunectes species*

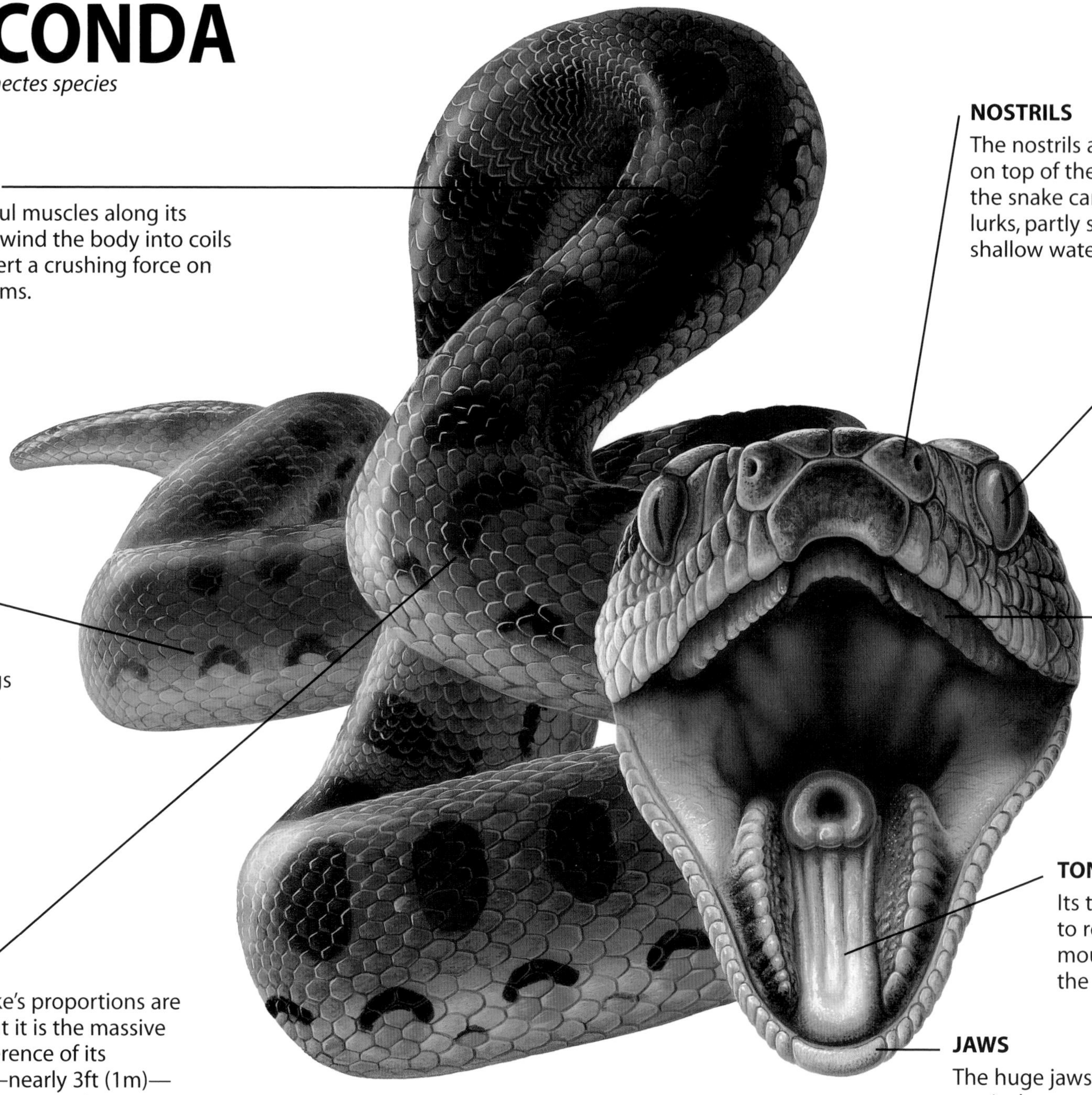

**COILS**

Powerful muscles along its length wind the body into coils and exert a crushing force on its victims.

**NOSTRILS**

The nostrils are positioned on top of the flat head so the snake can breathe as it lurks, partly submerged, in shallow water.

**EYES**

The snake's vertical pupils allow it to take in the maximum available light, so it can hunt at night.

**COLORING**

The muddy coloring and blotchy markings help to camouflage the anaconda in the murky shallows.

**TEETH**

The jaws are lined with many backward-pointing teeth. There is a double row of teeth on the upper jaw and a single row on the lower jaw.

**TONGUE**

Its tongue transfers airborne scents to receptors in the roof of the mouth. When not in use, as here, the tongue retracts into a sheath.

**GIRTH**

The snake's proportions are huge, but it is the massive circumference of its middle—nearly 3ft (1m)—that is so astounding.

**JAWS**

The huge jaws spring back to create an almost vertical gape, and dislocate so that the snake can swallow prey wider than its body.

Stalking its prey in the swamps and rivers of tropical South America, the giant anaconda is a living legend—the main source of terrifying reports of monster-sized jungle serpents. Sleek and deadly, the anaconda is too bulky to move easily over dry land, but in water it's a streamlined assassin. Gliding swiftly and silently, it strikes like lightning, catching its victims in the shallows or close to the water's edge.

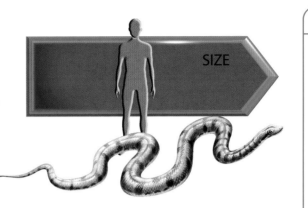

SIZE

## KEY DATA

| | | |
|---|---|---|
| LENGTH | Usually up to 19ft (6m), but possibly up to 27ft (8.5m) | The anaconda ranges across most of the tropical rainforest of South America, east of the Andes, from Venezuela in the north to Paraguay in the south. It is also found on the offshore island of Trinidad. Its favored habitats are swampy savannah, streams, rivers, and lakes. |
| WEIGHT | Up to 551lb (250kg) | |
| PREY | Small to medium-sized mammals, birds, reptiles, and fish | |
| LIFESPAN | Up to 30 years in captivity | |

**1** An anaconda lurks submerged in a stream, until it detects the movement of a caiman. Approaching unseen, the snake grabs the caiman with its powerful jaws and throws its muscular coils tightly round its quarry.

**2** Steadily increasing the pressure, the anaconda squeezes the life out of its prey. Once the caiman is dead, the snake dislocates its jaw and slowly engulfs its victim.

## Did You Know?

● A graceful and economical swimmer, the anaconda often simply drifts downstream in search of new hunting grounds, before gliding into shallow water near the bank.

● The anaconda is most active at night. During the day it prefers to rest in shallow water or drape over low-hanging branches, where people passing by sometimes mistake it for trailing vegetation.

● When mating, as many as 12 male anacondas at a time wrap themselves around a big female. This huge living, "breeding ball" can stay knotted for up to four weeks. Each male makes tiny movements as it tries to inch itself into the best position to mate—and wrestle the competition out of the way.

● Anacondas give birth to live young, producing 30 to 80 offspring at a time. At 28in (70cm) in length, each newborn animal is about the length of a full-grown adder.

# RINGHALS
**Latin name:** *Hemachatus haemachatus*

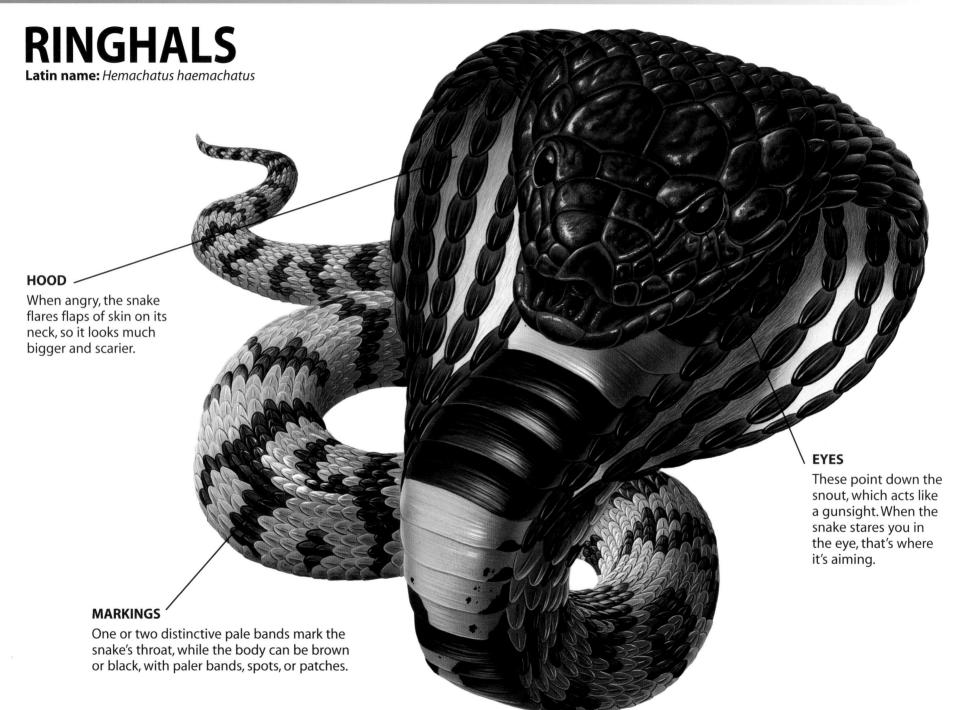

**HOOD**

When angry, the snake flares flaps of skin on its neck, so it looks much bigger and scarier.

**EYES**

These point down the snout, which acts like a gunsight. When the snake stares you in the eye, that's where it's aiming.

**MARKINGS**

One or two distinctive pale bands mark the snake's throat, while the body can be brown or black, with paler bands, spots, or patches.

Armed with specially adapted fangs, this boldly marked African serpent sprays venom in an enemy's face. A well-aimed spurt leaves you reeling in pain, screaming, and clutching your eyes. A ringhals doesn't spray people as a matter of course: venom is too precious. If disturbed, it prefers to try to scare the intruder, or play dead until they go away— but this last ploy doesn't always work…

SIZE

**1** A ringhals sunbathing on open ground feels the footsteps of an approaching boy. With nowhere to hide, the snake flops on to its back and freezes as if it were dead. Feigning death is a way of repelling predators that prefer their meat live and kicking—but this time the sham backfires spectacularly.

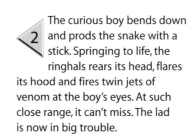

**2** The curious boy bends down and prods the snake with a stick. Springing to life, the ringhals rears its head, flares its hood and fires twin jets of venom at the boy's eyes. At such close range, it can't miss. The lad is now in big trouble.

## KEY DATA

| | |
|---|---|
| LENGTH | Up to 5ft (1.5m); average 3ft (1m) |
| PREY | Mainly small mammals, birds, and amphibians |
| WEAPONS | Fixed fangs primed with nerve-attacking venom |
| DEFENSES | Spits venom at eyes, which can result in blindness |

The ringhals is found in eastern parts of southern Africa, as far north as the eastern highlands of Zimbabwe. It ranges from lowland swamps to dry, mountain slopes up to 7378ft (2500m) above sea level.

## Did You Know?

● "Ringhals" is sometimes spelled "rinkhals" and is Afrikaans for "ring neck"— a reference to the pale band or bands on the snake's throat.

● Spitting snakes probably evolved their unusual means of defense for the same reasons rattlesnakes most likely evolved rattles. Painful sprays and noisy rattles are both good ways of stopping big animals such as buffalo accidentally trampling you to death. And by not always having to bite in self-defense, the snakes reduce the risk of losing their fangs.

● Africa has many elapid snakes (snakes with fixed, front fangs), all venomous, but the ringhals is the only one that gives birth to live young—up to 50 at a time.

● Dangerous though it may be, the ringhals faces an array of mortal enemies, especially when young. One extra-large African bullfrog was once found to have consumed an entire litter of 16 newborn snakes.

# BUSHMASTER

**Latin name:** *Lachesis muta*

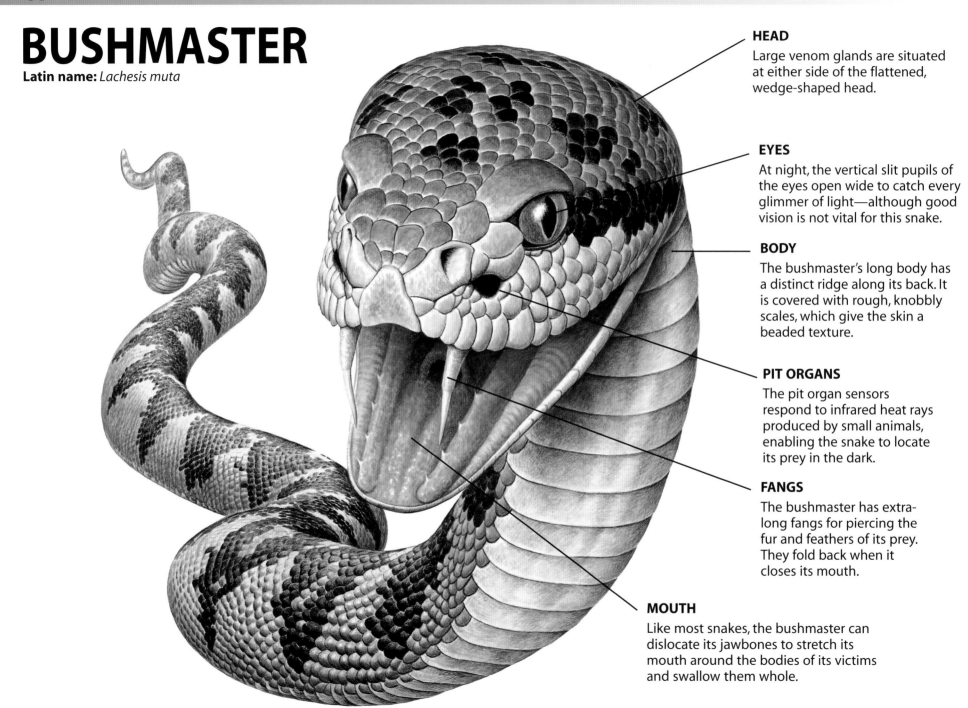

### HEAD
Large venom glands are situated at either side of the flattened, wedge-shaped head.

### EYES
At night, the vertical slit pupils of the eyes open wide to catch every glimmer of light—although good vision is not vital for this snake.

### BODY
The bushmaster's long body has a distinct ridge along its back. It is covered with rough, knobbly scales, which give the skin a beaded texture.

### PIT ORGANS
The pit organ sensors respond to infrared heat rays produced by small animals, enabling the snake to locate its prey in the dark.

### FANGS
The bushmaster has extra-long fangs for piercing the fur and feathers of its prey. They fold back when it closes its mouth.

### MOUTH
Like most snakes, the bushmaster can dislocate its jawbones to stretch its mouth around the bodies of its victims and swallow them whole.

The fallen leaves beneath the trees of the American rainforest conceal a fearsome killer: a huge viper armed with extra-long fangs that inject a caustic venom. Instead of giving birth to live young like other pit vipers, a female bushmaster lays eggs. And while most snakes leave their young to fend for themselves, she guards her eggs fiercely. The female bushmaster will carry out a lightning defensive strike if anyone comes close to her nest.

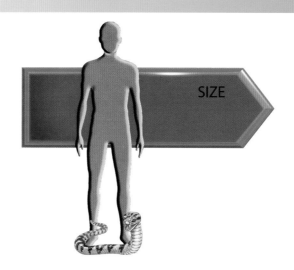

SIZE

## KEY DATA

| | |
|---|---|
| LENGTH | 7 ft 6in–11ft 6in (2.4–3.5m) |
| WEIGHT | |
| PREY | Small mammals, |
| DIET | birds, and reptiles |
| ATTACK BREEDING | Single bite, injecting venom |
| EGGS LIFESPAN | Average 12 per brood |
| LIFESPAN | Unknown |

The bushmaster lives in areas of lowland rainforest and the surrounding fields and cleared areas. Its range stretches south from Costa Rica in Central America, across most of South America north of the Amazon Basin from western Ecuador and Peru. It is also found in the coastal forests of eastern Brazil.

**1** Despite the warmth of the rainforest, the female's eggs take about two months to develop and hatch. She remains coiled around them on the forest floor for much of this time, guarding her clutch from potential enemies such as rats or other snakes.

**2** The female is particularly aggressive at this time, and any intrusion triggers her defensive instincts. When she is alerted by the footsteps of a local farmer strolling close to her nest, she breaks from cover and slithers rapidly to the attack.

**3** Before the farmer can react, she bares her great fangs and plunges them deep into his leg, pumping in a large dose of her corrosive venom. This destroys flesh and blood vessels, and if no antidote is available, may ultimately be fatal.

## Did You Know?

● The bushmaster's most important sense organs are the heat-sensitive pits behind its nostrils. Covering its eyes has little effect, but when the pits are plugged, it can barely hunt.

● Although the bushmaster kills larger prey with venom, it frequently swallows smaller animals alive.

● When the bushmaster wants to warn away an enemy it thrashes at nearby plants with its tail, making a sound a bit like a rattlesnake with the burr-like arrangement of scales at the tip. It often tries this before it bites, as it prefers to save its venom.

● In some areas, the bushmaster is known as the pineapple snake, because of its rough, lumpy scales. Its Latin name translates as "silent fate," as the snake sometimes strikes without any audible warning.

● Unlike many pit vipers, the bushmaster is more heavily marked on its back rather than its flanks.

# CORAL SNAKE

**Latin name:** *Micrurus species*

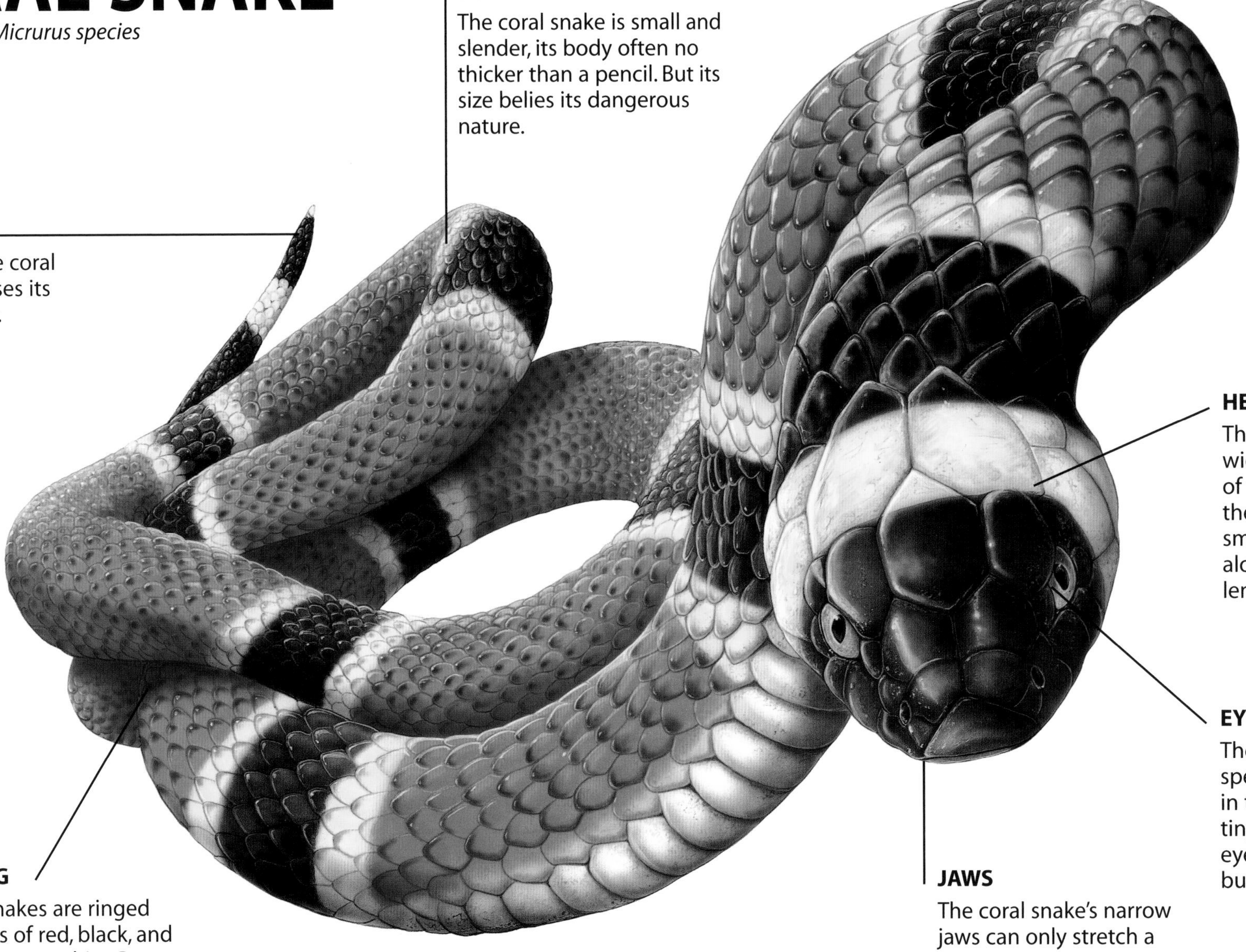

**BODY**

The coral snake is small and slender, its body often no thicker than a pencil. But its size belies its dangerous nature.

**TAIL**

If attacked, the coral snake often uses its tail as a decoy.

**HEAD**

The head is barely wider than the rest of the body, making the coral snake smoothly cylindrical along its entire length.

**EYES**

The coral snake spends most of its life in the dark, and has tiny, inconspicuous eyes like those of burrowing snakes.

**JAWS**

The coral snake's narrow jaws can only stretch a limited distance, so it feeds on relatively small animals.

**COLORING**

All coral snakes are ringed with bands of red, black, and either yellow or white. But the precise combination of colors and widths varies from species to species.

Ringed with gleaming bands of brilliant color, the coral snake is an alluring sight. But don't be fooled by its beauty—anyone touching its slender coils runs the risk of a lethal bite. The coral snake's jaws limit its biting chances. It usually nips fingers or toes, and must hang on for several moments to inject a full dose of venom with its tiny fangs. But even though the fangs are relatively small, a full dose is quite enough to kill.

SIZE

## KEY DATA

| | | |
|---|---|---|
| LENGTH | Average 20–39in (50–100cm); occasionally up to 5ft (1.5m) | The only front-fanged snakes in the Americas, their range stretches from southern USA to northern Argentina. There are 61 species, living in a range of habitats: dry deserts, grassy fields, wetland margins, and dense forests. The greatest species variety is found in the hardwood rainforests of Central and South America. |
| PREY | Other snakes, lizards, frogs, birds, and insects | |
| WEAPONS | Small, fixed, venomous fangs at the front of the mouth | |
| LIFESPAN | Up to 7 years | |

**1** All seems tranquil in the leafy suburbs as a woman reaches down to collect some timber from a woodpile in her garden. But she fails to notice a telltale flash of color: the tail of a coral snake hiding among the logs. Disturbed from its slumbers, the snake initially slips farther into its refuge in an effort to avoid the intrusion—but it can only wriggle so far.

**2** Stretching her hand down one last time, the woman grips a final piece of wood. But as her fingers brush against the snake, it strikes in an instant, sinking its fangs into the tip of her finger. Screaming with pain, she pulls her arm violently back, only to find the serpent still hanging from her finger.

## Did You Know?

● The coral snake's bright colors have earned it various alternative names, including "harlequin snake" and "candy-stick snake." Other names such as "American cobra" reflect the darker side of its character.

● The record size for a coral snake is held by the Amazonian species *Micrurus spixii*, which occasionally grows to 5ft (1.5m) in length.

● If threatened at close range, the eastern coral snake *Micrurus fulvius* not only diverts attention from its head by raising and writhing its tail, but also expels air from its tail vent, making a bubbly, popping sound.

● In North America, coral snakes are the only venomous snakes to lay eggs instead of bearing live young.

● As well as eating other snakes, coral snakes happily eat each other. In the breeding season this can lead to problems, as a pair are as likely to end up fighting as they are mating.

# CARPET PYTHON

**Latin name:** *Morelia spilota variegata*

## SCALES

Despite its size, the carpet python is amazingly skilled at climbing trees. It can even climb vertically up a tree trunk, using the large, flat scales on its belly to anchor itself to the bark.

## BODY

The carpet python is a powerful snake, but it has a thin body compared to other constrictors.

## TEETH

This snake has a formidable set of razor-sharp teeth, in several rows.

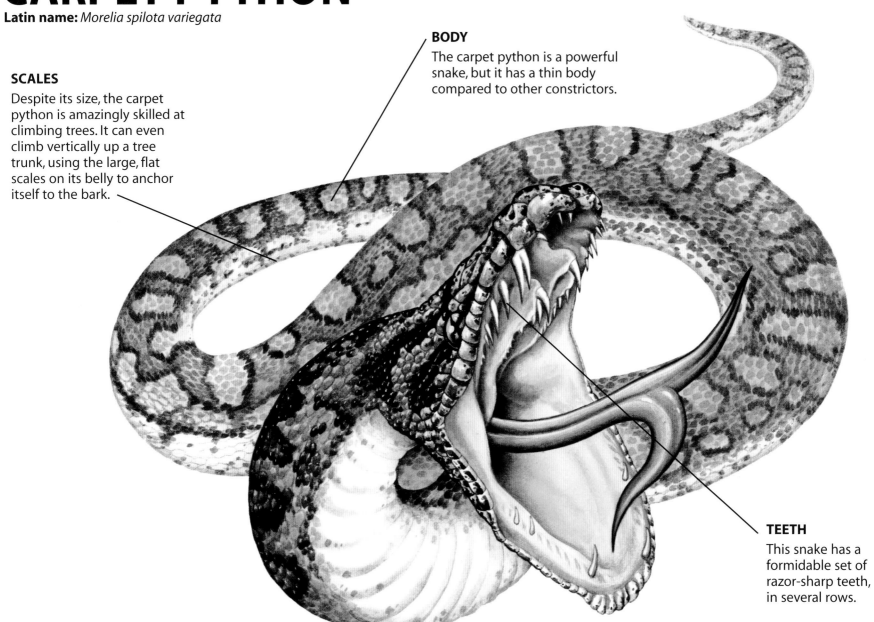

The carpet python is not quite as large as some other constrictors, but it spells trouble for possums and other creatures. In the night, a carpet python rests in a tree. A possum does not notice the well-camouflaged python, but the python senses its prey through smell and body heat. With dozens of sharp teeth, it chomps down on the possum and coils around it for a deadly squeeze.

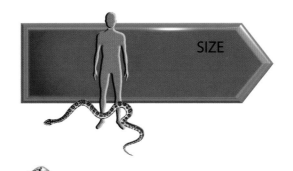

SIZE

### KEY DATA

| | |
|---|---|
| LENGTH | Between 4ft 6in (140cm) and 6ft 3in (190cm) |
| WEIGHT | No information available |
| PREY | Variety of birds and mammals, including marsupials |
| LIFESPAN | Between 20 and 30 years in captivity. |

The carpet python is widespread in much of Australia and New Guinea. There are several closely related species of carpet pythons throughout this vast range.

**1** Carpet pythons can be found in many kinds of environments, from wooded grasslands to thick jungle. They do not live, however, in places without trees or bushes.

**2** These snakes can be a variety of colors and patterns. They are often beige or brownish, with beautiful patterns of dark patches and stripes. Some are almost pink, and others are yellowish. Scientists think this variety comes from the snakes adapting to the many kinds of environments in which they live.

**3** The python has good camouflage. It can lie hidden for hours, waiting patiently to ambush its prey. The snake mainly feeds on birds and mammals, especially possums.

### Did You Know?

● A female carpet python lays its eggs in secluded places, such as hollow logs or holes in trees. It then coils around the eggs to protect them. The snake warms the eggs by contracting the powerful muscles in its body.

● The python can lay almost 20 eggs. How warm an egg gets determines if the baby snake will be male or female.

● Because they have beautiful markings and are mostly mild-mannered, carpet pythons have become popular as pets. As with most snakes, however, you must always be careful where you put your fingers during feeding time!

● Carpet pythons get their name from their colorful markings, which resemble the designs of oriental carpets.

# ASIAN COBRA
**Latin name:** *Naja naja*

**NECK**
Specially elongated ribs support the flaps of skin along the creature's neck that give the snake its hood.

**HOOD MARKINGS**
The hood may bear a single eyespot or a pair. Alternatively, it may bear a horseshoe shape or a banded pattern.

**FANGS**
The cobra's fangs are fixed in place at the front of its mouth, and thus always ready to make a stabbing bite.

**BODY**
Smooth-scaled and cylindrical, the Asian cobra is equally well-adapted to moving around in fields as well as near areas of human habitation.

**COLOR**
The cobra's coloring varies, but it is usually yellowish, black, or dark brown, with lighter markings on the throat.

As if having a deadly bite isn't scary enough, this viciously venomous snake spreads out its hooded neck to make itself look even bigger and more menacing. Asian cobras often make their homes near human habitations or in cultivated areas, turning up in villages, towns, and cities. Here they lurk threateningly among building foundations or debris—ready to strike at any intruders.

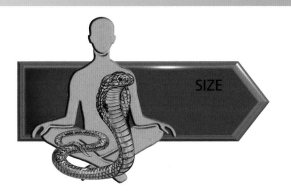

SIZE

## KEY DATA

| | |
|---|---|
| LENGTH | Up to 6ft 6in (2m) |
| NUMBER OF SUB-SPECIES | 7 |
| PREY | Snakes, lizards, and other reptiles, frogs, birds, and their eggs, small mammals and large insects |
| WEAPONS | Venom-primed fangs |
| TYPICAL ATTACK | Single strike |
| TOXICITY | Neurotoxic venom causes breathing and heart difficulties |

The Asian cobra is found throughout southern and southeastern Asia, from India, Pakistan and Sri Lanka east to southern China and south to the Malay archipelago and the islands of the Philippines.

**1** In a Sri Lankan paddy field, rice-pickers are hard at work. Unknowingly, one woman moves too close to a resting Asian cobra, which rears up in a typical threat posture just out of her sight.

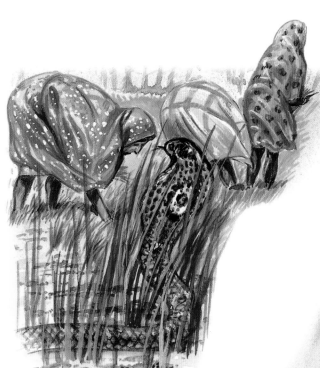

**2** The woman does not see the snake and so carries on picking. Mistaking this for a sustained threat, the cobra feels it has no other option but to strike, sinking its fangs into the picker's lower arm. The woman's screams bring fellow workers rushing to her side, but unless they can get urgent medical help, she is doomed.

## Did You Know?

● When Portuguese settlers established trading outposts in India early in the 16th century, they encountered a snake that they called *Cobra de capello*, meaning "snake with a hood." In time, British travelers and traders used the name cobra for any hooded snake they found in Asia and Africa.

● In India, people sometimes organize fights between cobras and their natural enemies, mongooses, for public entertainment.

● Some cobras squirt their venom straight into an enemy's eyes from several feet away, instead of biting. The toxins cause pain and temporary blindness when they score a hit.

# BLACKNECK COBRA

**Latin name:** *Naja nigricollis*

## HEAD

When the blackneck spits at an intruder it uses its snout rather like a gunsight, peering down its long nose to aim with unnerving accuracy.

## THROAT

The snake's latin name nigricollis means "black neck," and refers to the black bands running across its throat.

## HOOD

Like most cobras, the blackneck can spread the long ribs of its neck, stretching the loose skin to create a menacing "hood."

## COLOR

Blacknecks are usually dull brown with a yellowish belly, but they can vary greatly in color. One subspecies is banded with black and white, and another is rusty-red—especially in areas of reddish soil.

Accidentally disturb this venomous snake and what seems like plenty of space between you and it, is no guarantee of safety, for it has a devilish way of defending itself. Most of us enjoy playing with water-pistols, but this snake goes way too far with the squirters, especially if you catch it unawares in the African bush. It's capable of emitting a devastating spray of venom that can travel impressive distances—so watch out…

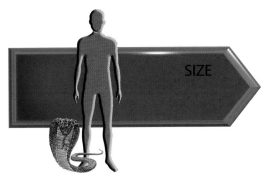

SIZE

## KEY DATA

| | |
|---|---|
| LENGTH | Up to 9ft (2.8m) |
| PREY | Small mammals, birds, eggs, frogs, toads, lizards, snakes, insects |
| VENOM | Both cytotoxic (kills cells) and neurotoxic (affects nervous system) |
| TYPICAL ATTACK | Rapid bite injects venom into prey |
| TYPICAL DEFENSE | Spreads hood, squirts venom—usually at the intruder's face |
| LIFESPAN | 22 years in captivity |

The blackneck spitting cobra and its various subspecies are widespread across much of mainland Africa, and are also found on several offshore islands. They lurk in a broad range of habitats, from thick woodland to dry scrub and semidesert, only avoiding areas of dense rainforest and the most arid desert regions.

1 Rumbling along in their safari jeep, two tourists make their way across the grassy savannah of Kenya. Soon, one of them spots a snake dozing in the sun, and believing themselves safe in the confines of their jeep they pull up for a closer look. Unfortunately, they've disturbed a blackneck cobra, which rears up angrily and spreads its hood in threat.

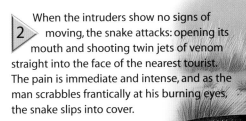

2 When the intruders show no signs of moving, the snake attacks: opening its mouth and shooting twin jets of venom straight into the face of the nearest tourist. The pain is immediate and intense, and as the man scrabbles frantically at his burning eyes, the snake slips into cover.

## Did You Know?

● Baby blackneck cobras are only about 10in (25cm) long on hatching, and usually need several weeks to perfect their spitting skills. But some have been known to start spraying venom while only half-out of the egg.

● Captive blacknecks soon stop bothering to spray venom, but they can keep you on your toes. In 1999, a zoo-keeper in San Antonio, Texas, was trying to feed a blackneck when the snake lunged past the rodent in his tongs and bit his hand instead. Fortunately, he lived to tell the tale.

● If you're sprayed by a blackneck you should quickly flush your eyes with water. If none is available, you can use beer, milk, or urine instead.

# TIGER SNAKE

**Latin name:** *Notechis scutatus*

## BODY

The body is thicker and stouter than that of many other snakes. The tiger snake flattens its entire body when basking in sunshine or when threatened.

## HEAD

The head is flat and blunt, widening out behind the eyes but merging back into the body without forming a distinct neck.

## COLORING

The snake has 40 to 50 yellow or cream cross-bands along its back. These contrast with the background color, which may be brown, olive, or green.

When this snake flattens its neck and hisses, it's time to beat a retreat, for the enraged beast is just moments away from unleashing a devastating strike. And its venom is often lethal. One of the most tragic tiger-snake deaths was that of a nine-year-old boy from Victoria. Playing truant from school one day, he went off into the bush on his own…

SIZE

## KEY DATA

| | |
|---|---|
| LENGTH | Usually 3ft (1m), but occasionally reaches 6ft 6in (2m) |
| PREY | Mainly frogs; also lizards, rodents, and birds |
| WEAPONS | Venom-primed, ¼in (3–3.5mm) fangs |
| LIFESPAN | Over 17 years in captivity |

The tiger snake occurs throughout much of Victoria, eastern New South Wales, and adjacent parts of South Australia and Queensland. These areas are the most heavily populated parts of the country, which accounts for the large number of victims over the years.

**1** The boy's hobby was snake-catching, but this time he met more than he bargained for. As he sauntered along the track he accidentally stepped on a tiger snake, which instantly launched a vicious counterattack, biting him hard on the lower leg.

**2** Afraid of getting into trouble, the boy didn't go for help immediately, and the venom soon weakened and disoriented him so that he couldn't find his way home.

## Did You Know?

● Deaths from tiger snake bites used to be quite common, especially in remote areas. Today, fatalities are rare, due to tiger snake antivenom. Available since 1929, it was the first antivenom for animal toxins to be widely distributed in Australia.

● The tiger snake has some immunity to the toxins produced by other venomous snakes in Australia. The bite of a death adder, which is dangerous to humans, has little effect on the rugged tiger snake.

● A normal brood of young for a female tiger snake numbers 30 to 40. They are born live after hatching from eggs kept inside their mother's body. Even larger broods can occur, with extremes of up to 80 young per female.

● A tiny drop of tiger snake venom may be fatal to humans.

● The tiger snake often climbs trees to prey on vulnerable nestling birds.

# KING COBRA

**Latin name:** *Ophiophagus hannah*

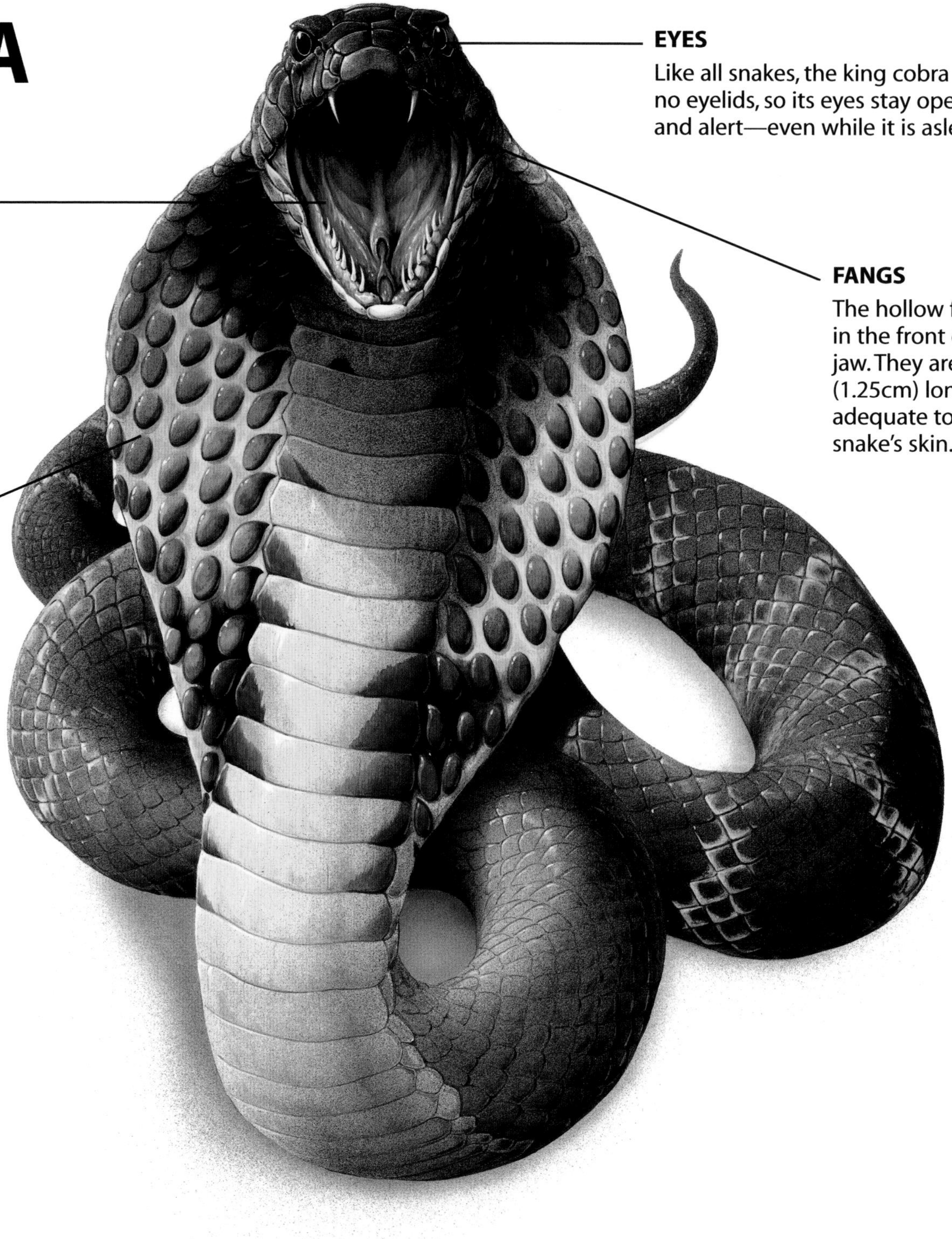

**EYES**

Like all snakes, the king cobra has no eyelids, so its eyes stay open—and alert—even while it is asleep.

**MOUTH**

The cobra's jawbones are only loosely connected, so it can stretch them far apart to engulf large prey whole.

**FANGS**

The hollow fangs are fixed in the front of its upper jaw. They are about ½in (1.25cm) long—more than adequate to pierce another snake's skin.

**HOOD**

The snake flares its hood by flexing its neck ribs.

Coming face to face with a king cobra is a terrifying experience. Rearing angrily above your head, this venomous giant won't hesitate to strike if you don't back off immediately. More people fall victim to the fangs of the king cobra in each passing year, as more of its forest home is cut down to make farmland. Far from medical aid, few of those bitten have any hope of surviving.

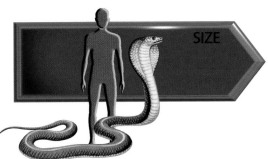

SIZE

Planting seed in a newly cleared patch of forest, a lone village boy disturbs a full-grown female king cobra guarding her nest. Instantly she rears off the ground, hissing loudly, flaring her hood, and swaying, to assess the distance to the boy's face. Terror-struck, he staggers back, but the cobra moves with him, advancing on her coils. As he turns to run, she strikes like lightning, injecting a lethal dose of venom—leaving him to die far from home.

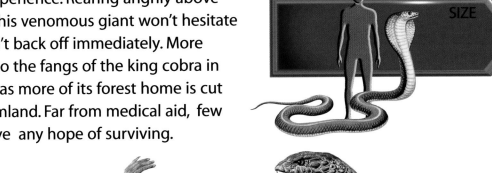

## KEY DATA

| | |
|---|---|
| LENGTH | Up to 18ft (5.7m), but 11ft 6in–12ft 6in (3.5–4m) on average |
| WEIGHT | 5–6kg |
| PREY | Mainly other snakes, including venomous ones; some lizards |
| TYPICAL ATTACK | Single bite |
| VENOM | Nerve toxins injected by fangs; fatal unless treated rapidly with antivenin |
| LIFESPAN | About 20 years |

The king cobra lives in tropical and subtropical forests, and dense scrub across the Indian subcontinent and southern and southeastern Asia, including southern China and the Philippines.

## Did You Know?

● The longest recorded king cobra measured 17ft 6in (5.5m) when captured in Malaysia in 1937. Shipped to London Zoo, it grew to 18ft (5.7m). When World War II began in 1939 its keepers destroyed it, in case the zoo was bombed and it escaped.

● The king cobra is immune to the venom of its own kind, so if one bites another, the venom has no effect.

● A zookeeper once foolishly put a king cobra in a cage overnight with six smaller cobras. By the following morning, it had eaten the lot.

● After one large meal, the king cobra can go for several weeks without needing to hunt again.

# FIERCE SNAKE

**Latin name:** *Oxyuranus microlepidotus*

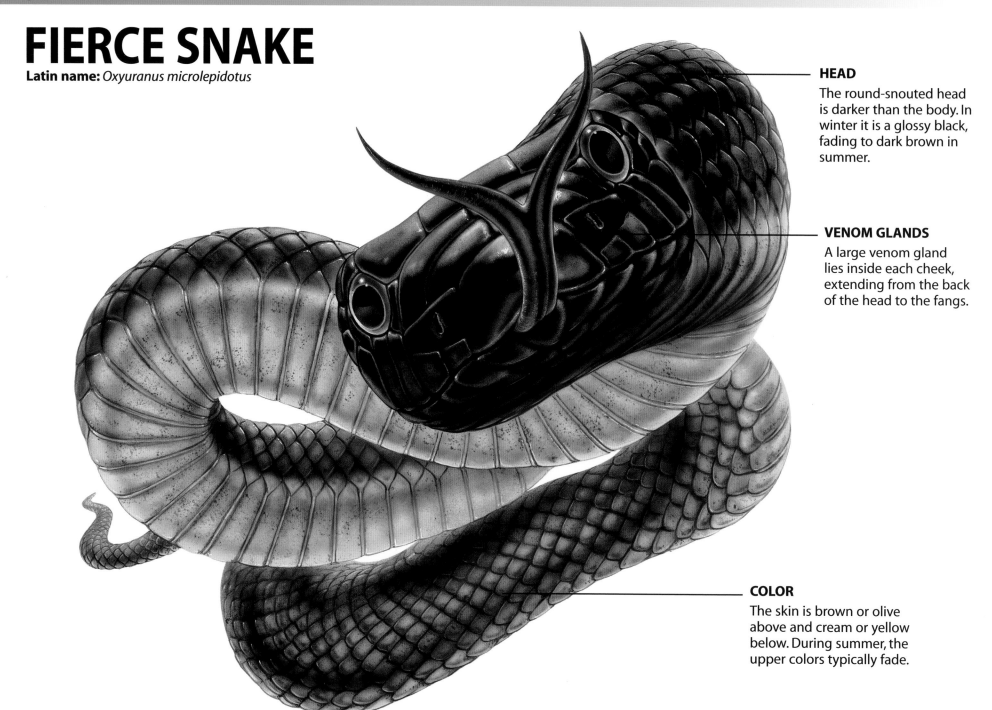

**HEAD**

The round-snouted head is darker than the body. In winter it is a glossy black, fading to dark brown in summer.

**VENOM GLANDS**

A large venom gland lies inside each cheek, extending from the back of the head to the fangs.

**COLOR**

The skin is brown or olive above and cream or yellow below. During summer, the upper colors typically fade.

A world-champion killer, the fierce snake injects prey animals with a venom so strong that it kills in seconds. On the few occasions that it bites people, death can be equally swift. The fierce snake does not have to reach full size to be dangerous. Reptile enthusiasts—herpetologists—who keep specimens can get a nasty shock from young snakes that appear quite harmless.

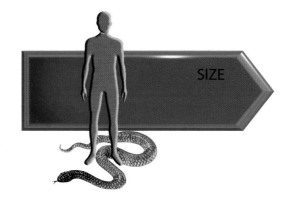

SIZE

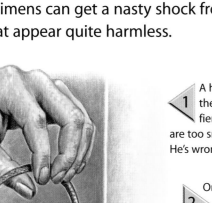

1 A herpetologist thinks the three-week-old fierce snakes he's bred are too small to cause harm. He's wrong…

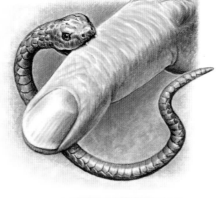

2 On being handled, a baby snake instinctively jabs its tiny fangs into one of the man's fingers. The snake may be just a tiddler, but its venom glands are already primed with terrible toxins.

3 As the venom takes effect and he starts feeling sick, the herpetologist becomes increasingly scared. So he should be, for without urgent antivenom treatment he could die, even from the bite of such a small specimen. Eventually he calls for an ambulance, but his nervous system is done for and he collapses before the call is finished.

## KEY DATA

| | |
|---|---|
| LENGTH | Up to 8ft (2.5m) |
| PREY | Rodents, small marsupials |
| WEAPONS | Venom-primed fangs |
| VENOM | Coagulants clot a victim's blood, neurotoxins destroy the nervous system, and myolysins attack muscles |

The fierce snake lives on the fringes of Australia's interior desert, in parts of Queensland, New South Wales, Northern Territory, and South Australia, to the west of the mountains known as the Great Dividing Range.

## Did You Know?

● "Discovered" by naturalists in the late 19th century near Adelaide, the fierce snake was barely seen again until 1967. The man who found it then was bitten twice on the thumb. He mistook the culprit for a brown snake, so when rushed to hospital, he received the wrong antivenom. Luckily he eventually recovered, but not before his heart had stopped beating twice.

● This snake is also known as the small-scaled snake or inland taipan, after its closest relative, the taipan, which lives in warm, coastal regions of Australia and New Guinea.

● The venom of the taipan is not as potent as that of the fierce snake, but it can still be lethal for humans. In truth, the taipan is the deadlier snake, since it often occurs around human settlements and bites are relatively common. In Papua New Guinea's Central Province, four out of every five reported snake bites are the work of taipans.

# TAIPAN

**Latin name:** *Oxyuranus scutellatus*

## VENOM

Large venom glands near the taipan's eyes produce a devastating mixture of nerve toxins and tissue-destroying enzymes, which runs down narrow tubes to the tip of the hollow fangs.

## JACOBSON'S ORGAN

As in all snakes, openings in the roof of the taipan's mouth lead to the Jacobson's organ, which analyzes scent particles gathered from the air by the taipan's flickering tongue.

## BODY

The taipan's long, narrow body is well suited to its active lifestyle and enables it to strike from a distance.

## FANGS

At up to $\frac{1}{3}$in (12mm), the taipan's rigid fangs are exceptionally long for a fixed-fang snake, and they are also unusually strong.

One of the world's most dangerous snakes, the taipan strikes swiftly and repeatedly, plunging its fangs deep into its victim to inject large amounts of deadly venom. Even stout boots give little protection from the taipan's long, strong fangs, which shear straight through leather to pierce the flesh underneath. And way out in the Australian outback, the effects of its bite are likely to be lethal.

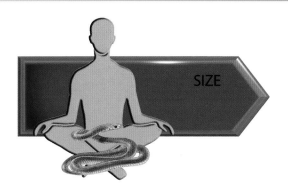

SIZE

**1** As a farmer wanders along out in the bush, he disturbs a taipan. Unable to retreat under cover, the enraged snake hurls itself at the intruder, striking several times with incredible speed and ferocity.

**2** A particularly aggressive bite forces the snake's long fangs through the farmer's boot and thick sock into his leg, pumping venom into his bloodstream. Soon, he will be gripped by bouts of agonizing pain and nausea, and if he can't reach a hospital for a shot of antivenom, he will die from slow suffocation.

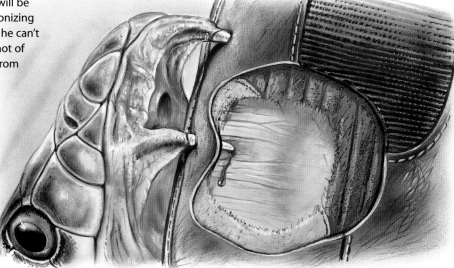

## KEY DATA

| | |
|---|---|
| LENGTH | 6–12ft 6in (2–4m) |
| PREY | Small mammals |
| WEAPONS | Long, venomous fangs |
| TYPICAL ATTACK | Multiple strikes |
| LIFESPAN | 7–9 years |

The taipan is found in southern New Guinea and throughout northeastern Australia, from the fringes of the Kimberley Plateau to the Queensland coast near Brisbane. It inhabits a variety of habitats, from dry plains to open woodland, but although this snake is widespread, it is relatively scarce.

### Did You Know?

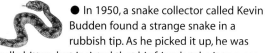

● In 1950, a snake collector called Kevin Budden found a strange snake in a rubbish tip. As he picked it up, he was badly bitten, but insisted that his friends take it to a serum laboratory. Thanks to him, taipan antivenom was discovered, but Kevin died that day.

● In mythical tales, the aboriginal people of Wikmunkan know Taipan as a gigantic serpent that stretches across the sky like a rainbow.

● One of the taipan's victims was a young boy, who died 10 minutes after receiving six bites on his thigh.

● The antivenom for a taipan bite usually saves lives—but in rare instances it causes an extreme allergic reaction in humans known as anaphylactic shock. This can kill.

● Taipans are often kept as "pets" by snake enthusiasts in Australian cities, but as few city doctors keep stocks of taipan antivenom, it is a particularly dangerous hobby.

# MULGA
**Latin name:** *Pseudechis australia*

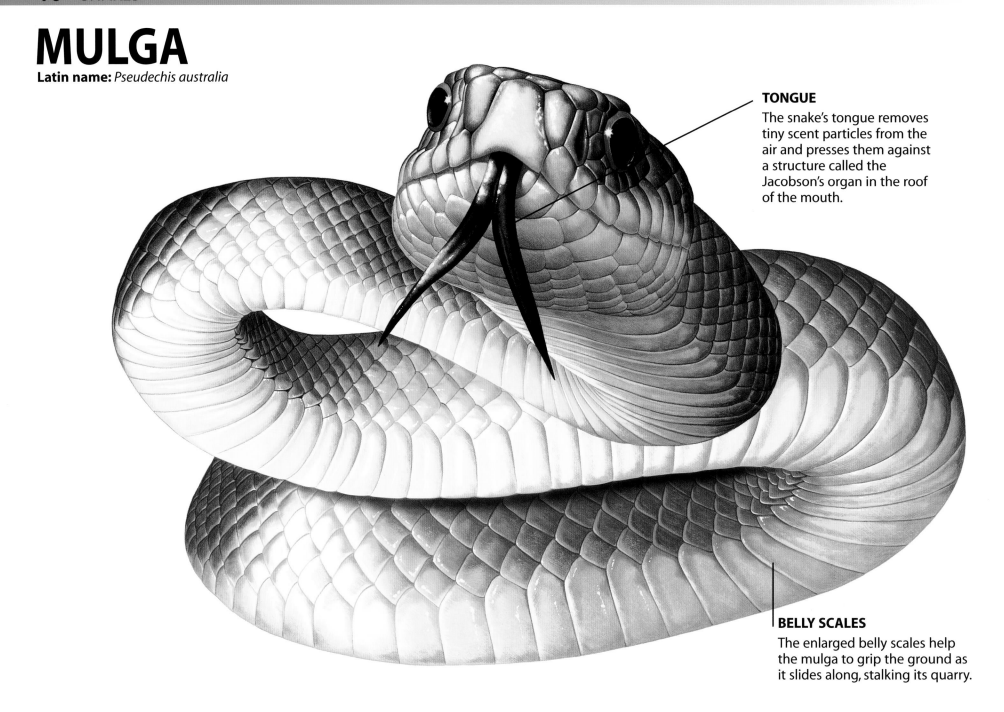

**TONGUE**
The snake's tongue removes tiny scent particles from the air and presses them against a structure called the Jacobson's organ in the roof of the mouth.

**BELLY SCALES**
The enlarged belly scales help the mulga to grip the ground as it slides along, stalking its quarry.

This lurking killer produces more venom than any other Australian snake. Its toxins paralyze all the muscles, including the heart, and cause death unless bite victims get a quick jab of antivenom. The deadly mulga often gets mistaken for a brown snake—a costly error for anyone who is bitten by the reptile and needs an urgent injection of antivenom to survive.

SIZE

## KEY DATA

| | |
|---|---|
| LENGTH | Up to 10ft (3m) Average 5ft (1.5m) |
| PREY | Mainly lizards, rodents, and other small mammals, frogs, birds, and other snakes |
| WEAPONS | Sharp fangs primed with muscle-attacking venom |
| LIFESPAN | Unknown |

The mulga is the most widespread of all the many Australian snakes. It is found in a variety of habitats throughout most of mainland Australia, being absent only from southeastern parts of the mainland, the extreme south of Western Australia, and the island of Tasmania.

**1** A man is busily at work on his car early one morning, blissfully unaware of the mulga that has taken refuge under the bonnet in order to warm itself after a cool night.

**2** The man reaches for a tool —and then yelps with pain as the snake lunges and bites him. He glimpses the reptile before it slides away — just enough to see that it is brown.

**3** In hospital, the man describes the snake to doctors, who inject him with brown-snake antivenom. When it has no effect, they try others, including those for death adder and tiger snake. Unless they realize their mistake soon, the victim has only a little longer to live…

## Did You Know?

● The mulga is under threat from an unlikely quarter: the cane toad (*Bufo marinus*) which just gets eaten by it. To the mulga, the toad looks like a delicious snack—but unfortunately it is deadly poisonous. The cane toad was introduced to Australia in the 1930s, and the native animals have yet to come to terms with it.

● The mulga is "milked" for its venom to make antivenom medicine. A milked mulga provides an average yield of 2½ grain (180mg). However, in 1986 one mulga yielded 20 grain (1350mg)—currently the world record for snake venom.

● The mulga tolerates a wider range of habitats than other Australian snakes, from desert to rainforest. It shelters in any crevice including rabbit holes, deep cracks in the soil, hollow logs, and under rocks. It's not averse to hiding in farmhouses—much to their inhabitant's alarm!

# RED-BELLIED BLACK SNAKE

**Latin name:** *Pseudechis porphyriacus*

**NECK**

When disturbed, the red-bellied black snake not only rears and hisses, but also makes itself appear even more intimidating by raising its head and flaring its neck just like a cobra.

**EYES**

The snake has keen eyesight at close range, on land and in water, to judge a strike.

**TONGUE**

The snake tracks prey on land by flicking its tongue in and out to "taste" the air for scent trails.

**BODY**

The flexible, muscular body is perfect for swimming, climbing trees, or wriggling down narrow burrows.

**COLOR**

The snake's purple-black back camouflages it in the shadows of undergrowth.

A stealthy killer with a lethal bite, this eastern Australian serpent has a clear and simple way of warning enemies to back off: it rears up to display the distinctive red belly that gives it its name.

A naturally wary creature, the red-bellied black snake slips away into the safety of the undergrowth at the slightest sound of danger. But it can't resist a comfy place to spend the night, even when there are people close by.

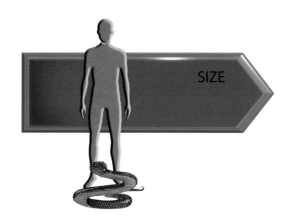

SIZE

## KEY DATA

| | |
|---|---|
| LENGTH | Up to 8ft (2.5m). Average 5ft (1.5m) |
| PREY | Rodents, lizards, snakes, frogs, fish, and birds |
| WEAPONS | Venom-primed fangs |
| TOXICITY | Has killed children |
| LIFESPAN | About 20 years |

The red-bellied black snake lives in eastern Australia and some areas along the southern coast. It prefers damp habitats with plenty of prey, such as swamps, rivers, and temperate rainforests. At night the snake retreats into a dark burrow or under a log so that it can rest and digest its latest meal in peace.

**1** A snug sleeping bag is just what you need after a long day trekking in the bush. It's also a tempting bed for a red-bellied black snake that has been hunting all day, and as a young camper prepares for a night under the stars, a tired red-belly slips into the bag alongside her.

**2** The instant the girl's bare feet touch the snake, the trapped red-belly reacts by sinking its fangs into her flesh. Leaping from the sleeping bag, the snake clinging to her right leg, she shrieks in terror and pain—and staggers dangerously close to the roaring campfire.

## Did You Know?

● Keeping an adult red-bellied black snake in the same tank as a juvenile one is never a good idea. Red-bellies are notorious cannibals and the larger snake is more than likely to devour its roommate.

● Doctors administer tiger snake antivenom to bite victims of the red-bellied black snake, though the red-belly is less venomous than its more famous relative. When milked, the average red-belly yields sufficient venom to kill 500 mice, the average tiger snake enough to kill 6000.

● The wily red-belly often hides under water to escape predators, and cold water slows down its bodily processes enough for it to stay submerged for more than an hour before it has to surface for air.

● The female of the species bears between five and 40 live young each year. The babies are born in clear, sticky sacks, struggling free within in the first few hours of life.

# BROWN SNAKE

**Latin name:** *Pseudonaja species*

## SENSES

A brown snake's keen eyes can detect a lizard scuttling along up to 96ft (30m) away. As it hunts, the snake repeatedly flicks out its forked tongue, tasting the air for telltale traces of nearby prey.

## FANGS

A sheath of tissue covers and protects each hollow fang. It slides up out the way as the fang pierces a victim's skin.

## MOUTH

An attacking brown snake opens its jaws wide so that it can bite down as hard as possible with its sharp but tiny fangs.

## NECK

When angry, a brown snake spreads its neck like a cobra flaring its hood: the brown snakes' Latin name, *Pseudonaja*, means "false cobra."

Some snakes kill prey with savage bites of their venom-dripping fangs. Others squeeze victims to death with ever-tightening, slithering coils. The deadly brown snakes of the Australian bush do both.

Like a hired hitman the brown snake takes no chances, making quite certain of the kill. If one catches a rat sniffing around for food, inevitably the rodent finishes up nestling in the satisfied serpent's belly.

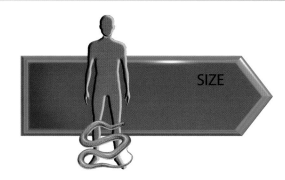

SIZE

## KEY DATA

| | |
|---|---|
| LENGTH | Up to 7ft 6in (2.4m), depending on species |
| PREY | Lizards, mice, rats, eggs, frogs, and toads |
| VENOM | Potent brew of nerve and other toxins |
| LIFESPAN | 10–15 years |

Together, the seven species of brown snake live throughout mainland Australia, except in the most densely forested areas. The deadliest species, the Eastern brown snake (*Pseudonaja textilis*), is found in southern New Guinea as well as in eastern Australia.

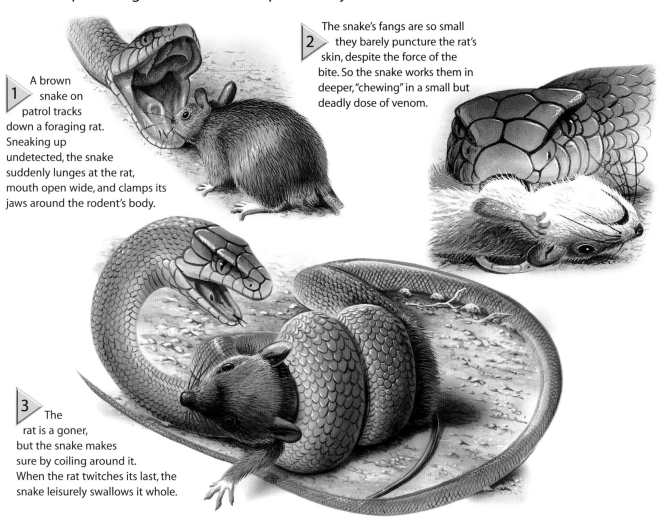

**1** A brown snake on patrol tracks down a foraging rat. Sneaking up undetected, the snake suddenly lunges at the rat, mouth open wide, and clamps its jaws around the rodent's body.

**2** The snake's fangs are so small they barely puncture the rat's skin, despite the force of the bite. So the snake works them in deeper, "chewing" in a small but deadly dose of venom.

**3** The rat is a goner, but the snake makes sure by coiling around it. When the rat twitches its last, the snake leisurely swallows it whole.

## Did You Know?

● The world's deadliest snake is thought to be the saw-scaled viper (*Echis carinatus*) of Africa, the Middle East, and India. This small but aggressive and venomous snake probably kills more people than any other: up to 8000 a year in Asia alone.

● Australia has more species of venomous snake than any other country: about 120—over twice the number of non-venomous species. At least 20 are highly dangerous to humans. Even so, you are more likely to be struck by lightning than bitten by a snake in Australia.

● In 1979, in the state of Victoria, a brown snake bit a young greyhound that was being trained for a career in racing. Only prompt action by a vet, who immediately administered antivenom and oxygen, saved the greyhound's life. After making a full recovery, the dog went on to win substantial prize money—running under the name Full of Venom.

# ASIAN PYTHON

**Latin name:** *Python molurus*

**TAIL**

By winding its strong tail around the branch of a tree, the python can reach across to snatch a bird or lizard off another branch—or hang down to grab prey on the ground.

**EYES**

The vertical, slit pupils open wide like those of a cat to gather the dim light when the snake sets out to hunt at sunset.

**BODY**

Thick, muscular, and sinuous, the snake can constrict large, struggling prey, and its ribcage can open wide to make room in its stomach for the meal.

**SKIN**

Contrasting markings mingle with light-dappled trees and grass. This hides a young python from eagles and other enemies, as well as concealing it from prey.

One of the biggest and strongest snakes in the world, the mighty Asian python is a massively built beast with the muscle power to constrict the life out of you—before swallowing you whole.

The Asian python attacks people rarely—but it does happen. An excellent climber, it often basks in a treetop by day then dangles from a low branch at dusk, waiting quietly for prey to pass below.

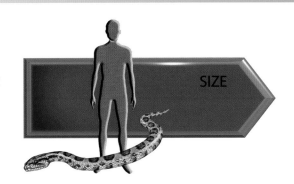

SIZE

As night falls over a remote village in India, a woman walking along the path on the edge of the forest fails to spot a fully grown Asian python hanging from an overhead branch. Ninety-nine times out of a hundred, the snake would let her go by — but not tonight. The python hasn't fed for weeks, and such a large meal is too good an opportunity to miss…

## KEY DATA

| | |
|---|---|
| LENGTH | Up to 21ft (6.5m) |
| WEIGHT | 220lb (100kg) or more |
| DIET PREY | Mainly mammals; some birds, and reptiles |
| BREEDING | |
| WEAPONS | Constricting coils |
| LIFESPAN | |
| LIFESPAN | Up to 40 years |

The Asian python lives in the tropical lowlands and hills of southern Asia, in forested, grassy, and swampy areas. Now rare, it ranges from the Indian subcontinent through Burma (Myanmar), Thailand, Cambodia, Laos, and Vietnam to southeastern China.

## Did You Know?

● Each year, the Asian python needs to eat only its own weight in food. It may eat most of this in one go then spend months not feeding.

● The Asian python isn't native to southeastern Asia. It probably got there by escaping from the baskets of traveling Indian snake-charmers.

● There are two races of Asian python: the Indian python and the darker, bigger, and more common Burmese python. In captivity, the Burmese python becomes quite docile—making it the most popular snake among exotic dancers!

● An 18ft-long (5.7m) Asian python was once found with a fully grown leopard inside its stomach.

● Uniquely, the female Asian python keeps her eggs warm by wrapping her coils around them and twitching her muscles. She does this for 60–90 days, during which time she may lose half her bodyweight.

# RETICULATED PYTHON

**Latin name:** *Python reticulatus*

**BODY**

The reticulated python is long and muscular, but its body is more slender than other constrictors. A reticulated python can weigh half as much as an anaconda of the same length.

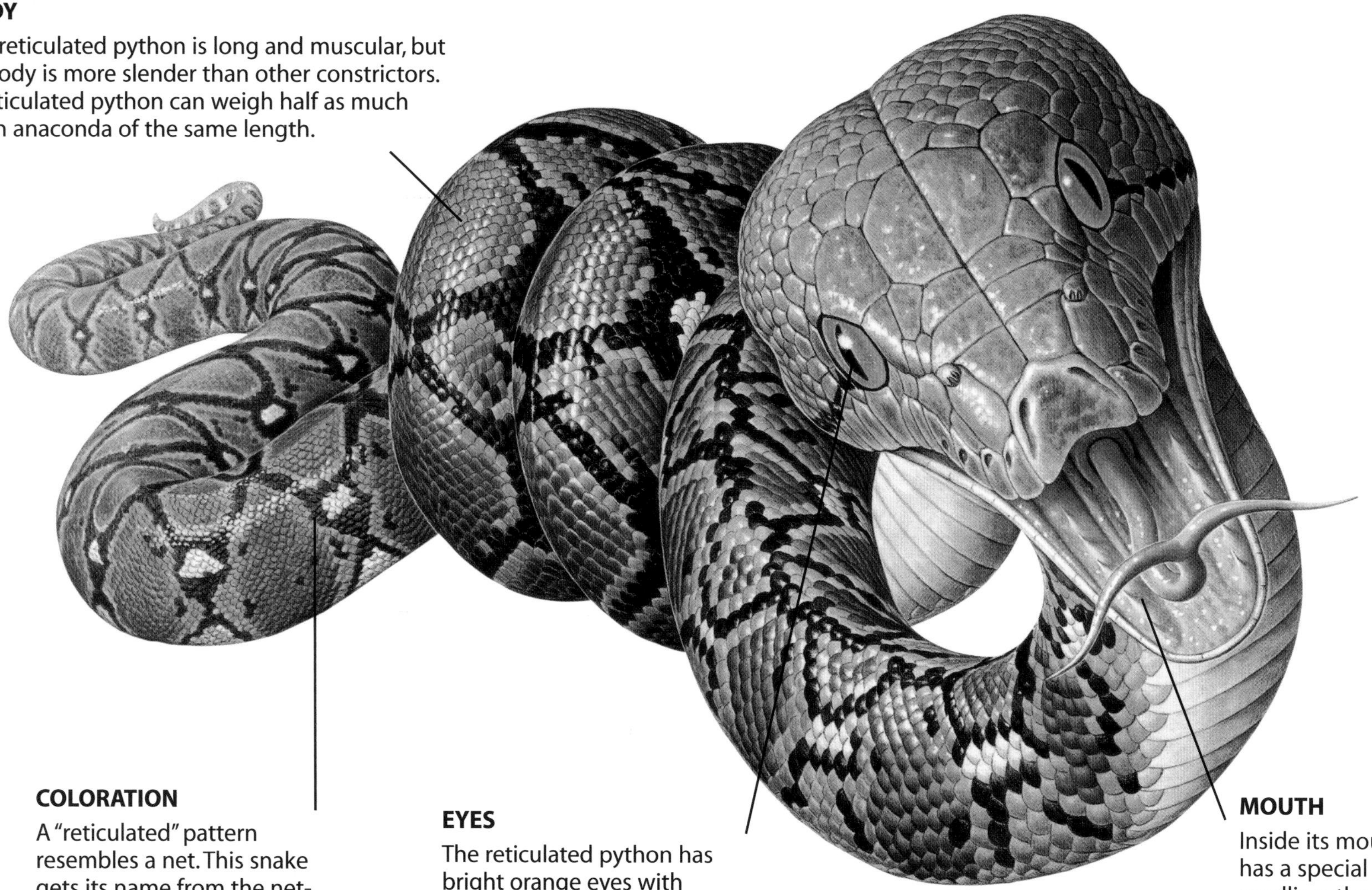

**COLORATION**

A "reticulated" pattern resembles a net. This snake gets its name from the net-like pattern on its body. It is usually light brown or yellowish in color.

**EYES**

The reticulated python has bright orange eyes with vertical pupils, which allow it to see very well at night.

**MOUTH**

Inside its mouth, the snake has a special organ for smelling, the Jacobson's organ. It smells by flicking out its tongue, and then touching Jacobson's organ to pick up a scent.

When it comes to length, few snakes can top the reticulated python. Other snakes, such as the anaconda, are heavier, but this snake is considered the world's longest, growing nearly as long as a school bus. Like the anaconda, it is a constrictor, so it kills by squeezing prey until they suffocate. It often eats small animals, such as birds, but it eats larger prey, too, including deer, pigs, and dogs. There have even been reports of reticulated pythons having a person for dinner!

SIZE

## KEY DATA

| | |
|---|---|
| LENGTH | Average 3–6 m (10–20 ft); occasionally more than 9m (30 ft) |
| PREY | Birds, mammals such as rodents, deer, pigs, goats, and dogs. |
| WEAPONS | Sharp teeth and constricting coils of powerful body. |
| LIFESPAN | Up to 20 years |

The reticulated python is common throughout much of Southeast Asia. It is also found on many of the larger Indonesian islands.

**1** Reticulated pythons can be held in captivity. The snakes are kept in large terrariums, where the temperature and humidity can be controlled. They are usually fed dead chickens or rabbits. A python senses the dead rabbit in the air with its Jacobson's organ.

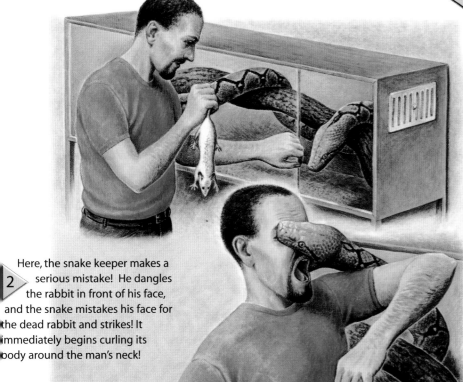

**2** Here, the snake keeper makes a serious mistake! He dangles the rabbit in front of his face, and the snake mistakes his face for the dead rabbit and strikes! It immediately begins curling its body around the man's neck!

## Did You Know?

● The reticulated python is one of the few constrictor snakes that is dangerous to people. On rare occasions, children and even small adults have been killed and swallowed by a giant reticulated python!

● A reticulated python has about 100 very sharp teeth. It actually has fangs, though it is not venomous.

● This constrictor can eat some very big meals. With its jaws unattached, it opens wide to swallow an entire animal. A tube in its mouth lets in air when its mouth is full.

● Like many snakes, reticulated pythons do not give birth to live young, but instead lay eggs. A female reticulated python lays 25 to 100 eggs.

● A young reticulated python starts out long and quickly gets even longer. Out of the egg, a baby can be 2ft (60cm) long. It can grow 2ft or more each year.

# MASSASSAUGA
**Latin name:** *Sistrurus catenatus*

**EYES**
In sunlight, the pupils contract to vertical slits, but they open wide at night to admit as much light as possible.

**RATTLE**
Smaller than that of a typical rattlesnake, its rattle, when shaken, warns enemies to keep well away.

**TONGUE**
The long forked tongue gathers scent particles and passes them to a sensor (the Jacobson's organ) inside the mouth, where they can be analyzed and identified.

This North American serpent usually avoids people, preferring to hide in the dark, waiting for small prey. But if cornered, it rapidly delivers an agonizing bite that its human victims will not forget. The massassauga lurks among rocks, its mottled coloring making it hard to see. A rider's horse can easily step on it, inviting painful retribution as the snake strikes back with long, venom-laden fangs.

SIZE

**1** As they slowly make their way along a drying riverbed in the Midwest, neither horse nor rider notice a massassauga lying among the sun-warmed pile of rocks in their path.

**2** The horse treads on the snake's tail and the massassauga rears up and plunges its fangs into the animal's leg. The snake is lifted into the air as the horse rears up in terror, pitching its rider onto the ground.

## KEY DATA

| | |
|---|---|
| LENGTH | 20–30in (50–80cm) |
| WEIGHT | 2–3lb 3oz (1–1.5kg) |
| LIFESTYLE | Nocturnal ambush hunter |
| WEAPONS | Hinged fangs and powerful venom |
| TOXICITY | Attacks blood and nervous system. Painful to humans —not usually fatal |
| PREY | Small mammals, birds' eggs; some reptiles and amphibians |
| LIFESPAN | Up to 20 years |

There are three subspecies of massassauga—the eastern, western, and desert populations. They inhabit a band of territory in the USA, stretching from the Great Lakes in the northeast down as far as the Mexican border.

### Did You Know?

● Unlike the western and desert massassaugas, which keep to arid areas, the eastern subspecies also inhabits damp meadows, swamps, and bogs for part of the year.

● The massassauga is becoming quite rare, because farmers have drained many of its swampland strongholds and ploughed up the wild prairies for agricultural land.

● Although it feeds mainly on small mammals such as mice and voles, the massassauga also enjoys the eggs of ground-nesting birds such as quail. Even swamp-dwelling types avoid frogs, and reptiles such as lizards and snakes, unless their preferred prey is in short supply.

# AFRICAN TWIG SNAKE

**Latin name:** *Thelotornis capensis, T. kirtlandii*

## HEAD

The twig snake has a lance-shaped head, which increases its resemblance to a leaf.

## BODY

The slender body is supported by a strong, yet flexible spine, and protected by scaly skin.

## EYES

The pupils are horizontal and elongated, which extends them toward the snout. This enables the twig snake to see straight forward with both eyes, giving range-finding binocular vision. Like all snakes it has no eyelids.

## JAW

Like most snakes, the twig snake has a specially modified jaw that can be stretched around prey much larger than its own head. The long, grooved fangs are situated near the back, where the jaw muscles exert the most leverage.

## COLOR

Apart from its green head, the forest twig snake is a dull gray-brown with darker speckles.

## TAIL

The twig snake can curl its long whip tail around branches for extra support as it attacks its prey.

Sneaking through the branches, the impossibly slender twig snake looks too fragile to take on prey. But its venom is deadly enough for its predatory purpose. The forest twig snake attacks anything it can eat, but its favorite targets are tree-dwelling chameleons and geckos. Disguised as a branch or vine, it hides in the foliage, ambushing luckless lizards that come too close.

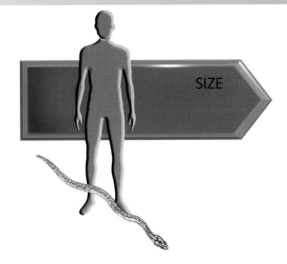

SIZE

**1** As a forest twig snake hangs motionless from a branch, a two-horned chameleon creeps into view. Despite its sharp eyesight, the chameleon doesn't spot the slender predator above. Carefully, the twig snake sways its head, checking the distance to its prey. Then it strikes.

## KEY DATA

| | |
|---|---|
| LENGTH | 4–6ft (1.2–1.8m) |
| PREY | Mainly lizards, frogs, young birds, and small snakes |
| WEAPONS | Grooved "back-fangs" laden with venom |
| TYPICAL ATTACK | Single bite, then chewing action to introduce venom |
| EGGS | 4 to 12 |
| LAYING TIME | Normally midsummer; eggs take up to 3 months to hatch |
| LIFESPAN | Unknown |

Between them, the two species of twig snake inhabit most of Africa south of the Sahara. The forest twig snake (*Thelotornis kirtlandii*) prefers the tropical forests of Central and West Africa, while the savannah twig snake (*T. capensis*) inhabits the savannah and coastal bush of southeastern Africa.

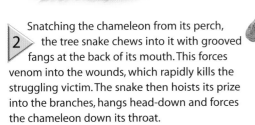

**2** Snatching the chameleon from its perch, the tree snake chews into it with grooved fangs at the back of its mouth. This forces venom into the wounds, which rapidly kills the struggling victim. The snake then hoists its prize into the branches, hangs head-down and forces the chameleon down its throat.

## Did You Know?

● In some parts of Africa, people fear the twig snake because they think it can fly through the air and pierce their skin like an arrow.

● Twig-snake venom is modified saliva, loaded with protein-destroying enzymes. Although bites are rare, several people have died from kidney failure after being bitten.

● When a twig snake is alarmed it resorts to a cobra-like threat display, inflating its neck to reveal bold, dark markings on the stretchy skin.

● Twig snakes normally wait in ambush for their prey, but they also search the trees for birds' nests and devour any nestlings they find.

# ASIAN PIT VIPER
**Latin name:** *Trimeresurus species*

**EYES**
These face forward, giving stereoscopic vision to judge the distance to a target.

**TONGUE**
The tongue picks up particles of scent and then passes them to an organ in the mouth for analysis.

**BELLY SCALES**
Wider scales along the belly stretch apart and contract alternately, helping the viper wriggle along.

**SKIN**
These vipers come in various colors and patterns, and like other snakes, they shed their skin as they grow.

**TAIL**
As tree dwellers, most Asian pit vipers depend on their strong, gripping tail to anchor them safely high above the ground.

Sliding effortlessly through the foliage, the Asian pit viper homes in unerringly on its doomed prey. It kills with a single, lightning strike, stabbing viciously with its long fangs and delivering a fatal dose of venom. In cooler months, the Sri Lankan pit viper also hunts by day, often slithering into local tea plantations in search of prey. And as workers pick the tea by hand, they run a high risk of startling the snake and provoking a painful bite.

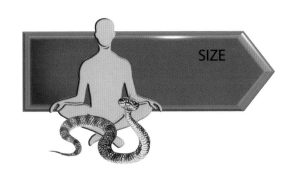

SIZE

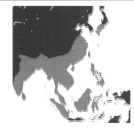

## KEY DATA

| NUMBER OF SPECIES | More than 30 |
|---|---|
| LENGTH | Young 4¾–6in (12–15cm), adult 18in–6ft 6in (45cm–2m), depending on species |
| WEAPONS | Folding fangs that inject a mixture of tissue- and blood-destroying toxins |
| PREY | Mice and rats, other small mammals, birds, and their chicks, frogs and lizards |
| LIFESPAN | Up to 20 years |

Asian pit vipers inhabit much of India and southeastern Asia, from Nepal, eastern China, Bangladesh, Burma (Myanmar), Thailand, Cambodia, Laos, and Vietnam to Malaysia, Sumatra, and Borneo. Some species live on islands such as Sri Lanka, the Nicobar and Andoman islands, and in the Philippines.

**1** A woman makes her way across a tea plantation, pulling off the tips of leaves and throwing them into her basket. But although she stays alert, she fails to spot the Sri Lankan pit viper in a nearby bush, coiled with its green scales almost invisible among the foliage.

**2** Increasingly alarmed by the disturbance, the pit viper readies itself in anticipation as the woman moves closer. She reaches into an adjacent bush and—wham!—the snake shoots out its head and sinks its fangs deep into her wrist.

## Did You Know?

● Asian pit vipers are related to American rattlesnakes, and some species coil up and vibrate their tails in warning if cornered in the open.

● Male and female Siamese palm vipers differ greatly in size and habits; the slim males live in trees, while the heavy females stay on the ground.

● Japan's Ryukyu Islands are home to several species of Asian pit viper—and with one in 500 of the human population being bitten every year, they also have the highest recorded incidence of snake bites in the world.

● Tiger pit vipers are often found in swampy coastal areas, and will readily swim through salty water.

# ASP VIPER

**Latin name:** *Vipera aspis*

**MARKINGS** —————————————

Although usually gray or brown, the asp viper can also be a brighter orange, copper, or yellow, often with a greenish tinge. Blotches break up its outline.

**EYES**

As the viper closes in on a victim, its forward-facing eyes judge the range.

**SHAPE** ————

The male is more slender than the female, and 4–6in (10–15cm) longer.

**JAWS**

The jaws gape wide just before the snake sinks its fangs into a victim.

**HEAD**

This snake has the typically wedge-shape head and upturned snout of a true viper.

This European serpent is a genuine "snake in the grass." With its short fuse and life-threateningly toxic bite, the asp viper can shatter the peace of a balmy summer's afternoon in a split second. The asp viper is sitll common on farms in southern Europe where people work the land by hand. Unfortunately, its sleepy habits may result in unexpected encounters with farm workers, sometimes  with potentially fatal consequences.

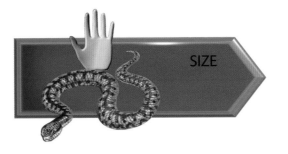

SIZE

## KEY DATA

| | | |
|---|---|---|
| LENGTH | 20–29in (50–75cm) |  |
| PREY | Small mammals, lizards, and young birds | |
| WEAPONS | Venom-primed fangs | Ranging across most of Switzerland, France, and Italy, and parts of Spain and Germany, the asp viper lives wherever it can find plenty of warm sunshine and concealing cover. Its haunts include fields of grass, mountain meadows, woodland glades, quarries, and even garbage dumps. |
| TOXICITY | Can kill you | |
| LIFESPAN | Up to 20 years | |

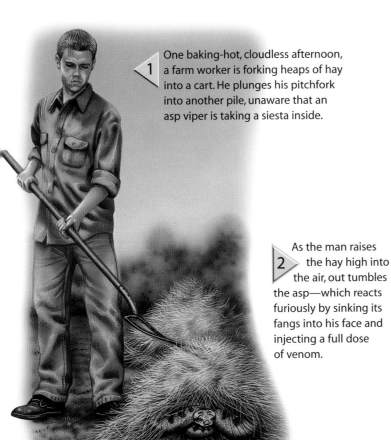

**1** One baking-hot, cloudless afternoon, a farm worker is forking heaps of hay into a cart. He plunges his pitchfork into another pile, unaware that an asp viper is taking a siesta inside.

**2** As the man raises the hay high into the air, out tumbles the asp—which reacts furiously by sinking its fangs into his face and injecting a full dose of venom.

## Did You Know?

● The asp viper often dwells high up the sides of mountains, above the treeline, especially on south-facing slopes. Particularly hardy individuals live at altitudes up to 9840ft (3000m).

● When fall comes the asp viper hibernates, retiring into holes in the ground, hollow tree-trunks, and crevices in walls. Several vipers may share the same shelter. If the weather is warm they may emerge as early as February, but they don't usually do so until late March.

● Each year, hundreds of asp vipers take refuge in unlit bonfires, fall asleep in them and perish when the piles are set ablaze.

● In Italy, the asp viper is to blame for nine out of 10 snake bites.

● Asp vipers in captivity rarely lose their natural hostility toward humans, and readily lash out with their fangs if their keepers are rash enough to try to handle them.

# EUROPEAN ADDER

**Latin name:** *Vipera berus*

**ZIGZAG**

The adder typically has a dark zigzag down its back. This hides it from enemies like birds of prey by breaking up its outline. But the "black adder" is so dark all over that its zigzag can barely be seen.

**EYES**

The adder has vertically slit pupils. These are usual in snakes that hunt at night, as the adder does in warm southern parts of its range.

**SEXES**

The male is usually gray and black, the female a shade of brown.

**TONGUE**

This is the snake's main sensory organ, constantly flicking in and out between its fangs to "taste" the air for prey.

The sinister hiss of a cornered adder gives fair warning that this is a snake to treat with all due respect, for it comes armed with a blood-destroying venom that can kill. Shy and elusive, the adder would rather slip away from trouble, but if it is backed into a corner, tormented, or trapped, it will bite. For the old, the weak and the young, the effects of a full dose of venom can prove lethal.

SIZE

## KEY DATA

| | | |
|---|---|---|
| LENGTH | Female up to 25½ in (65cm); male up to 24 in (60cm) | |
| PREY | Voles, mice, lizards, frogs, and nestlings | |
| VENOM | Can have severe, sometimes fatal, effects on humans | The adder lives throughout northern Europe, apart from Ireland, and throughout most of Scandinavia. Its range extends east across Asia to northern China, and south to northern Italy and Greece. |
| LIFESPAN | Up to 20 years | |

**1** One glorious summer's day at the seaside, an adder sunbathes drowsily on a sand dune, away from the noisy crowds on the beach. Hour after hour, it dozes blissfully. Then a young girl decides to take a short cut across the dunes. This takes her right into the adder's sunning spot…

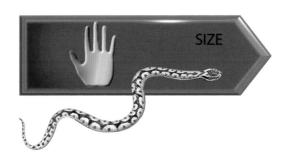

**2** The girl treads on the sleepy adder's coils. Unable to escape, the snake reacts by striking at her leg, sinking its long fangs deep into her flesh.

## Did You Know?

● Sometimes the adder "freezes" when disturbed, as if playing dead, until the danger passes—but more often it hisses before slinking away.

● When two male adders compete to mate with a female they often settle the matter by ritual combat. They rear up with their bodies entwined and try to push each other over. The duel—known as "the dance of the adders"— may last half an hour before one gives up, exhausted.

● When the adder basks in the sun, it flattens its body to expose as much of its skin as it can.

● The adder is the only species of snake in the world that is found inside the Arctic Circle.

● Stirling Moss, the famous racing driver, was bitten by an adder in 1999. He made a full recovery.

● If the snake finds a nest of mice or birds, it may eat the whole family.

# Lizards

*The world of lizards is full of amazing variety. They may all be cold-blooded reptiles, but they are not all the same. Lizards survive in different ways, and they come in many shapes, sizes, and colors.*

Ground chameleons hide from predators by blending in with leaves and bark, while Panther chameleons warn away intruders by turning brilliant colors. Some lizards are ingenious escape artists. The basilisk lizard can literally walk on water! If attacked, a leaf-tailed lizard will jump from a tree and curl up, and then hit the ground like a bouncing ball. Other lizards are covered in spiky scales, so they are hard to eat. Some lizards bluff their way out of trouble. The bearded dragon has a flap of spiky skin on its throat, which it inflates to scare off attackers. If cornered, the regal horned lizard shoots blood from its eyeballs! Lizards also find food in different ways. Jackson's chameleon zaps insects by shooting out its long, sticky tongue. The gliding lizard flies from tree to tree in search of a meal.  Some lizards are truly dangerous. The Gila monster injects a toxic venom into its victims. Monitors tear their victims to pieces with sharp claws and teeth. The fearsome Komodo dragon is the world's largest lizard—it can grow longer than a car.  For lizards, there is no single way to survive.

# MARINE IGUANA

**Latin name:** *Amblyrhynchus cristatus*

## CREST

Like some prehistoric movie monster, the iguana has a saw-like crest of horny spines extending along its back and tail, with longer spines on the nape of its neck.

## SKIN

Tough, scaly skin prevents the iguana from being dashed to pieces against the rocks. Although usually black, some males flush red and green during the breeding season.

## NOSE

A special excretion gland opens into each nostril, so the iguana can eject excess salt from its system in a spray of salty water.

## MOUTH

A mouthful of sharp, three-cusped teeth help the marine iguana scissor its way through springy seaweed.

## FEET

Strong toes and extra-long claws enable the marine iguana to keep its grip on the slippery rocks as it feeds in the pounding surf.

It can be a hard-knock life on the rocky fringes of the Galapagos, miles from anywhere, but the marine iguana can usually find plenty to eat in the sea. It nibbles seaweed from rocks exposed at low tide, or dives deep to find richer pickings underwater. Caught between the ocean and the bare volcanic shores of its remote island home, this unique black lizard spends much of its life shuffling between the baking rock and the cold blue water.

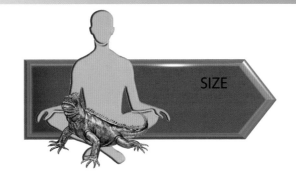

SIZE

**1** A peckish male iguana heads toward the sea to feed. Gripping with its long, curved claws, it clambers like a mountaineer down to the spray-spattered rocks close to the ocean's edge. Braced against the titanic force of the waves, it gnaws at the salty seaweed. Its short, flattened snout enables it to nuzzle right up to the rocks, scraping the weed away with rows of small, saw-edged teeth.

**2** Later, the iguana abandons the rock and dives into the booming surf, feet clamped against its sides. It uses its long, flattened tail to drive itself down, sweeping it from side to side with powerful strokes.

**3** By slowing its body processes down, until its heart beats only five times a minute, the iguana can save on oxygen and stay down for up to an hour, or until the cold forces it back to the sunny rocks.

## KEY DATA

| | | |
|---|---|---|
| LENGTH | Up to 4ft (1.4m) | The marine iguana lives only on the Galapagos, a group of volcanic islands in the eastern Pacific. These lie right on the equator, about 600 miles (1000km) off the coast of Ecuador in South America. The marine iguana is found in coastal areas, diving into the sea to feed. |
| WEIGHT | Up to 28lb (12.5kg) | |
| DIET | | |
| DIET | Seaweeds; occasionally small marine animals | |
| BREEDING | | |
| BREEDING | Buries 2 or 3 eggs on beach | |
| LIFESPAN | | |
| LIFESPAN | Usually 20 years; max. 40 | |

### Did You Know?

● As the marine iguana grows, its skin continually peels away. Local crabs clamber on to its back to pick off bits of nutritious dead skin.

● After a dip in the sea, the marine iguana becomes thoroughly chilled and its internal organs no longer work properly, so it must warm up again before it can digest its food.

● During the breeding season in January and February, marine iguanas become much more aggressive and males fight for their own territory. Rushing at each other with heads down, they battle for up to an hour.

● At night, marine iguanas huddle together in groups to keep warm.

● The naturalist Charles Darwin originally thought the marine iguana could breathe underwater. To test his theory, he tied one to a brick and left it underwater for two hours. (Don't try this at home.) By the time he hauled it out, it was dead.

# GREEN ANOLE

**Latin name:** *Anolis carolinensis*

**TOES** —————————————————

The lizard's toes have sticky pads to give a secure grip on smooth and vertical surfaces.

**SKIN** ——————

Peppered with expandable color cells, the anole's skin changes color with temperature and background, as well as its state of mind.

**EYES**

Since it hunts mainly by sight, and always in daylight, the green anole has large, keen eyes.

**DEWLAP**

The expandable dewlap creates a flash of bright color when the male anole wants to show off to a female or scare a rival male away from his territory.

**JAWS**

Unlike a snake, the anole cannot expand its jaws to accommodate large prey, so it limits itself to small prey.

When a male green anole decides to announce himself, he unfolds a bright pink throat flap to flash a colorful, coded message to any other anole in the neighborhood. A male green anole is very jealous of his territory, and won't tolerate any trespassers. A confrontation between rivals can lead to big trouble if they're evenly matched and neither anole is willing to lose face by backing down.

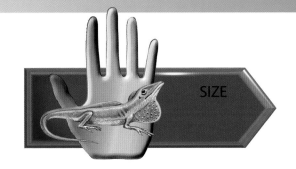

SIZE

## KEY DATA

| | |
|---|---|
| LENGTH | 5–8in (13–20cm) |
| LIFESTYLE | Lives in trees; active by day |
| PREY | Mainly insects and spiders |
| DEFENSES | Cunning chameleon-like camouflage |
| LIFESPAN | 5–10 years |

The green anole is the only anole native to the USA, where it lives in several southeastern states, ranging from southern Virginia in the east to the eastern third of Texas in the west, and to the tip of Florida in the south. It favors sunny, open woodland and scrub.

1 ▷ At the sight of another male moving into his territory, a furious green anole turns broadside on, bobs his head vigorously, flares his bright pink dewlap and bristles up the crest on his back—all to make himself look as big and fierce as possible. But the intruder is just as big as the defending male, and keeps on coming, clearly fancying his chances.

## Did You Know?

● If a green anole accidentally tumbles out of a tree it adopts a "skydiving" posture to slow its fall.

● The green anole quenches its thirst by lapping raindrops on leaves.

● While an anole's color usually matches its background or indicates its mood, it also reflects its health. A sick anole looks very drab indeed, literally fading away until it dies.

● There are over 110 species of anole on separate Caribbean islands.

● As it grows, the green anole must slough, or shed, its old skin several times each year, from snout to tail-tip.

2 ▷ The two lean, mean lizards square up face to face, and much head-bobbing, dewlap-flaring, and crest-bristling ensues. But still neither will back down, so they launch into furious combat, biting and scratching as each anole tries to oust the other from the territory. Eventually one will concede and scurry away to lick his wounds.

# BASILISK LIZARD

**Latin name:** *Basiliscus species*

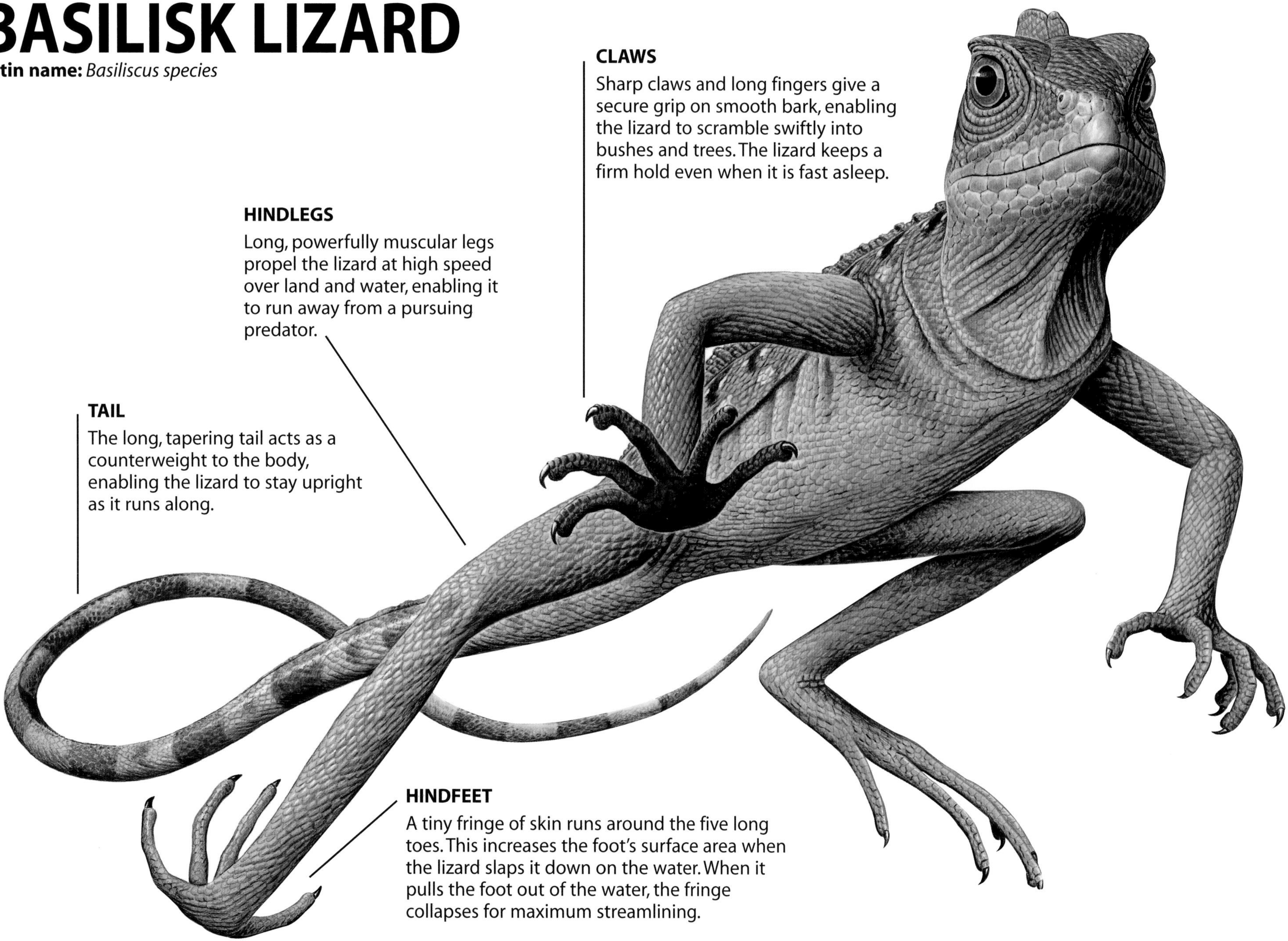

**CLAWS**

Sharp claws and long fingers give a secure grip on smooth bark, enabling the lizard to scramble swiftly into bushes and trees. The lizard keeps a firm hold even when it is fast asleep.

**HINDLEGS**

Long, powerfully muscular legs propel the lizard at high speed over land and water, enabling it to run away from a pursuing predator.

**TAIL**

The long, tapering tail acts as a counterweight to the body, enabling the lizard to stay upright as it runs along.

**HINDFEET**

A tiny fringe of skin runs around the five long toes. This increases the foot's surface area when the lizard slaps it down on the water. When it pulls the foot out of the water, the fringe collapses for maximum streamlining.

Named after the mythical monster that sported a similar head-crest, the basilisk lizard of the Americas has an amazing way of escaping enemies when young and light on its feet. It runs on water! Fleeing a hungry snake, most lizards would be trapped if they found a river blocking their path, but not the basilisk lizard. It just keeps on running, taking the water in its stride—provided that the lizard weighs no more than 7oz (200g).

SIZE

### KEY DATA

| | |
|---|---|
| LENGTH | Depending on species, male up to 3ft (1m), female 2ft (60cm) (*B. vittatus* and *B. galeritus* are smaller) |
| WEIGHT | Some males up to 20oz (600g), females 10oz (300g) |
| DIET | Insects and other invertebrates, (worms, scorpions, and shrimps), plus small animals (lizards, nestling birds, fish, mice); sometimes fruit and flowers |

The basilisk lizard ranges from southern Mexico south through Central America to western Venezuela, Ecuador, and Colombia. There are four species: *Basiliscus basiliscus, B. vittatus, B. plumifrons* and *B. galeritus*.

| | |
|---|---|
| LIFESPAN | Up to 7 years or more |

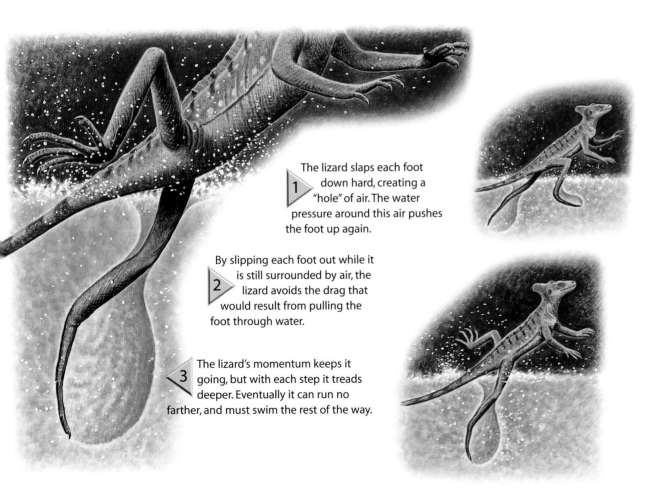

1 The lizard slaps each foot down hard, creating a "hole" of air. The water pressure around this air pushes the foot up again.

2 By slipping each foot out while it is still surrounded by air, the lizard avoids the drag that would result from pulling the foot through water.

3 The lizard's momentum keeps it going, but with each step it treads deeper. Eventually it can run no farther, and must swim the rest of the way.

### Did You Know?

● The mechanics of the basilisk lizard's ability to run on water were not understood until the 1990s, when they were explained by James Glasheen and Thomas McMahon of Harvard University in the USA.

● To run on water, an 176lb (80kg) person would have to top 62mph (100km/h) and have the leg-strength of 15 people.

● In South America the basilisk lizard is known as the Jesus Christ lizard, after the Biblical account of Christ walking on the Sea of Galilee.

● Some experts think the basilisk lizard identified widely as *Basiliscus galeritus* isn't a separate species at all, but the juvenile of *B. basiliscus*.

# GROUND CHAMELEON
**Latin name:** *Brookesia species*

**TONGUE**
Inside the mouth lurks a sticky, telescopic tongue, capable of launching swiftly forward to snatch prey.

**TAIL**
Ground chameleons usually lack the long, gripping tail of bigger tree-dwelling species, and are often called stub-tailed chameleons.

**TEXTURE**
Small spines and nodules cover much of *Brookesia peramata*'s skin, breaking up its outline and increasing its resemblance to bark.

**LIMBS**
Despite its delicate limbs, a ground chameleon can grip firmly using its opposing toes. Some species also have double claws and spiny soles for extra hold.

**COLOR**
Ground chameleons lack the bright hues and spectacular color changes of many species; their drab camouflage colors alter only slightly whatever their mood or surroundings.

Look again at that dead leaf on the forest floor or that sliver of bark on a stem, for it might be a ground chameleon standing motionless as if frozen to the spot. Ground chameleons are fiercely territorial, and they never waste time with the ritual head-nodding and color flushes of larger species. Their warning signal is immediate and aggressive, and if it fails, a serious showdown follows.

ACTUAL SIZE

Neither male is prepared to back down, so finally a fight ensues. Launching themselves at one another, the males bite ferociously and grapple with their spindly limbs. The battle will end only when one of them runs away or is seriously injured.

▽ 2

## KEY DATA

| | |
|---|---|
| LENGTH | 1¼–4in (3–10cm), depending on species |
| PREY | Small insects |
| DEFENSES | Effective camouflage and the ability to stand totally motionless for hours |
| WEAPONS | Long, sticky tongue |

The 24 known species of ground (or stump-tailed) chameleon belong to the *Brookesia* genus. Most of these occur only in the rainforests, mountains, and remote islands of Madagascar, although a few species can be found in the highland savannahs and tropical forests of central Africa.

### Did You Know?

● In Madagascan folklore the ground chameleon is regarded with dread. Many people are terrified of stepping on the little beast when it is hidden underfoot, for according to tradition, anyone who crushes or touches a ground chameleon risks subsequent ill-health and even death.

● *Brookesia karchei* has probably the most limited range, existing only on the remote Marojejy mountain massif in northern Madagascar.

● It's difficult to keep ground chameleons in captivity, as they need both humid conditions and dry sites where they can sun themselves. Most demanding of all, they require a constant supply of tiny insects to satisfy their appetites.

● Although *Brookesia stumpffi* is known as the dead-leaf chameleon, it is just as hard to spot when it rests on a slender twig.

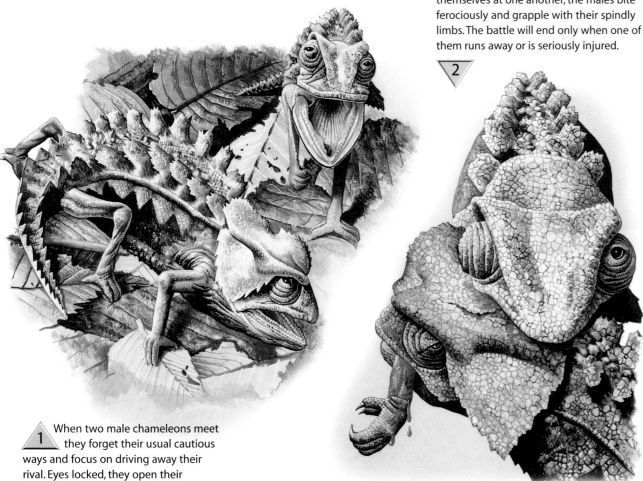

△ 1 When two male chameleons meet they forget their usual cautious ways and focus on driving away their rival. Eyes locked, they open their mouths wide and sway in rising anger.

# JACKSON'S CHAMELEON

**Latin name:** *Chamaeleo jacksonii*

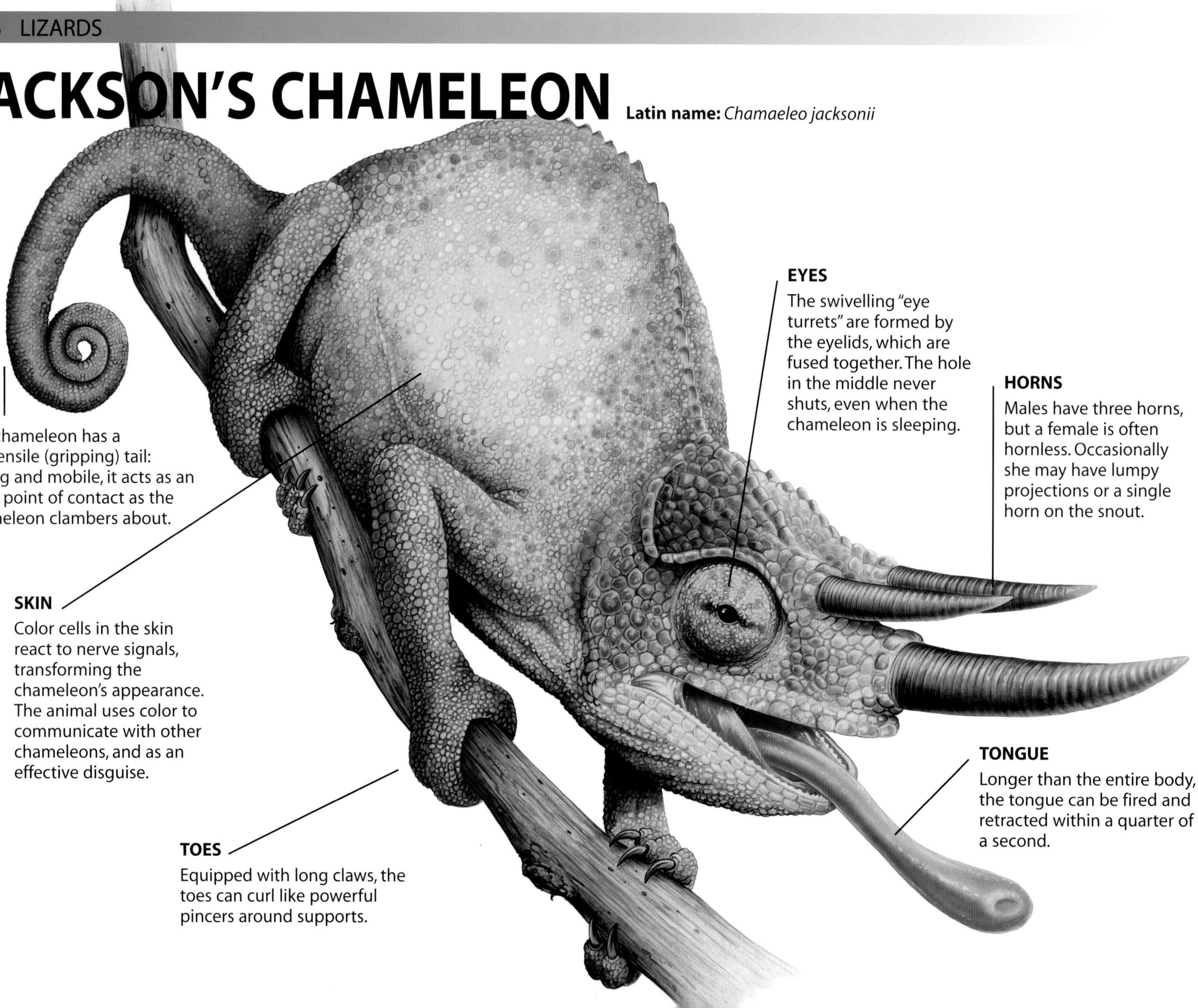

**EYES**

The swivelling "eye turrets" are formed by the eyelids, which are fused together. The hole in the middle never shuts, even when the chameleon is sleeping.

**HORNS**

Males have three horns, but a female is often hornless. Occasionally she may have lumpy projections or a single horn on the snout.

**TAIL**

The chameleon has a prehensile (gripping) tail: strong and mobile, it acts as an extra point of contact as the chameleon clambers about.

**SKIN**

Color cells in the skin react to nerve signals, transforming the chameleon's appearance. The animal uses color to communicate with other chameleons, and as an effective disguise.

**TONGUE**

Longer than the entire body, the tongue can be fired and retracted within a quarter of a second.

**TOES**

Equipped with long claws, the toes can curl like powerful pincers around supports.

This spike-faced reptile stalks its prey with such slow precision that the lightning speed of its final attack comes as an explosive surprise. It outwits any potential prey with a deadly combination of ice-cool stealth and sophisticated weaponry. The chameleon steals up on prey with infinite care. As it closes in, its eyes swivel forward and lock on target, calculating the distance to its victim. Then, in a flash, it unleashes its secret weapon: its tongue.

**1** The chameleon's tongue is a long tube with circular muscles running round it, longitudinal muscles along its length, and a club-like tip coated with sticky mucus. At rest the tongue is retracted on to a spike of gristle like a pushed-up sleeve.

**2** As the chameleon nears the target, the tip of its tongue often protrudes from its mouth as it readies for action. The chameleon "fires" by squeezing the circular muscles, shooting its tongue forward with amazing speed.

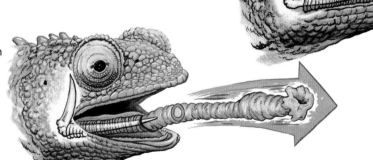

**3** Within 1/20th of a second the tip of its tongue has stuck fast to the prey. Retracting the tongue's long muscles reels it back into its mouth in another 1/5th of a second.

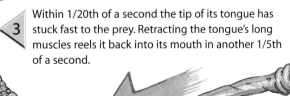

SIZE

| KEY DATA | | |
|---|---|---|
| LENGTH | 6–13in (15–32cm) from the nose to the tip of the tail | |
| TONGUE | Up to 12in (30cm) fully extended | Jackson's chameleon lives in trees and bushes in parts of the East African highlands around Nairobi, including the western slopes of Mount Kenya, the Aberdare Mountains of Kenya, and the Usambara Mountains of Tanzania. |
| HORNS | Up to 2in (5cm) | |
| DIET | Insects, spiders, and scorpions | |
| LIFESPAN | Average lifespan 5–6 years; up to 10 years in captivity | |

## Did You Know?

● Many chameleons are strongly territorial, staying in the same tree for weeks on end to defend it against other chameleons.

● Some chameleons can grow to 2ft (60cm) long, regularly preying on small mammals and even birds.

● In experiments chameleons have proved good at tackling mazes—a reflection of their ingenuity in setting up ambushes in the wild.

● Reptiles use the heat of the sun to warm their blood. Dark colors absorb heat more easily than paler colors, so by turning darker, the chameleon can rapidly warm up and become active.

# PANTHER CHAMELEON

**Latin name:** *Chamaeleo pardalis*

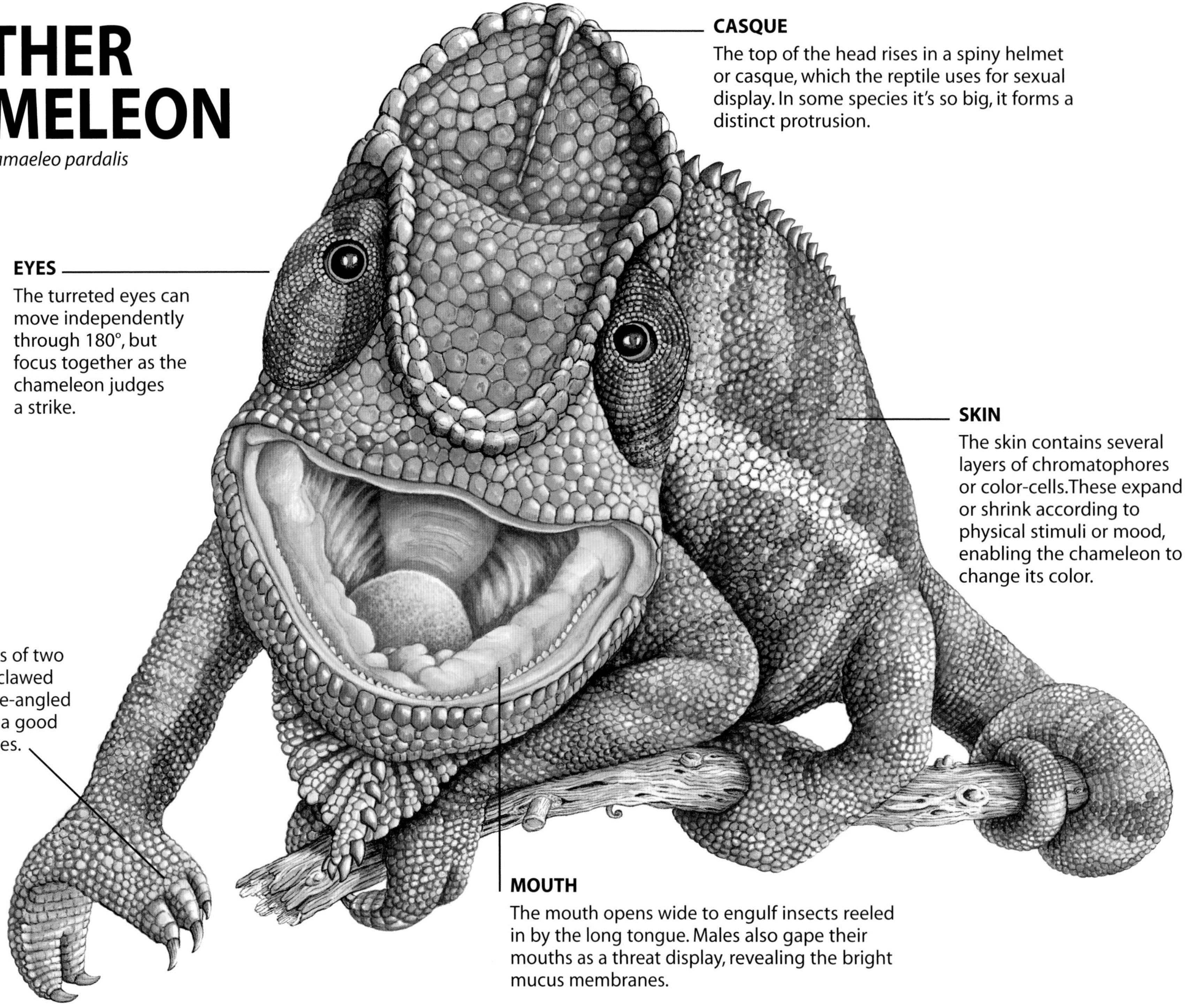

**CASQUE**

The top of the head rises in a spiny helmet or casque, which the reptile uses for sexual display. In some species it's so big, it forms a distinct protrusion.

**EYES**

The turreted eyes can move independently through 180°, but focus together as the chameleon judges a strike.

**SKIN**

The skin contains several layers of chromatophores or color-cells. These expand or shrink according to physical stimuli or mood, enabling the chameleon to change its color.

**TOES**

Grouped in sets of two and three, the clawed toes act as wide-angled pincers, giving a good grip on branches.

**MOUTH**

The mouth opens wide to engulf insects reeled in by the long tongue. Males also gape their mouths as a threat display, revealing the bright mucus membranes.

M any chameleons roam the forests of Madagascar, but this chameleon is one of the largest and most colorful. It also produces brilliant body displays when agitated. A male panther chameleon is fiercely territorial, using color and patterning to identify its own species and as a way of warning off intruders. So when two males meet, the color display can be spectacular.

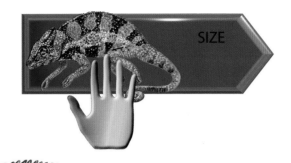

SIZE

## KEY DATA

| | | |
|---|---|---|
| LENGTH | Male up to 20in (50cm); female up to 14in (35cm) | |
| WEAPONS | Long, sticky tongue and powerful jaws | Panther chameleons inhabit the coastal rainforests of Madagascar, and they often turn up in cultivated fields and areas of degraded forest and scrub around villages. Small populations also live on several offshore islands such as Nosey Bé and Nosey Mangabe, as well as Réunion and Mauritius in the Indian Ocean. |
| PREY | Insects of all sizes, from small bugs to large locusts and jungle moths | |
| ENEMIES | Birds of prey (hawks, kites, and owls) and snakes | |
| EGGS | Up to 50, several times a year | |
| LIFESPAN | About 2 years in the wild and 4 years in captivity | |

**1** As a large male panther chameleon strolls along a twig he comes face-to-face with an intruder. Recognizing a rival male, he reacts aggressively, and this activates color cells in his skin.

**2** Hissing in anger, the dominant male changes from cool green to an intimidating mix of flaring red and orange. His smaller rival is in no mood for a fight, and toning his own color to a muddy hue, signals his defeat and beats a hasty retreat.

## Did You Know?

● Panther chameleons inhabit several smaller islands off the shores of Madagascar, and these populations often have a different basic coloring from the rest. Those from the popular resort of Nosey Bé for example, are usually bright turquoise or blue.

● Panther chameleons often halt the traffic in Madagascar as they wander unhurriedly across roads, for the local people have a strong fady or taboo against harming them.

● A chameleon's tongue is as long as its body, and it catches prey by trapping victims on the sticky pad at the tip. What's more, it can shoot out its tongue and retract it with a meal attached in only 0.3 seconds.

# FRILLED LIZARD

**Latin name:** *Chlamydosaurus kingii*

**FRILL**

This is a U-shaped flap of skin, open at the back of the neck and supported on each side by two bony rods.

**SCALES**

Spiny scales cover the whole body to protect the lizard.

**CLAWS**

These are sharp and strong for climbing trees and for digging nest burrows in the breeding season.

**TAIL**

Held out straight, the long, tapering tail acts as a balancing rod when the lizard is on the move.

The bizarre frilled lizard scampers around like a scaled-down dinosaur and tries to bluff its way out of trouble with the help of its truly spectacular neckwear. The ground's a risky place to be for a frilled lizard. In the open, it's exposed to the unwelcome attentions of all manner of predators, from snakes and wildcats to birds of prey. Small wonder the lizard has evolved an elaborate escape strategy.

SIZE

## KEY DATA

| | |
|---|---|
| LENGTH | Head and body about 10in (25cm); tail up to 20in (50cm) |
| WEIGHT | Up to 1lb 8oz (700g) |
| WIDTH OF FRILL | 8–12in (20–30cm) |
| DIET | Caterpillars, termites, spiders, beetles, and ants; some lizards, mice and other small animals |
| LIFESPAN | About 5 years in the wild; up to 10 years in captivity |

The frilled lizard is found in northern Australia and southern New Guinea. At one time it lived only in Australia; it might have drifted to New Guinea by sea on natural rafts, or walked across during one of the Ice Ages, when sea levels were much lower.

1 Confronted by a predator, the frilled lizard's first reaction is to "freeze'"and hope that its enemy won't see it. As long as it stays stock-still, its camouflaged coloring helps it blend in remarkably well with its surroundings.

2 If that ruse fails, the lizard raises its huge frill and hisses repeatedly. To add to the effect, it gapes its jaws, baring its teeth and the bright pink or yellow skin inside its mouth.

3 If the frill fails to frighten and the predator comes closer, the lizard rears up on its hindlegs and lashes the air with its claws, jaws, and tail. But if this performance doesn't fool its foe, it abandons all attempts at bluff and promptly runs away.

## Did You Know?

● Male frilled lizards have bigger and brighter frills than females. They raise them to intimidate each other in fights over territories and also to impress potential mates.

● The male is thought to grip the female with his teeth while mating.

● The frilled lizard sometimes hops like a kangaroo—especially when cornered, in a desperate last effort to scare away its attacker.

● Rich in blood vessels, the frill may help the lizard warm itself up in the sun and cool itself down in a breeze. Some prehistoric reptiles had large plates and "sails" on their backs, probably for the same reason.

# SUNGAZER LIZARD

**Latin name:** *Cordylus species*

**CREST**

This backward-pointing fringe of scales, fused to the skull, deters an attack from the rear.

**HEAD**

The sungazer's wedge-shaped skull is hinged at the back, enabling the lizard to raise the crest of spiny scales when danger threatens.

**SCALES**

The head, body, legs and tail bristle with spiky scales, making the lizard a very hard creature to swallow.

**BUILD**

The sungazer has a thickset, flattened body for wedging against the walls of its burrow.

**TAIL**

Like a medieval knight swinging a mace, the sungazer lashes its spiky tail furiously to drive away attackers.

**LEGS AND FEET**

Muscular legs and sharp claws enable the lizard to scramble over rocks and excavate a long burrow in hard, dry soil.

Clad from head to tail in a scaly, spiny suit of armor, the sungazer lizard of southern and eastern Africa defends itself stubbornly if a marauding enemy dares to disturb its slumbers in the sun. The sungazer's body can be a tempting sight to a hungry predator, but the lizard's flesh is well protected. When an enemy tries to take a bite out of the prickly reptile, the attacker often ends up the worse for the encounter

**1** A roving jackal spots a sungazer lizard out foraging and immediately bounds toward it, confident of an easy meal. But with its life in peril, the normally slow-moving lizard sprints back toward its burrow as fast as its legs will carry it, with the surprised jackal hot on its heels.

**2** The sungazer makes it back just in time, but instead of retreating deep into the hole, it stops in the entrance. The lizard puffs up its body and raises the spiny scales on its head and back, jamming itself fast, then lashes its tail furiously from side to side—swiping the jackal full in the face and giving it a bloodied nose.

SIZE

## KEY DATA

| | |
|---|---|
| LENGTH | 6–16in (15–40cm), depending on species (*Cordylus giganteus* is the largest) |
| PREY | Mainly small invertebrates such as spiders, beetles, termites, and grasshoppers; occasionally smaller lizards |
| LIFESPAN | Up to 25 years in captivity |

There are some 20 species of sungazer lizard. They are found in dry lowland and upland areas of southern and eastern Africa, wherever the soil is suitable for burrowing —from South Africa in the south to Angola in the west and Ethiopia in the north.

### Did You Know?

● Sungazer lizards give birth to live young—usually one or two, once a year— instead of laying eggs. The newborn are about a quarter as long as their mother. They start life ready-armored, but their spiky scales are soft to begin with, so that they don't harm their mother's body.

● Should a predator manage to seize hold of the sungazer's tail, the lizard has a last-ditch tactic to save itself. Like many other lizards, it can shed its tail, leaving the aggressor clutching the bloody limb while it scuttles for cover. The lizard then slowly grows a new tail.

● Sungazers that live in upland areas, such as *Cordylus giganteus* of South Africa, have to endure cold winters with occasional frosts and snowfalls. They survive by staying in their burrows night and day and entering a state of torpor: a sort of semihibernation in which they slow all their body systems right down.

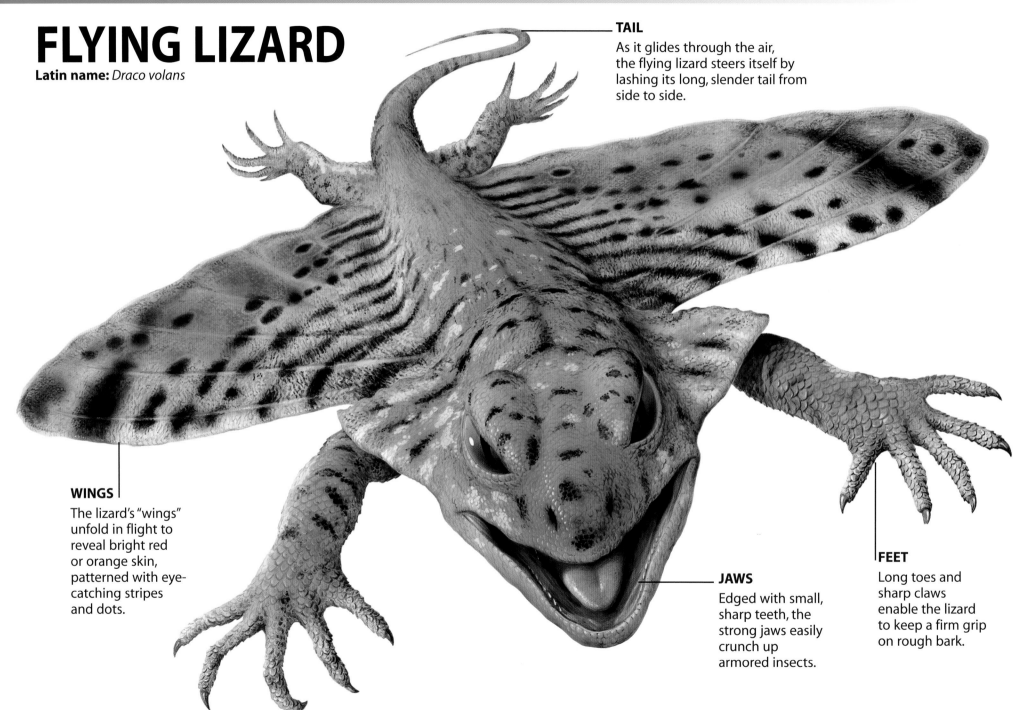

# FLYING LIZARD

**Latin name:** *Draco volans*

**TAIL**
As it glides through the air, the flying lizard steers itself by lashing its long, slender tail from side to side.

**WINGS**
The lizard's "wings" unfold in flight to reveal bright red or orange skin, patterned with eye-catching stripes and dots.

**JAWS**
Edged with small, sharp teeth, the strong jaws easily crunch up armored insects.

**FEET**
Long toes and sharp claws enable the lizard to keep a firm grip on rough bark.

When a flying lizard runs into trouble, it simply leaps into the air, spreads its amazing "wings" and glides to safety on the bark of another rainforest tree. As it forages through the rainforest in search of prey, the flying lizard uses its gliding skills to travel from tree to tree. Its wings are more efficient than they look, enabling it to swoop with pinpoint accuracy and make a perfect landing.

SIZE

**1** A flying lizard is climbing toward the tree canopy when it finds a plump beetle hiding in a crevice. Scraping at the bark with its claws, and probing with its tongue, the reptile digs the juicy insect out and crunches it up with obvious relish.

Despite its size, one beetle isn't enough to satisfy the lizard's appetite, so the hungry reptile decides to search another tree. Leaping headfirst into space, it spreads its vivid wings and glides effortlessly through the air. **2**

As the lizard approaches a **3** nearby tree, it flattens its body to slow its descent and adjusts its direction by steering with its tail. Then, with a final upward swoop, it lands, gripping the bark with its claws before scampering up the trunk to look for prey.

## KEY DATA

| | | |
|---|---|---|
| LENGTH | About 8in (20cm) | |
| PREY | Insects and spiders | |
| WEAPONS | Sharp teeth and claws | |
| DEFENSES | Camouflaged skin and the ability to "fly" | The flying lizard *Draco volans* lives in the rainforests of southeastern Asia, from the Philippines in the north, through Malaysia and Indonesia. It is one of about 40 similar species, and they're all found in the same region. |
| LIFESPAN | Up to 10 years | |

## Did You Know?

● The only reason why any flying lizard visits the forest floor is when a female lays a batch of eggs, which she buries in the soil. So, barring flying accidents, a male could spend his whole life up in the trees.

● The lizard is incapable of soaring flight, and must leap from a height.

● A flying lizard can cover up to197ft (60m) in a single glide, enabling it to flit between the forest trees without once coming down to ground level.

● The flying lizards are part of a family known as the chisel-toothed lizards or "agamids," which includes more then 350 species from the tropics of Africa, Asia, and Australia.

● Flying lizards can tell each other's sex by the color of their fan-like dewlaps. The male's dewlap, for example, may be brilliant yellow while that of the female is sky blue.

# MEXICAN BEADED LIZARD

**Latin name:** *Heloderma horridum*

**TAIL**

During summer the beaded lizard's tail grows steadily fatter as it stores supplies of fat, becoming thinner again in winter as the lizard converts it into energy.

**TONGUE**

The forked, flicking tongue gathers scent molecules from the air and transfers them to the Jacobson's organ in the roof of the beaded lizard's mouth.

**JAWS**

Armed with sharp, curved teeth, the heavily muscled jaws close with a vice-like grip. Bulges on the lower jaw house big venom glands.

Never tease this clumsy, sprawling lizard, for it may retaliate with a vice-like bite. What's more, its venomous saliva causes instant, agonizing pain, made worse by the sheer force of its grip. Few predators mess with a beaded lizard, for it bites with ferocious force when antagonized, injecting quantities of cobra-like venom. No one who has suffered its agonizing bite is likely to forget the pain—if they survive…

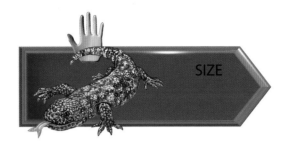

SIZE

## KEY DATA

| | |
|---|---|
| LENGTH | Up to 3ft (1m) |
| PREY | Mainly young mammals, bird and lizard eggs, and reptiles |
| DEFENSES | Clamping, venomous bite |
| VENOM | Kills by attacking the lungs |
| LIFESPAN | 20 years or more |

The Mexican beaded lizard lives in forests and thorn scrub along the Pacific coast of Mexico (as far north as Sonora) and in southeastern Guatemala. Three subspecies are also found in Mexico, while a fourth is isolated in the Motagua Valley of Guatemala.

**1** Two students on a camping trip in Mexico settle down under the stars, unaware that a beaded lizard is dozing nearby. Soon, it emerges to hunt, crawling right over one of the boys. As he tries to brush the lizard away, it clamps its jaws around his hand and bites deeply.

**2** As venom pours into the wound, the boy tries to prise the lizard's jaws apart, but to no avail.

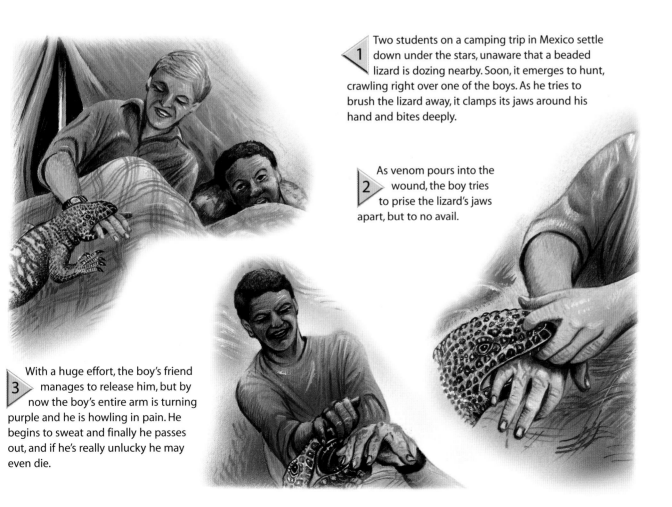

**3** With a huge effort, the boy's friend manages to release him, but by now the boy's entire arm is turning purple and he is howling in pain. He begins to sweat and finally he passes out, and if he's really unlucky he may even die.

## Did You Know?

● Male beaded lizards often fight in the mating season, but as they are immune to each other's venom, their bites rarely cause serious damage.

● Sometimes, the Mexican beaded lizard climbs trees to steal eggs from birds' nests. It's a cautious climber, though, so any bird nesting more than 10ft (3m) above ground is reasonably safe.

● The most common subspecies of beaded lizard, *Heloderma horridum horridum*, is called the escorpion in Mexico. *Heloderma horridum alvarezi*, a completely black subspecies, is known as the escorpion negro.

● Although the beaded lizard's venom is similar to that of a cobra, containing neurotoxins that attack the nervous system, it has a slightly different composition. The lizard's venom seems to attack mainly the lungs rather than the heart, and in many mammals, the heart continues beating up to half an hour after the victim has stopped breathing.

# GILA MONSTER

**Latin name:** *Heloderma suspectum*

**MOUTH**

The tongue transfers samples of the air to a special sensory organ in the roof of the mouth.

**EYES**

The small eyes are inefficient, so the Gila monster relies on other senses until it gets close enough to pounce on its prey.

**JAWS**

The heavily built jaws are equipped with strong muscles and lined with long, sharp teeth. Two glands at the back of the lower jaw produce the monster's venomous saliva.

**COLORS**

The color patterns of the Gila monster are an effective camouflage in the hard-edged shadows and light of the desert.

**SCALES**

The skin is covered with bony, bead-like scales that don't overlap. They make a tough armor and reduce moisture loss in the dry desert air.

**LEGS**

Short, strong legs with large, spreading feet and long, sharp claws help the lizard clamber about on rocks and subdue lively prey.

The Gila monster looks too sluggish to be dangerous, but this lumbering desert lizard has an agonizingly painful bulldog bite laced with powerful venom. Gila monster venom is fatal to most small animals, be they reptiles, rodents, or rabbits—although the lizard can usually rely on its initial devastating bite to snuff out any resistance before the venom begins to take effect.

SIZE

## KEY DATA

| | | |
|---|---|---|
| LENGTH | 16–22in (40–55cm) | The Gila monster is found in parts of the states of New Mexico, California, Nevada, Arizona, and Utah in the southwestern USA. It also occurs in the state of Sonora in northwestern Mexico. It lives mainly in deserts and chaparral (dry scrubland). |
| WEIGHT | 10–12lb (4–5kg) | |
| PREY | Eggs, small lizards, and young mammals | |
| LIFESPAN | About 20 years in the wild; up to 40 years in captivity | |

**1** Tasting the air repeatedly with its flicking forked tongue, a Gila monster relentlessly tracks down a small snake—one of its favorite foods. As the monster waddles in for the kill, mouth agape, the cornered snake rears on its coils, staring helplessly down the throat of its enemy.

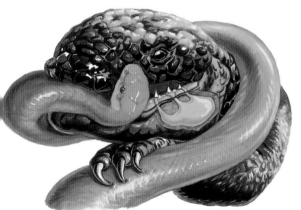

**2** With one bite, the monster grabs the snake's neck in its jaws, puncturing holes and crunching bones. Venom (shown here in blue) flows up its grooved lower teeth and floods the wound. The snake wraps itself around the lizard's head, but a pinning claw soon puts a stop to that.

**3** Stricken by shock and paralyzing pain, the snake can do nothing to prevent the Gila monster's claws slowly and deliberately juggling it into position to swallow it headfirst. Powerless to resist, the snake finds itself on a last, one-way journey—straight down the Gila monster's throat in a series of great gulps.

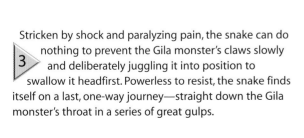

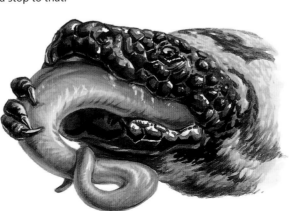

## Did You Know?

● Rival male Gila monsters often bite each other as they fight over females, but luckily for them they are immune to each other's venom.

● The Gila monster's mouth is full of nasty bacteria, so when it bites, the wound often becomes badly infected. This can be almost as dangerous as the monster's venom.

● Captive Gila monsters have lived for up to three years without eating, apparently surviving on the reserves of fat stored in their tails.

● No one knows why, but the Gila monster's venom appears to have little effect on frogs.

● The Gila monster takes its common name from the Gila River area of southwestern Arizona.

● So many Gila monsters have been collected to sell as exotic pets that the creature is now rare in the wild and protected by law.

# GREEN IGUANA

**Latin name:** *Iguana iguana*

**CREST**

A row of elongated scales forms a crest down the back, and is used for visual display.

**EYES**

The iguana has keen eyesight and sees colors, while the parietal organ between its eyes registers levels of light.

**JAWS**

Powerful muscles operate the jaws, which are studded with sharp teeth.

**DEWLAP**

Both sexes have a dewlap or throat fan for displaying to rivals and mates, and pet iguanas extend this if they are upset.

**TAIL**

Like many lizards, the iguana can shed its tail to distract predators—but when it grows again, it may not be serrated like the original.

**CLAWS**

Curved claws give a good grip as the iguana scampers nimbly up trees.

**HINDLEGS**

Pores on the underside of the thighs secrete a grey waxy substance that the green iguana uses to scent-mark its territory.

Dragons may be the stuff of legend but there are several lookalikes in real life, including the huge green iguana, whose jagged throat fan and spiny crest have earned it roles in monster movies. Green iguanas spend much of their time lying about, so keeping one might seem easy—but no! Adult males are unpredictable, and in the mating season they are so territorial they may even attack their owners…

SIZE

## KEY DATA

| | | |
|---|---|---|
| LENGTH | Tail more than 4–5ft (1.5m); total more than 6ft 6in (2m) | Originally, the green iguana was found in forested areas from central Mexico south through Central America into northern South America—including Trinidad and Tobago and several smaller Caribbean islands. Recently, humans have also introduced it into Hawaii and southwestern USA. |
| CREST | Male up to 3in (8cm) high; female smaller | |
| DIET | Juvenile eats insects; adult mainly fruit, leaves, flowers | |
| BREEDING | Lays 20 to 40 eggs | |

**1** Perched high on a bookshelf, a big male iguana surveys its "territory"—and takes exception to the sight of its owner sprawled in a chair below.

**2** Hoping to warn the "intruder" away, the iguana bobs its head up and down threateningly, but its owner just gazes blankly at his television.

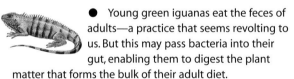

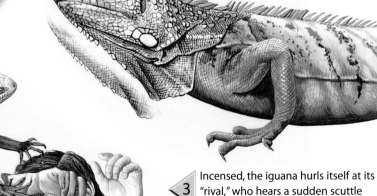

**3** Incensed, the iguana hurls itself at its "rival," who hears a sudden scuttle and turns to see his pet flying toward him, claws outstretched. He tries to shield himself, but the great lizard lands right on his head, inflicting a painful series of bites and scratches.

### Did You Know?

● Young green iguanas eat the feces of adults—a practice that seems revolting to us. But this may pass bacteria into their gut, enabling them to digest the plant matter that forms the bulk of their adult diet.

● A green iguana can change its color considerably. In captivity and under artificial light it is often dull green, gray or brown, but in the wild it may appear brilliant, almost fluorescent green or bright orange.

● Due to its size and appearance, the green iguana often plays the role of dinosaurs in science fiction films.

● In 2000, in Britain, a baby died from salmonella food poisoning after coming into contact with the feces of a pet lizard. Subsequently, a public health warning advised children and pregnant women to avoid pet reptiles.

● Like most reptiles, the green iguana is voiceless, although it emits loud, gurgling hisses if cornered.

# THORNY DEVIL

**Latin name:** *Moloch horridus*

**FALSE HEAD**

This spiny knob looks like a false head. It can distract a predator from attacking the true head.

**TAIL**

The armored tail is typically held off the ground when the animal walks.

**SPINES**

Thorny spines with broad bases and sharp tips coat the entire body.

**LEGS**

Long legs stretch out sideways away from the troublesome spines to lift the lizard's body clear of the surface. They move in a typically jerky, "clockwork" gait.

Close-up, the thorny devil looks fierce with its body grossly distorted by humps, ridges, and sharp spines—but its tiny size and awkward, jerky movements expose it to attack. If the thorny devil finds there's no time to hide, it sits tight and relies on its bizarre suit of armor to bewilder and repel hungry enemies.

SIZE

## KEY DATA

| | | |
|---|---|---|
| LENGTH | 3–4in (8–11cm) | |
| LENGTH OF TAIL | ³⁄₄–1¹⁄₂in (2–4cm) | |
| WEIGHT | 1–3oz (35–90g) | The thorny devil's |
| DIET | Small insects, mostly ants | stronghold is in the interior of Australia, wherever the climate is hot and dry, and the soils sandy. Conditions are friendlier in coastal parts of its range—for example, in the Great Australian Bight to the south. |
| LIFESPAN | Probably up to 20 years | |

**1** A thorny devil plods over the sands in search of ants, unaware that its own tracks are being stalked. It is being quickly caught up by a blue-tongued lizard, one of several hefty desert reptiles that occasionally attack thorny devils. With nowhere to hide, the devil must call on its defenses. Before the blue-tongue gets a bite in, the thorny devil stops still in its tracks, tucks its head down between its forelegs, and presents its "false head."

**2** The enemy investigates what appears to be the hard, spiny, and certainly inedible head of its intended meal. Baffled, it walks away, leaving the wily devil to survive another hostile day.

## Did You Know?

● Though hatchling thorny devils of different sexes are much the same size, after about a year the females start to grow faster than the males. By the time they are adult, females are visibly longer and stouter. The biggest are nearly twice as heavy as the largest males.

● Small twigs, tiny flowers, and insect eggs have been found in the stomachs of thorny lizards. These objects were probably the cargo of ants at their moment of capture on the lizard's tongue.

● Female thorny devils dig nest burrows in the sand. A pregnant animal tunnels down about 10in (25cm) then makes an abrupt bend. At the end, she hollows out a nest chamber. After laying, the lizard leaves the chamber filled with air but seals off the tunnel with sand as she backs out. After hatching from the egg, each baby devil claws its way to the surface.

# REGAL HORNED LIZARD

**Latin name:** *Phrynosoma solare*

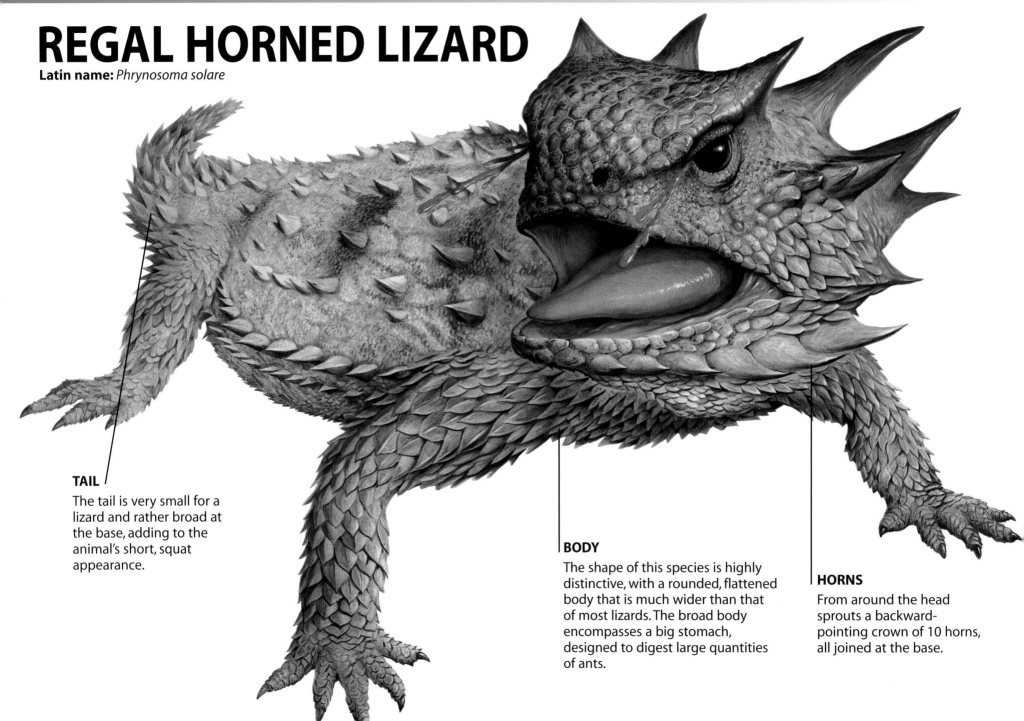

**TAIL**

The tail is very small for a lizard and rather broad at the base, adding to the animal's short, squat appearance.

**BODY**

The shape of this species is highly distinctive, with a rounded, flattened body that is much wider than that of most lizards. The broad body encompasses a big stomach, designed to digest large quantities of ants.

**HORNS**

From around the head sprouts a backward-pointing crown of 10 horns, all joined at the base.

Clad in its thorny armor, the regal horned lizard has a shocking and gory surprise in store for any determined attacker. If provoked enough, the beast shoots fine jets of blood from its eyes. The regal horned lizard dwells in thinly vegetated desert habitats with little cover to hide in. So luckily for it, the creature has evolved this startlingly effective defense against passing predators.

SIZE

## KEY DATA

| | |
|---|---|
| LENGTH | Up to 5in (13cm) |
| DEFENSES | Camouflage, bloated size, armored spikes, and eyes that can squirt blood |
| WEAPONS | Fast, sticky tongue |
| PREY | Small insects, especially harvester ants |

The regal horned lizard is found only in the rocky wastes of the Sonoran Desert region of northwestern Mexico, Arizona, and New Mexico.

**1** A striped skunk catches wind of a regal horned lizard and trots along to investigate. As the skunk approaches through the scrub and sand of the desert, the lizard has little chance of escape. Instead, it turns to face the oncoming mammal and sits tight, holding its armored body stiff and immobile, and ominously closing its eyelids in preparation to launch its horrible, gory defense.

**2** The skunk moves up close and sizes up the lizard, which seems transfixed in resting pose. Little does the aggressor know that behind those eyelids blood pressure is building up. Suddenly, fine streams of blood from ruptured vessels shoot through tiny pores in the beast's lower eyelids, hitting the skunk right in the face. The startled aggressor quickly retreats.

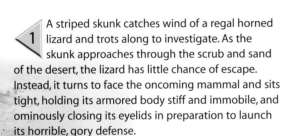

## Did You Know?

● There are 14 species of horned lizard in all. Because of their squat appearance and static postures, they are often known in the USA as "horned toads." This name is very confusing, though, because they are reptiles and not amphibians, while there are true amphibians called horned toads that live in the forests of southeastern Asia.

● When young horned lizards hatch from their eggs they receive no help or protection from their parents at all and have to learn how to hunt for food from scratch. Often a juvenile lizard's first action is to bury itself in the sand to avoid the immediate attentions of any nearby predators that are on the prowl.

● Because they have to spend so much time feeding by day, you might think horned lizards are in danger of overheating in the strong sunshine. Like most other desert animals, though, horned lizards have a high tolerance of high temperatures.

# BEARDED DRAGON

**Latin name:** *Pogona species*

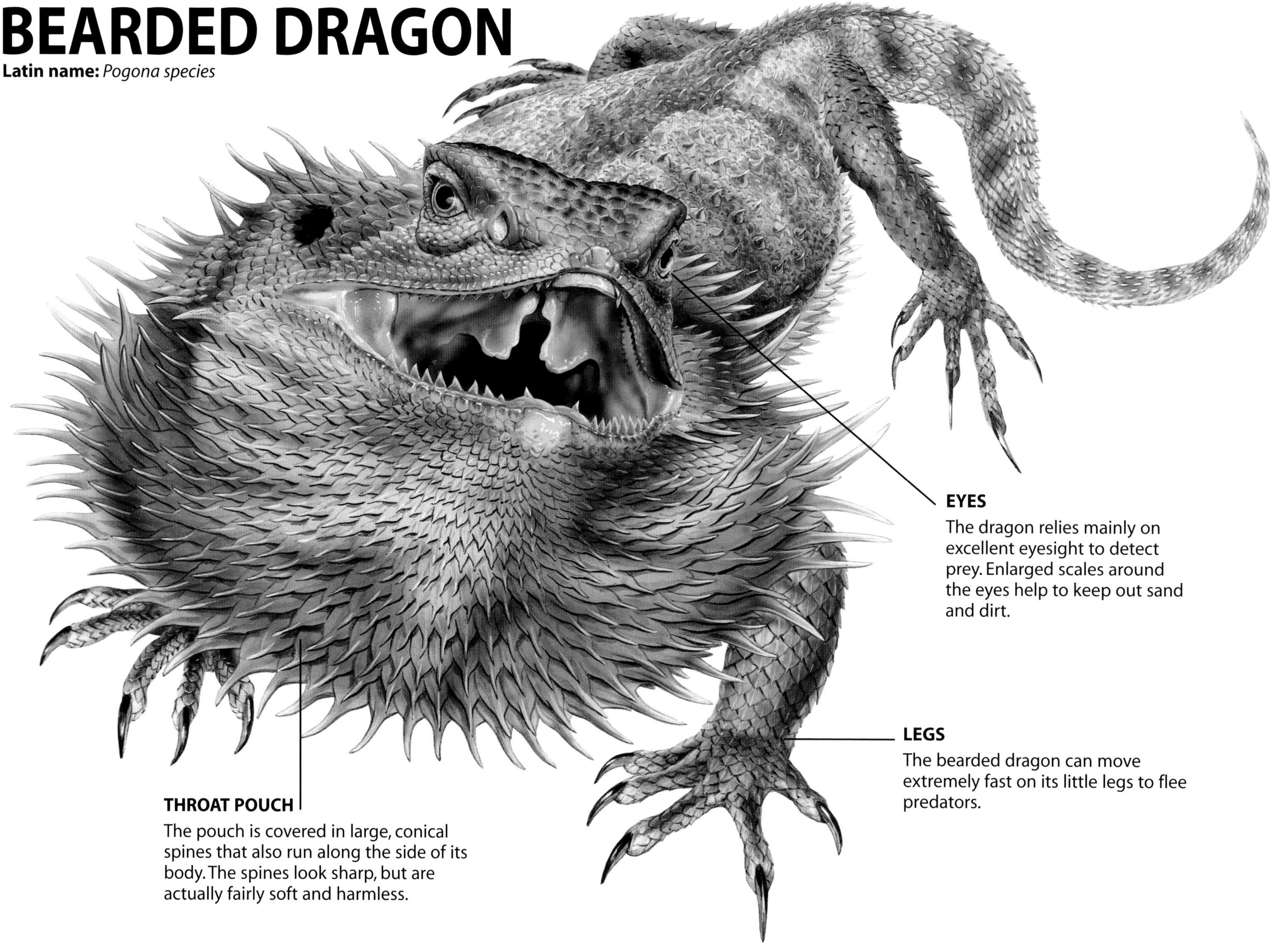

**EYES**

The dragon relies mainly on excellent eyesight to detect prey. Enlarged scales around the eyes help to keep out sand and dirt.

**LEGS**

The bearded dragon can move extremely fast on its little legs to flee predators.

**THROAT POUCH**

The pouch is covered in large, conical spines that also run along the side of its body. The spines look sharp, but are actually fairly soft and harmless.

This Australian lizard puts on an impressive performance to scare off attackers and rivals—it puffs out its throat pouch to reveal a "beard" of sharp-looking spines. The bearded dragon normally keeps its scaly pouch folded against its body. When it is threatened, it inflates the pouch, making its spines stick out. If you've never seen such a spectacle before, the effect can be terrifying.

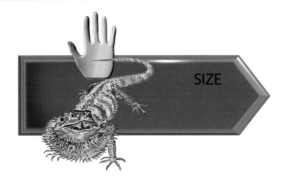

SIZE

1 As the sun rises in the sky, a chilly bearded dragon slowly climbs a fencepost in a suburban garden and perches at the top, basking in the rays. A little girl is walking across her parents' lawn when she suddenly spots the lizard and rushes over to get a closer look at the fascinating creature.

2 Alarmed by the girl's approach, the dragon reacts by puffing out its spiky pouch like a huge ruff. The sudden transformation shocks the toddler and sends her scampering back into her house, yelling with fright.

## KEY DATA

| | | |
|---|---|---|
| LENGTH | 18–24in (45–60cm), up to 8in (20cm) of which is the tail |  |
| DIET | Mainly insects and small reptiles, seeds, berries, fruit, and flowers | |
| DEFENSES | Threat display; fast running | |
| LIFESPAN | 5–6 years in captivity | |

The seven species of bearded dragon, are found all over Australia, apart from far northern and southern areas. They live in various habitats from wet coastal regions to arid semidesert, including grassland, forest, and thorny scrub.

## Did You Know?

● Two of the seven species of bearded dragon are beardless, and lack the spiny throat pouches.

● Before going to sleep, the bearded dragon digs itself into the sand to hide away from predators.

● During the mating season, the male bearded dragon puts on an impressive display, using its entire repertoire of gestures. The male may bite the female's neck during mating to stop her escaping—sometimes causing open wounds in her flesh.

● A female bearded dragon lays up to 35 eggs in a burrow. She digs with her front feet and scoops out loose soil with her rear feet.

● Baby bearded dragons hatch from 40 to 80 days after egg-laying. The young lizards cut their way out of the shells with a sharp projection, called an egg-tooth, on the tip of their snout. After hatching out, the babies scatter to avoid enemies.

# CHUCKWALLA

**Latin name:** *Sauromalus species*

**TRUNK**

Plumpness allows for efficient food-energy storage, and flatness enables the chuckwalla to enter narrow rock fissures.

**TAIL**

The tail grows back if lost, so the chuckwalla is ready to sacrifice it to a predator.

**SCALES**

Small, rough scales cover most of the body and give good grip in rocky crevices.

**LEGS**

Sturdy and muscular, the legs give the chuckwalla the power and agility to scramble across its vast territory and leap up on to large boulders and rocks.

**SKIN**

Around the neck and shoulders the skin is loose and wrinkly, so that when the lungs inflate, the skin unfolds to enable the trunk to expand considerably.

**FEET**

Long, strong claws enable the lizard to burrow deep into desert sand, climb bushes, and cling to rocks.

The desert-dwelling chuckwalla has an extraordinary trick for foxing predators—it scrambles into small rock crevices and then inflates its body, wedging itself in immovably. The chuckwalla's harsh rocky habitat offers little shelter, exposing it to the unwelcome attentions of birds of prey and coyotes, all eager for an easy meal. A nearby rock crevice is often its only hiding place.

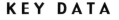
ACTUAL SIZE

**1** A hunting coyote surprises a chuckwalla patrolling its territory on the search for food. Despite the lizard's plumpness and size, it puts on an amazing turn of speed as it escapes to a rocky outcrop.

## KEY DATA

| | |
|---|---|
| LENGTH | Up to 24in (60cm) |
| WEIGHT | Up to 4–5lb (2kg) |
| DIET | Mainly the flowers, leaves, and buds of plants such as prickly pears; some insects as well when young |
| LIFESPAN | Up to 25 years |

The chuckwalla's main habitat spans the Mojave Desert in California and Sonora Desert in Mexico, where it thrives up to a maximum altitude of 4394ft (1370m). It is also found in parts of California, Nevada, Utah, Arizona, and Colorado, and in Mexico, Baja California, and some islands in the Gulf of California.

**2** Well inside a rock crevice, the chuckwalla gulps down air to expand its lungs, increasing its size by over 50 percent. Its rough-skinned body is firmly anchored to the rock, much to the frustration of the coyote.

## Did You Know?

● The chuckwalla is related to some 700 other species of iguanids, including the huge marine iguanas of the Galapagos Islands, which can grow to as long as 4–5ft (1.5m).

● The genus name *Sauromalus* is derived from Greek words meaning "flat lizard." The name chuckwalla comes from the language of the Native American Cahuilla Shoshone tribe of southeastern California.

● Chuckwalla meat was once prized by Native Americans, who dislodged the lizards from rock crevices by puncturing their lungs with a sharp stick to deflate them.

● When fresh water is unavailable, an island species of chuckwalla in the Gulf of California drinks salt water.

● The chuckwalla thrashes its tail when it's trying to escape capture. This may be a habit retained from prehistoric days when it may have had sharp spines along its tail.

# TUATARA

**Latin name:** *Sphenodon punctatus, S. guntheri*

**CREST**
Used for defense and display, the crest of enlarged scales is bigger on the male.

**SKIN**
The scaly, loose skin is soft to the touch. The small scales may have yellow spots.

**TAIL**
The end of the tail breaks off easily if a predator grabs it, allowing the tuatara to make a getaway. A new tail soon grows to replace the old one.

**LEGS**
The tuatara moves in a sprawling fashion on its strong, stout legs, with its belly leaving the ground only briefly.

**COLOR**
The tuatara varies from blackish-brown to dull olive-green, and can have a reddish tinge.

**EYES**
Unlike lizards, the tuatara has a third eyelid, known as a nictitating membrane, that closes horizontally.

**FEET**
Partially webbed, with five sharp claws, these are ideal for excavating burrows.

Not only can the New Zealand tuatara live for 100 years, it is the sole survivor of a group of reptiles that became extinct everywhere else in the world some 60 million years ago. An amazing discovery was made in 1867. Albert Günther, a naturalist from the British Museum, realized that the tuatara isn't a lizard at all. It is a surviving member of an ancient order of reptiles called the *Rhynchocephalia*.

SIZE

### KEY DATA

| | | |
|---|---|---|
| LENGTH | Male up to about 24in (60cm); female 18in (45cm) | |
| WEIGHT | Male up to about 2lb (1kg); female 1lb 2oz (500g) | |
| PREY | Insects, snails, worms, frogs, lizards, eggs, and chicks | |
| LIFESPAN | Up to 100 years or more | |

Once found throughout New Zealand's North and South islands, the tuatara is now restricted to about 30 small islands and rock stacks in Cook Strait and the Bay of Plenty. There are two species: Brother's Island tuatara (*Sphenodon guntheri*) and the Cook Strait tuatara (*S. punctatus*).

**tuatara skull**

**1** Albert Günther made his astonishing discovery when he studied the skull of the tuatara and found that it is radically different to the skull of any other living reptile. For one thing, the tuatara's chisel-like "teeth" are actually part of its jawbones. Also, the two large fenestrae (openings) in the skull behind each eye are both completely enclosed by bone.

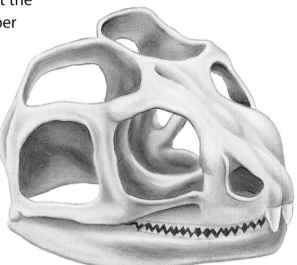

**lizard skull**

**2** Modern lizards have real teeth growing in sockets. As the teeth wear out or break off, new ones grow. Also, the lower fenestrae in a lizard's skull are open at the bottom. This allows the jaws to gape wider and engulf large prey.

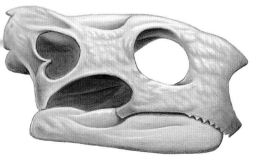

**tortoise skull**

**3** The small, strong, helmet-like skulls of tortoises and turtles have no fenestrae at all behind the eyes. Tortoises and turtles have no real teeth, either, but tear their food apart with their tough, beak-like jaws, which have a horny covering to protect the bone below.

### Did You Know?

● The tuatara usually drinks from small puddles of rainwater, but can survive for months on just dew and the moisture in its food.

● Because the tuatara needs so little energy to keep its vital body processes "ticking over," it functions well in temperatures as low as 33°F (6°C)—lower than any other reptile.

● The tuatara features heavily in the traditional carvings decorating the meeting houses of native Maori people—as a symbol of death or misfortune. In Maori mythology, the creature is associated with the fire goddess, who brought death into the world by killing her grandson.

● Look inside the burrow of a petrel or shearwater and you may see a tuatara sharing the seabird's home. It pays for its lodgings by keeping the burrow free of insects attracted to the bird's droppings. Ungratefully, it occasionally gobbles up the bird's eggs and chicks as well.

# SHINGLEBACK SKINK

**Latin name:** *Tiliqua rugosa*

**TAIL**
When food is plentiful, the shingleback skink stuffs its face as fast as it can, and stores some as excess fat inside its larder-like tail.

**EYES**
The skink has big eyes and keen vision, since it's active by day when there's lots of light. It spots distant danger as easily as it spies scuttling insects.

**SCALES**
These provide all-over protection against knocks and scrapes, and some defense against the teeth and claws of persistent enemies.

**JAWS**
Big and broad, the jaws are operated by powerful muscles to crush snails and beetles—and bite enemies.

**LEGS**
The skink has short legs and can't move very fast, so can't catch flying insects and other speedy prey.

**TONGUE**
This flap-like, vivid blue organ is the lizard's most astonishing feature—and it's supposed to be. One glimpse of it sends many an enemy running fast for cover.

This sluggish lizard might look easy meat for a passing predator, but it has a couple of tricks that can give an enemy quite a surprise. When not foraging, the shingleback skink likes to snooze in an abandoned animal burrow, or under a snug log or stone. A warm sheet of corrugated iron in a suburban backyard also suits its requirements perfectly…

SIZE

## KEY DATA

| | |
|---|---|
| LENGTH | Up to 16in (40cm) |
| WEIGHT | Up to 2lb (1kg) |
| DIET | Flowers, fruit, berries, insects, and snails |
| DEFENSES | Shows startling blue tongue |
| LIFESPAN | Up to 40 years |

The shingleback skink lives in southern Australia, in a variety of dry habitats to the west of the Great Dividing Range. It ranges from Victoria, New South Wales, and southern Queensland in the east, through southern South Australia to southern Western Australia.

**1** Happily helping his dad clear their backyard, a boy lifts a sheet of corrugated iron and comes face to face with a shingleback skink, which bares its blue tongue in alarm.

**2** Astonished by this unfamiliar sight, the boy reaches down to grab the harmless-looking lizard and show it proudly to his dad—only to receive a painful bite on the hand for his trouble.

## Did You Know?

● Most blue-tongued skinks give birth to litters of up to 25 live young, but the shingleback produces only two, or at most three. When born the young are relatively large and well developed, having been nourished inside the womb through a placenta, just like a human baby.

● In the spring mating season, rival male shingleback skinks may fight fiercely for females. Once they have mated, though, paired skinks often seek each other out year after year to renew their bond.

● The shingleback skink has many other local names in different parts of its range, including sleepy lizard, stumpy-tailed lizard, bog-eyed lizard (or boggi, for short), pine cone lizard, and even four-legged pine cone.

● The bite of a shingleback skink isn't venomous, but bacteria in the lizard's mouth sometimes infect the puncture wounds, turning them septic and painful.

# LEAF-TAILED GECKO

**Latin name:** *Uroplatus species*

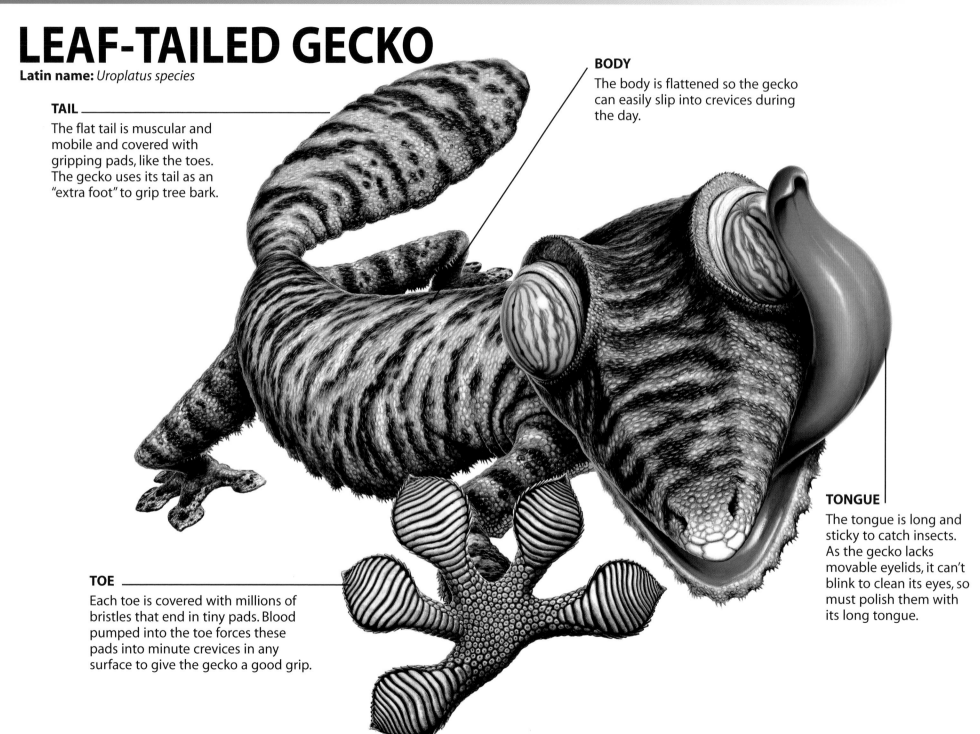

**TAIL**

The flat tail is muscular and mobile and covered with gripping pads, like the toes. The gecko uses its tail as an "extra foot" to grip tree bark.

**BODY**

The body is flattened so the gecko can easily slip into crevices during the day.

**TONGUE**

The tongue is long and sticky to catch insects. As the gecko lacks movable eyelids, it can't blink to clean its eyes, so must polish them with its long tongue.

**TOE**

Each toe is covered with millions of bristles that end in tiny pads. Blood pumped into the toe forces these pads into minute crevices in any surface to give the gecko a good grip.

With its bulbous eyes, gripping tail, and sticky toes, the Madagascan leaf-tailed gecko is one of the most versatile—and among the weirdest—of all lizards. Cornered by a killer high in a bush, some leaf-tailed geckos can bail out like a pilot leaping from a plane. Unlike a pilot, geckos are light enough to survive the fall without a parachute.

SIZE

1 Surprised high in its bushy home by a hunting fossa—a cat-like creature—a leaf-tailed gecko (*U. guentheri*) runs along its branch, looking for an escape route. With the fossa close behind, the gecko leaps for safety.

2 Curling itself into a protective ball in midair, the fleeing gecko plunges through leaves and branches toward the forest floor. It bounces twice on hitting the ground, but is totally unharmed by its desperate escape.

3 The gecko quickly unrolls, then scrambles into the dense undergrowth to hide from danger.

## KEY DATA

| | |
|---|---|
| LENGTH | Up to 8in (20cm) |
| PREY | Insects, spiders, and other small invertebrates |
| ENEMIES | Mammals, birds, and snakes |
| DEFENSES | Dives for cover; discards tail |
| LIFESPAN | Unknown |

Geckos in general are found in tropical and temperate areas all around the world, but the leaf-tailed species occupy a fairly small area. They are found only on the tropical island of Madagascar, in the Indian Ocean, off the east coast of Africa. Their preferred habitat is the high leaf canopy of the dense forest that covers much of the island.

## Did You Know?

● Scientists once thought geckos had suckers on their feet because they can climb glass. But using a microscope they noticed that most glass has minute crevices that the pads on a gecko's toes can grip on to. When the scientists used glass that was polished really smooth they found that geckos couldn't climb it.

● The leaf-tailed gecko is highly fastidious about personal grooming. After feeding it retires to a favorite spot to clean up by licking itself all over—including its eyes.

● In the breeding season, male geckos advertise to attract females and challenge rival males by making a series of noisy chirps and clicks that echo through the tropical night.

# SAVANNAH MONITOR

**Latin name:** *Varanus exanthematicus*

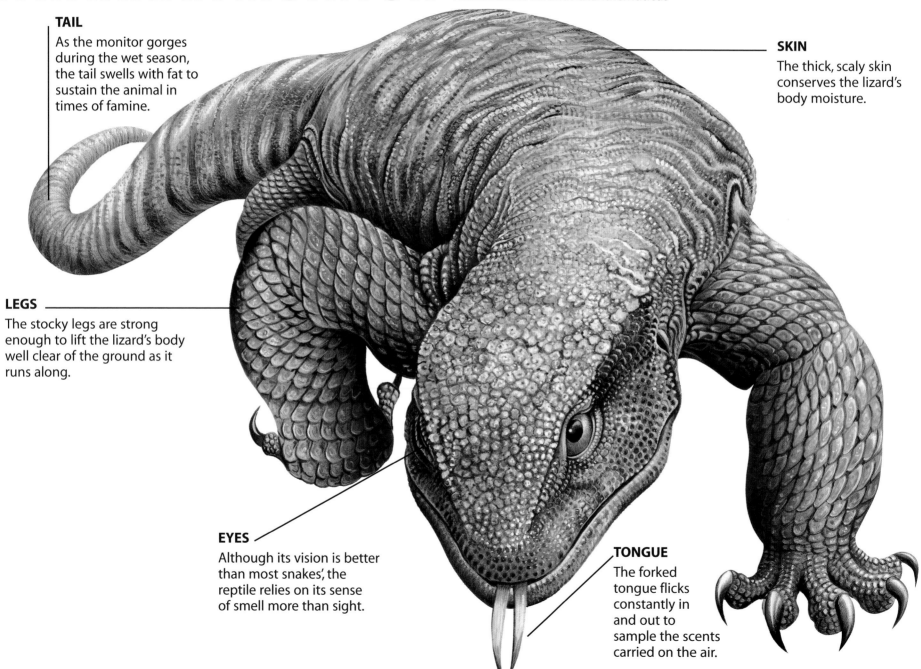

**TAIL**
As the monitor gorges during the wet season, the tail swells with fat to sustain the animal in times of famine.

**SKIN**
The thick, scaly skin conserves the lizard's body moisture.

**LEGS**
The stocky legs are strong enough to lift the lizard's body well clear of the ground as it runs along.

**EYES**
Although its vision is better than most snakes', the reptile relies on its sense of smell more than sight.

**TONGUE**
The forked tongue flicks constantly in and out to sample the scents carried on the air.

This shy, elusive creature likes to be left alone to gorge on small animals, so it can withstand the months of famine ahead. Large and placid, savannah monitors are popular pets, particularly in the USA. If they get used to being handled when young they can become tame, but they don't like surprises. A monitor that is alarmed can retaliate—so take care.

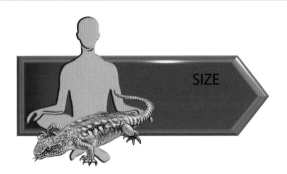

SIZE

## KEY DATA

| | | |
|---|---|---|
| LENGTH | 3–5ft (1–1.5m) | |
| WEIGHT | 4–10lb (2–4kg) | |
| PREY | Invertebrates, frogs, lizards, and small mammals | |
| WEAPONS | Teeth and claws | The savannah monitor lives in west and Central Africa, from Senegal to western Ethiopia, in the dry grasslands lying between the Sahara Desert and the equatorial rainforests. Similar species dwell throughout Africa, south of the Sahara. |
| LIFESPAN | Up to 30 years | |

**1** While visiting a friend, a father lifts his small son up to see the man's pet savannah monitor. The child reaches into the tank to stroke it.

**2** Startled by the intrusion, the monitor attacks. It seizes the child's thumb in its jaws and bites hard into the soft flesh. Then it rakes its sharp claws across the boy's fingers. Ouch!

## Did You Know?

● Savannah monitors are often caught and cooked as "bush chicken" in Ghana and Nigeria, and their skins are sold for leather to make shoes, handbags, and watchstraps.

● The savannah monitor's forked tongue gathers scent molecules from the air and transfers them to a special sensor, called the Jacobson's organ, in the roof of its mouth.

● The thick skin of the savannah monitor enables it to inhabit arid regions, many miles from the nearest river or waterhole, but it cannot survive long in a real desert, such as the Sahara. Although it lives in such dry terrain, the monitor is a surprisingly good swimmer.

● The savannah monitor has a cunning way of eating millipedes that defend themselves with acrid, foul-tasting fluids. The monitor just aggravates them by rubbing them with its chin so they discharge all their fluid, then it snaps them up.

# GIGANTIC LACE LIZARD

**Latin name:** *Varanus giganteus*

**TONGUE**
The lizard flicks its forked tongue in and out of its mouth like a snake to sample air for the scents that lead it to a tasty meal.

**TEETH**
The long, sharp, blade-like teeth curve back for a secure grip on struggling victims.

**THROAT**
If threatened, the lizard swells up its throat and makes an alarming hissing noise.

**TAIL**
Long and powerful, the tail makes a devastating weapon when the lizard finds itself in a tight corner.

**BODY**
The slender, elongated body weighs less than you might expect.

**CLAWS**
Sharp and hooked, the claws are ideal for tearing large prey apart. They also give the lizard a good grip when climbing trees.

**LEGS**
Strong enough to propel the lizard at high speed when it attacks prey, the legs are also armed with long, sharp claws.

The biggest of all Australian lizards, the gigantic lace lizard is a powerful killer armed with a fearsome set of serrated teeth and a thick tail that it swings like a club. Although mainly a creature of the outback, the adaptable gigantic lace lizard has learned to make use of the human landscape. On Barrow Island off Western Australia, it uses cars as cover to launch attacks on unwary seabirds.

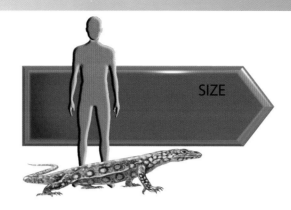

SIZE

### KEY DATA

| | | |
|---|---|---|
| LENGTH | Up to 8ft (2.5m) | |
| WEIGHT | Up to 26lb (12kg) | |
| DIET | Small mammals, lizards, snakes, birds, eggs | |
| WEAPONS | Sharp teeth and heavy tail | |
| LIFESPAN | 30 years | |

The gigantic lace lizard lives in the arid lands of central Australia, from the Queensland borders and Lake Eyre west, through the Simpson, Great Sandy and Great Victoria deserts, to the dry coast of Western Australia. Its smaller cousin, the lace lizard, lives on the east coast.

**1** Creeping behind the wheel of a car, a gigantic lace lizard ambushes a black-backed gull that is too preoccupied with finding its own food to notice any danger.

**2** The killer seizes the gull in its knife-like teeth and thrashes its head from side to side to stun the bird. Then it rips the gull apart and wolfs down the bloody chunks.

### Did You Know?

● In some areas, particularly in the Lake Eyre region, the gigantic lace lizard is known as the perentie, perentic, or perenthic. Its aboriginal name is echunpa.

● The instinct to climb trees when alarmed is so strong that these lizards have been known to climb people or horses by mistake!

● The gigantic lace lizard can swim quite well and, if necessary, can hide underwater for up to an hour before emerging.

● Scientists suspect that the gigantic lace lizard population has risen as its favorite prey animals —introduced European rabbits—have become more abundant.

● The gigantic lace lizard needs the sun to warm up its body before it can move around. As winter falls in May, it becomes too cold for the lizard so it finds a safe hiding place in which to hibernate until August.

# KOMODO DRAGON

**Latin name:** *Varanus komodoensis*

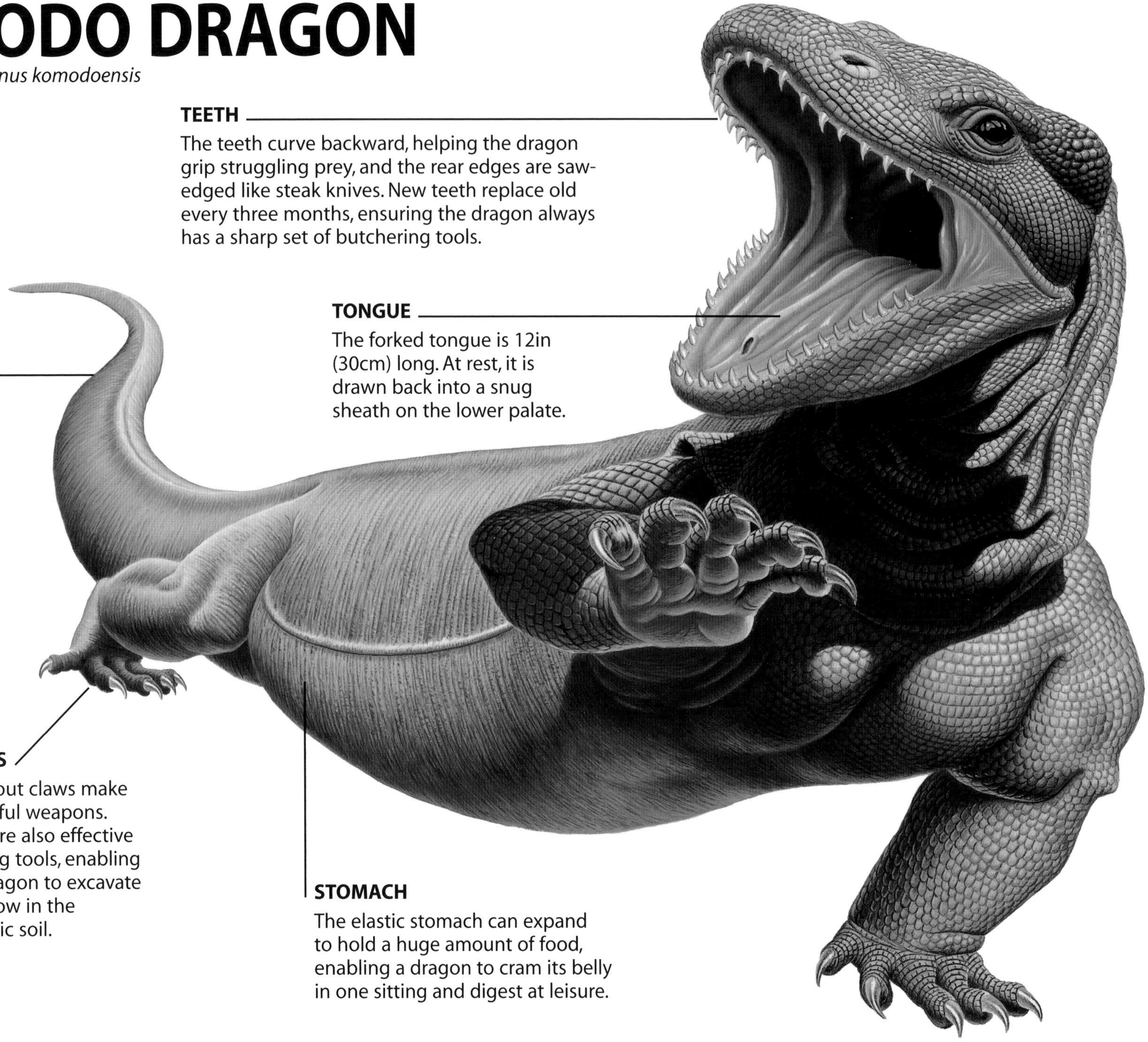

**TEETH**

The teeth curve backward, helping the dragon grip struggling prey, and the rear edges are saw-edged like steak knives. New teeth replace old every three months, ensuring the dragon always has a sharp set of butchering tools.

**TONGUE**

The forked tongue is 12in (30cm) long. At rest, it is drawn back into a snug sheath on the lower palate.

**SKIN**

A waterproof, scaly skin stops the dragon drying out in the tropical sun.

**CLAWS**

The stout claws make powerful weapons. They are also effective digging tools, enabling the dragon to excavate a burrow in the volcanic soil.

**STOMACH**

The elastic stomach can expand to hold a huge amount of food, enabling a dragon to cram its belly in one sitting and digest at leisure.

The awesome Komodo dragon is the biggest lizard in the world, with a mouthful of wickedly sharp teeth to match. This very real killer was once dismissed as a creature of the imagination. The Komodo dragon's specialty is the ambush. Lurking in the grass, it lunges powerfully at passing prey. Its first bite often kills outright—if not, the dragon simply bides its time. It tracks and watches its victim, waiting for it to die from blood poisoning.

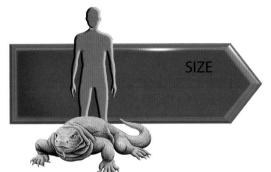

SIZE

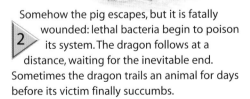

**1** A Komodo dragon surges from its hiding place to ambush a wild pig. If it can knock the pig off its feet, the end will be quick.

**2** Somehow the pig escapes, but it is fatally wounded: lethal bacteria begin to poison its system. The dragon follows at a distance, waiting for the inevitable end. Sometimes the dragon trails an animal for days before its victim finally succumbs.

**3** Weakened by infection, the pig finally falls into the dragon's jaws. The dragon shreds its body and devours the flesh in minutes. Sated, it returns undercover to digest its meal.

## KEY DATA

| | |
|---|---|
| LENGTH | Up to 11ft 6in (3.5m) |
| WEIGHT | 220lb (100kg) or more, depending on last meal |
| TEETH | Saw-edged, backward-curving blades, laden with toxic bacteria |
| DIET | Deer, pigs, goats, and other Komodo dragons —dead or alive |
| APPETITE | Can eat up to 80 percent of its own bodyweight in one sitting |
| LIFESPAN | Up to 50 years |

The Komodo dragon is found only on Komodo Island and a few nearby islands on the Lesser Sunda Islands. This tropical island group lies east of Java in southern Indonesia, very close to the Equator.

## Did You Know?

● The people of Komodo bury their dead in extra-deep holes to stop the dragons from digging up the corpses and eating them.

● Komodo dragons are excellent swimmers, and may visit nearby islands to gorge on wild goats.

● Western scientists first heard about the dragon in the early 1900s. A pilot crashed in the sea near Komodo, and swam to the shore. He returned home with tales of "giant reptiles." No one believed him until a later expedition confirmed his story.

● A dragon's bite may contain at least four poisonous bacteria for which there is no known antidote.

# NILE MONITOR

**Latin name:** *Varanus niloticus*

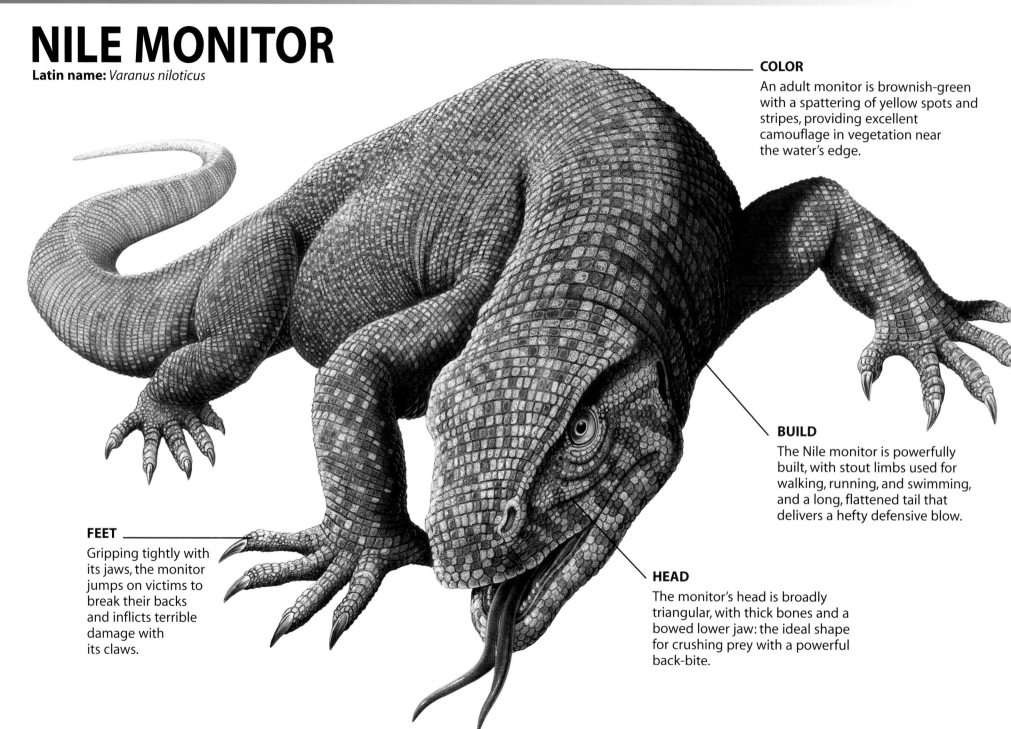

**COLOR**

An adult monitor is brownish-green with a spattering of yellow spots and stripes, providing excellent camouflage in vegetation near the water's edge.

**BUILD**

The Nile monitor is powerfully built, with stout limbs used for walking, running, and swimming, and a long, flattened tail that delivers a hefty defensive blow.

**FEET**

Gripping tightly with its jaws, the monitor jumps on victims to break their backs and inflicts terrible damage with its claws.

**HEAD**

The monitor's head is broadly triangular, with thick bones and a bowed lower jaw: the ideal shape for crushing prey with a powerful back-bite.

Gluttonous egg-thief and all-round bad neighbor, the Nile monitor is a big bully of a lizard—an aggressive predator with an appetite for just about anything it can catch. Eggs are a tasty treat for the Nile monitor, and it boldly raids the nests of massive Nile crocodiles. And although croc mums are notoriously aggressive, they may tolerate the marauding monitor with a mysteriously liberal attitude.

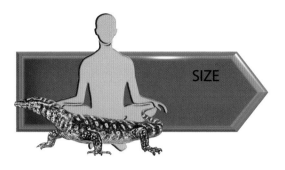

SIZE

1 After burying her eggs in the warm sand of a river bank, a female crocodile lurks nearby, watching for potential predators. When a mongoose comes sniffing too close, she reacts with customary anger, lunging savagely to chase the intruder away.

## KEY DATA

| | | |
|---|---|---|
| LENGTH | Up to 6ft 6in (2m) | |
| WEIGHT | 4–13lb (2–6kg) | |
| DIET | Mainly snails, insects, frogs, fish, eggs, and carrion | |
| WEAPONS | Claws, teeth, and lashing tail | |
| LIFESPAN | 15 years in captivity | |

The Nile monitor ranges across much of the African continent, except for the most arid areas to the north. Its favored habitats are watery spots around rivers, swamps, pools, lakes, and coasts—wherever there is permanent water. Consequently, many of its victims are aquatic of semi-aquatic creatures.

## Did You Know?

● When scavenging at a carcass the monitor often tries to swallow lumps that are far too big for its gullet. It may even end up bashing the bones against hard objects and tearing at the meat with its claws as it tries to break off the excess left hanging out of its mouth.

● The Nile monitor is an amazing egg-layer, producing regular clutches of up to 40 eggs. And as each weighs about 1¾oz (50g), a large batch can double the weight of an expectant mother.

● Sometimes, a female monitor makes crafty use of a termite mound as a nest chamber, breaking it open to drop her eggs inside. The termites quickly repair the hole, sealing the eggs in the safety of their warm nest.

● A little-studied subspecies of the Nile monitor lives in the rainforests of West Africa. Though seldom seen by locals, it is said to live in a huge burrow and to be so fierce that it is impossible to capture alive.

2 A little later, as she basks in the shallows, a Nile monitor creeps up, digs down and snatches one of the incubating eggs in its mouth. This time the croc stays put, watching with apparent disinterest as the thief retreats into the bush to swallow its booty.

# SALVADOR'S MONITOR

**Latin name:** *Varanus salvadori*

## TAIL

Long and gripping, the tail balances and supports the monitor as it climbs, and also forms a formidable whip. When walking, the lizard curls this vulnerable appendage into a spiral rather than trailing it along the ground.

## LEGS

Sturdy, heavily muscled legs enable Salvador's monitor to move at speed.

## SNOUT

As the monitor ages, the snout grows ever wider, and it is particularly bulbous in old males.

## CLAWS

Elongated toes with sharp, curved claws give the monitor an exceedingly firm grip, and it can cling to vertical tree-trunks by its hindfeet alone.

## TONGUE

Long and forked, the tongue collects scent molecules from the air, providing vital information about the monitor's surroundings, including the presence of prey.

Don't get on the wrong side of this moody monitor, it can inflict terrible wounds with its long, lashing tail and razor-sharp teeth and claws. Salvador's monitor is always edgy when it comes down from the treetops to cross wide clearings, and bolts for safety at the merest hint of danger. Unfortunately it can't see too well, so intruders should be especially cautious.

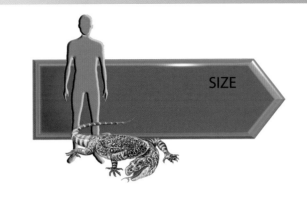

SIZE

1 A tourist visiting a forest reserve spots a giant monitor striding across a clearing and foolishly hurries over to take a photo. Startled by the noise, the lizard panics and dashes towards the closest upright shape it sees in search of an escape route.

2 As the massive reptile races toward him the man's jaw drops in horror, and a split second later the monitor leaps on to his chest and claws its way upward, its devilish talons ripping into his flesh. It's hard to tell which of the two is more shocked as they come face to face and topple over.

## KEY DATA

| | |
|---|---|
| LENGTH | 6ft–10ft (1.8–3m), of which the tail accounts for more than two thirds; females often smaller |
| WEIGHT | Up to 30lb (14kg) |
| PREY | Birds and their eggs, small mammals, reptiles and frogs |
| LIFESPAN | Over 20 years in captivity |

Salvador's monitor ranges across the tropical forests and mangrove swamps of the southern lowlands of New Guinea, off the northern coast of Australia. It is one of many extraordinary animal inhabitants, and spends most of its time up in the trees.

## Did You Know?

● Salvador's monitor is undeniably dangerous, but tales of giant lizards terrorizing soldiers and dragging off children are almost certainly false.

● Salvador's monitor is said to be one of the most intelligent of all lizards; ever alert and attentive to its surroundings, it soon discovers any escape routes from an enclosure.

● In 1878, the first specimen know to science measured only 5ft (1.65m) long, but the biggest on record was claimed to stretch a staggering 15ft (4.75m).

● Salvador's monitor grows longer than any of its relatives, but in terms of bulk it's no match for the Komodo dragon. A full grown Komodo may weigh as much as 220lb (100kg), seven times heavier than a typical adult monitor.

● Anyone approaching Salvador's monitor is wise to heed its threat behavior, for when the lizard inflates its throat and utters a loud hiss, it's a sure sign it's not happy.

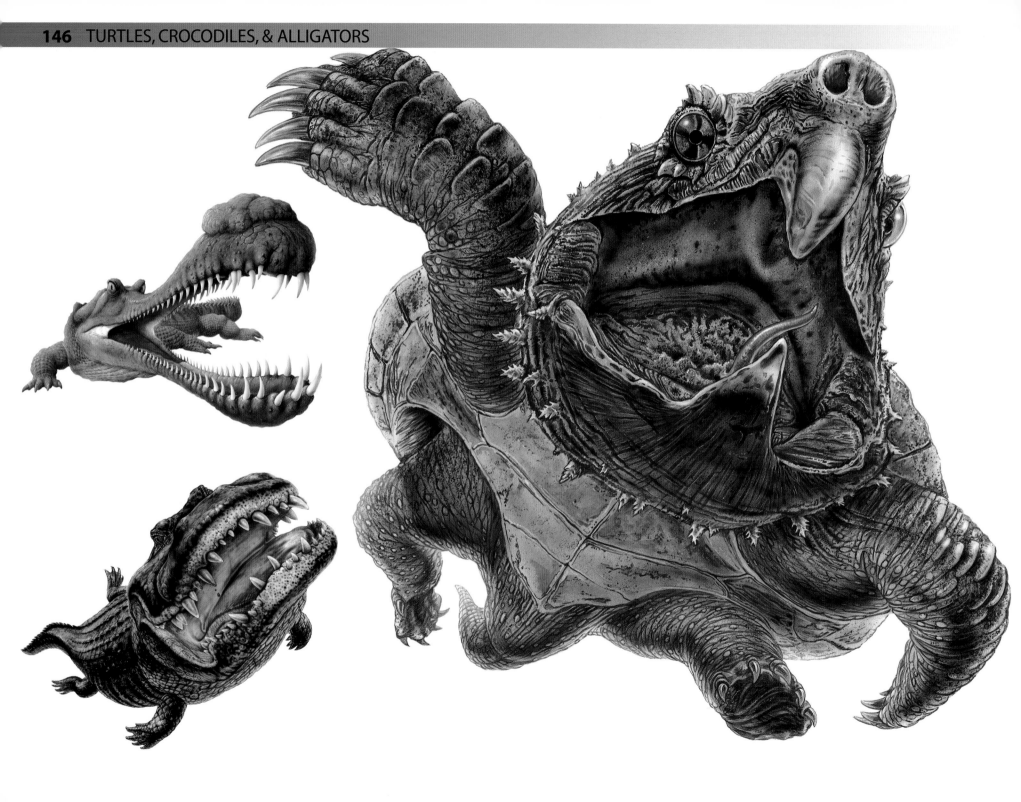

# Turtles, Crocodiles, & Alligators

*Turtles, crocodiles, and alligators are not much different from their ancient ancestors. These reptiles are well equipped for survival. They often live as long as people—or longer.*

The snapping turtle is a mean machine, with a sharp beak that crushes prey and a hard shell that protects it from enemies. The stinkpot turtle is smaller but just as vicious, and it sprays a smelly concoction on predators. More fearsome is the alligator snapping turtle, which has sharp claws and ugly spikes on its head. These reptiles pale in comparison to the mighty crocodile. The Nile crocodile is big, strong, and quick. It lurks in African rivers, only its eyes and nostrils visible above the water. When a large animal comes to the river's edge it strikes, dragging its prey to a watery death. The saltwater crococile is even more terrifying. Longer than most cars, it is the largest reptile in the world, and it can live for one hundred years. It also has no problem eating people! The alligator is somewhat smaller than the crocodile but no less deadly. Like the crocodile, it has sharp teeth and a long, powerful tail, and it hides in water waiting for its next meal. It can also take down large animals, including horses. Wherever they live, these reptiles have a proven track record for staying in the game.

# AMERICAN ALLIGATOR

**Latin name:** *Alligator mississippiensis*

**SNOUT**
An alligator's snout is distinctly broader and more rounded than that of a crocodile.

**EYES & NOSTRILS**
These are high-set, so the 'gator can lurk semisubmerged when hunting.

**TEETH**
The jaws are lined with a fearsome array of gleaming teeth that remain hidden when the mouth is closed.

**ARMOR**
A coat of tough, knobbly scales protects the whole body, but especially the back, where they form raised ridges.

**BODY**
This is big and hefty even by crocodilian standards, with short, sturdy limbs for lunging attacks.

**W**ithout warning, a huge, gaping mouth studded with sharp teeth erupts from the water. Another unwary animal falls victim to this swamp monster's terrible jaws. To a big hungry 'gator, any animal that strays into or close to its watery home is fair game. Even a horse isn't too large for a fully grown alligator to tackle—though the reptile prefers handy bite-sized meals…

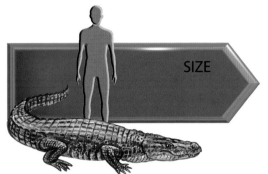

SIZE

## KEY DATA

| | | |
|---|---|---|
| LENGTH | Male up to 11–12ft (3.6m), female up to 7ft (2.3m) | The American alligator inhabits mainly protected wetland sites in the southeastern USA, mostly in the states of South Carolina, Georgia, Florida, Alabama, Mississippi, Louisiana, and Texas. The largest populations are in the Louisiana bayous (creeks), in the Florida Everglades and on the Mississippi River. |
| WEIGHT | | |
| DIET | | |
| WEIGHT | Up to 225kg (496lb) | |
| BREEDING | | |
| PREY | Fish, amphibians, reptiles, birds, and mammals, including domestic animals | |
| LIFESPAN | | |
| LIFESPAN | Up to 50 years in captivity | |

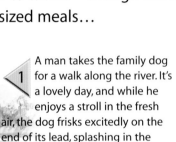

**1** A man takes the family dog for a walk along the river. It's a lovely day, and while he enjoys a stroll in the fresh air, the dog frisks excitedly on the end of its lead, splashing in the shallow margins and nosing at clumps of reeds.

**2** Suddenly, an enormous alligator bursts out of its hiding place in the weeds and seizes the dog in its jaws. Instinctively, the man holds on to the lead—which snaps like cotton as the 'gator crashes back into the water.

**3** The man watches helplessly as the 'gator swims off, leaving a bloody trail in its wake. While it finds a secluded spot to gulp down its prize, the man staggers home in a state of shock—heartbroken by his loss, yet realizing he has had a lucky escape himself.

## Did You Know?

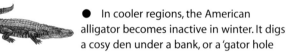

● In cooler regions, the American alligator becomes inactive in winter. It digs a cosy den under a bank, or a 'gator hole in muddy shallows, and stays there for up to four months, moving little and seldom eating. Sometimes the alligator gets frozen in its 'gator hole, but as long as there is a breathing hole it can survive until the ice thaws.

● The male alligator's roar carries for 492ft (150m). He often mistakes loud noises for the calls of rivals, hissing or bellowing at sounds such as those made by horns, jet engines, jackhammers, and pneumatic drills.

● It is often said the American alligator uses its powerful tail to sweep animals off riverbanks and into the water, but there is no firm evidence for this belief.

● Some female American 'gators are fiercely protective mothers and guard their young—mainly from other alligators—for several years.

# MATAMATA

**Latin name:** *Chelus fimbriatus*

**SHELL**

Conical scutes (horny shields) cover most of the matamata's shell, each well-marked with growth rings. The turtle spends so much time immobile that thick growths of algae may accumulate on its rough, ridged back, helping to break up its outline as it waits patiently on the riverbed.

**NOSE**

The tubular nose acts as a snorkel for sucking in air from the surface.

**MOUTH**

The matamata's broad, toothless jaws are designed for swallowing rather then chewing.

**FLESHY APPENDAGES**

Small flaps on the throat and head wave in the water like strands of weed, and may even act as worm-like lures for unsuspecting fish.

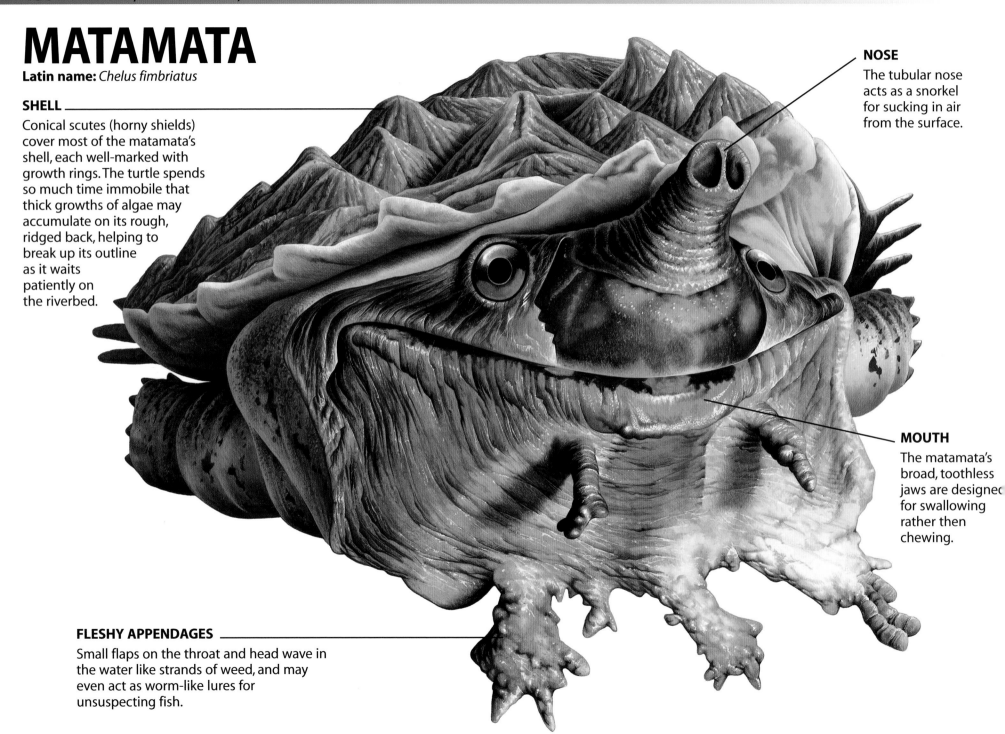

Any fish straying too close to this vacuum-powered villain is likely to find itself sucked on a surging current, straight into the creature's cavernous mouth. Although the matamata is chiefly a "sit-and-suck" predator, it occasionally "trawls" for prey by sweeping its long neck from side to side. It may even stir itself and plod along the bottom to corral small fish in the shallows.

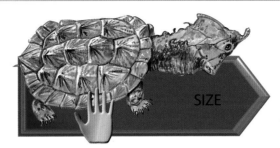

SIZE

## KEY DATA

| | |
|---|---|
| LENGTH | Shell up to 18in (45cm) |
| WEIGHT | Up to 5–6lb (2.5kg) |
| PREY | Fish, other water creatures, small birds, and mammals |
| WEAPONS | Wide, suctioning mouth |
| LIFESPAN | Up to 30 years in captivity |

Widely distributed in northern South America, especially the Orinoco and Amazon River basins. Most common in Brazil and Venezuela, but also found in northern Bolivia and eastern Peru, Ecuador, and Colombia. Matamata also live in the Guianas and Trinidad.

1 A matamata lies on the bed of a murky stream, looking like an algae-encrusted rock. Totally motionless, with just its flexible snout raised to the surface, it waits for a fish to swim into striking range.

2 But time passes and nothing palatable comes near, forcing the hungry turtle to change tactics. Slowly, it begins to walk across the streambed, herding some little fish toward a bank.

3 Now it's getting somewhere! Carefully, the turtle corners a few tiddlers, then with a thrust of its head, it opens its wide mouth and sucks them in. Snapping its jaws closed again, it expels the water through its lips and gulps its food down whole.

## Did You Know?

● Matamata is a South American Indian term, meaning "I kill." In Latin, the turtle's name, *Chelus fimbriatus*, translates as "fringed turtle."

● The matamata is a side-neck: one of a group of turtles that are unable to retract their heads into their shells if threatened. Instead, a side-neck moves its head sideways under the overhang at the front of its shell, leaving parts of its head and neck still vulnerable to attack.

● The matamata's neck is almost as long as its back. If humans were built the same way, the average person would have a neck almost 3ft (1m) long!

● Only a few turtles breathe air like the matamata. Others obtain their oxygen from the water, holding it in their mouths or their cloacal chambers (their reproductive and waste opening) while oxygen passes into the network of blood vessels inside. Soft-shelled turtles can also absorb oxygen through their shells.

# SNAPPING TURTLE

**Latin name:** *Chelydra serpentina*

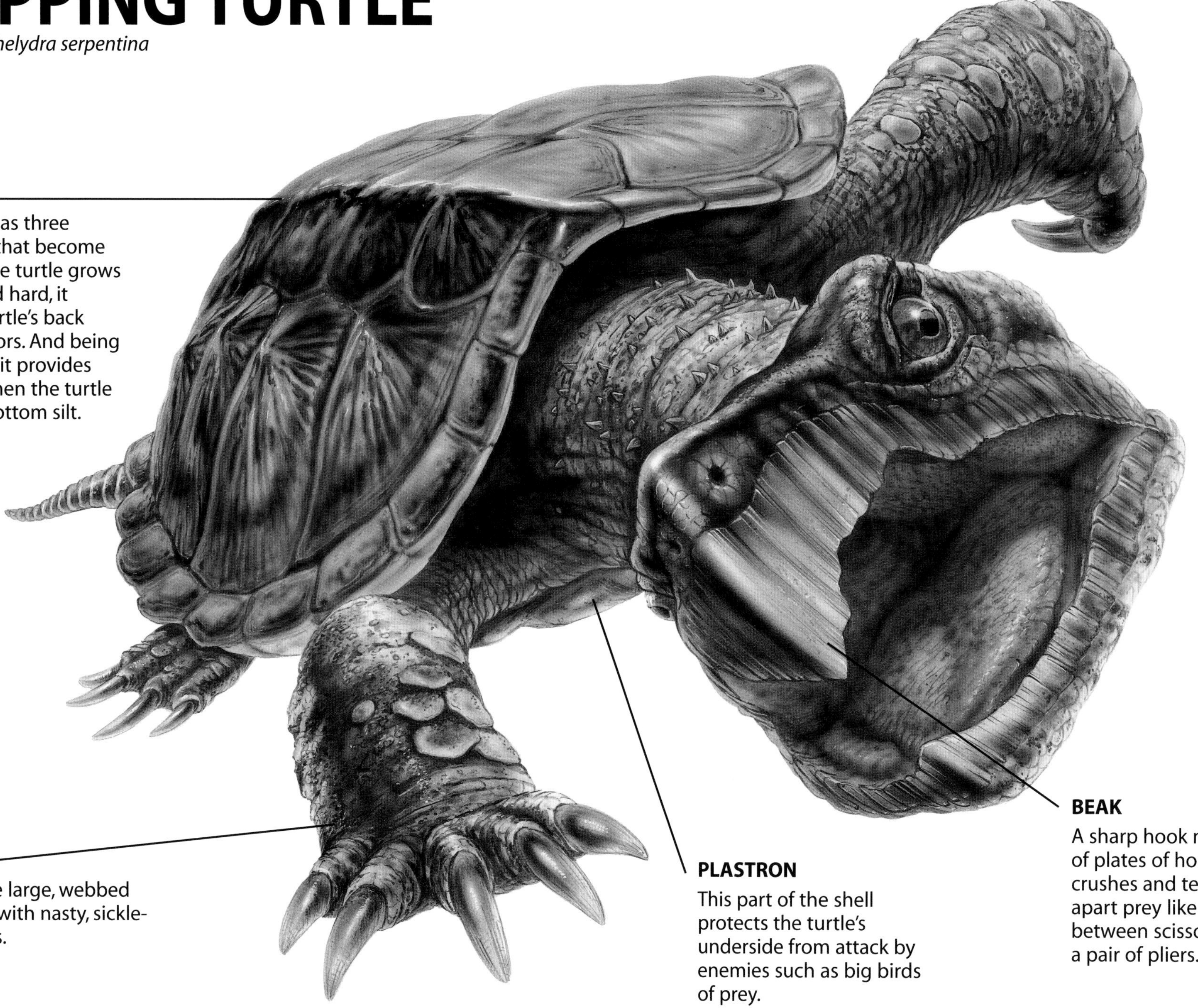

**CARAPACE**

The carapace has three knobbly keels that become smoother as the turtle grows older. Thick and hard, it protects the turtle's back against predators. And being a muddy color it provides camouflage when the turtle skulks in the bottom silt.

**FEET**

These are large, webbed paddles, with nasty, sickle-like claws.

**PLASTRON**

This part of the shell protects the turtle's underside from attack by enemies such as big birds of prey.

**BEAK**

A sharp hook made of plates of horn, this crushes and tears apart prey like a cross between scissors and a pair of pliers.

This American reptile is one mean critter, with a temper to match its sharp snapping beak. Few things are safe from its angry bite: not fish, not birds, and certainly not your fingers. A brutal end's in store for many creatures living in snapper-infested waters. One moment they're swimming along—the next, they're struggling to escape the vice-like hold of a vicious beak.

SIZE

At the bottom of a pond, a snapping turtle waits in the weed for the chance of a meal. A slow swimmer, it relies on surprise to secure its prey—like the moorhen that eventually paddles overhead. Instantly, the snapper launches itself skyward, seizes a dangling leg in its jaws and drags its frantically flapping victim beneath the surface. Even as the moorhen starts to drown and its struggles subside, the snapper begins ripping it apart and devouring it.

## KEY DATA

| | | |
|---|---|---|
| LENGTH | Up to 3ft (1m) or more from beak to tip of tail. | |
| WEIGHT | 14–16in (35–-40cm) shell | |
| DIET | | |
| WEIGHT BREEDING | Up to 35lb (16kg) or more | |
| DIET LIFESPAN | Almost any creature smaller than itself, plus carrion | |
| LIFESPAN | At least 47 years | |

The snapping turtle is the most widespread turtle in North America. It occurs as far north as the southern regions of the Canadian border states, and is common throughout the the USA east of the Rocky Mountains. Its range extends south through Mexico and Central America, as far as Ecuador in South America.

### Did You Know?

● When disturbed, the snapping turtle often releases a powerful musky scent. The older the turtle, the stronger the odor.

● The female snapper can store sperm inside her body for several years after mating before using it to fertilize her eggs.

● Although snapping turtles usually hibernate in mud in winter, they've been seen walking on frozen waters and swimming under the ice.

● A police service once used the snapping turtle's fondness for carrion in a bizarre exercise when a large specimen attached to a long line successfully discovered the underwater whereabouts of several murder victims.

● The snapper may have evolved its aggressive nature and sharp beak as a defensive measure, because the bottom part of its shell is too small to cover its head, legs and tail.

# NILE CROCODILE

**Latin name:** *Crocodylus niloticus*

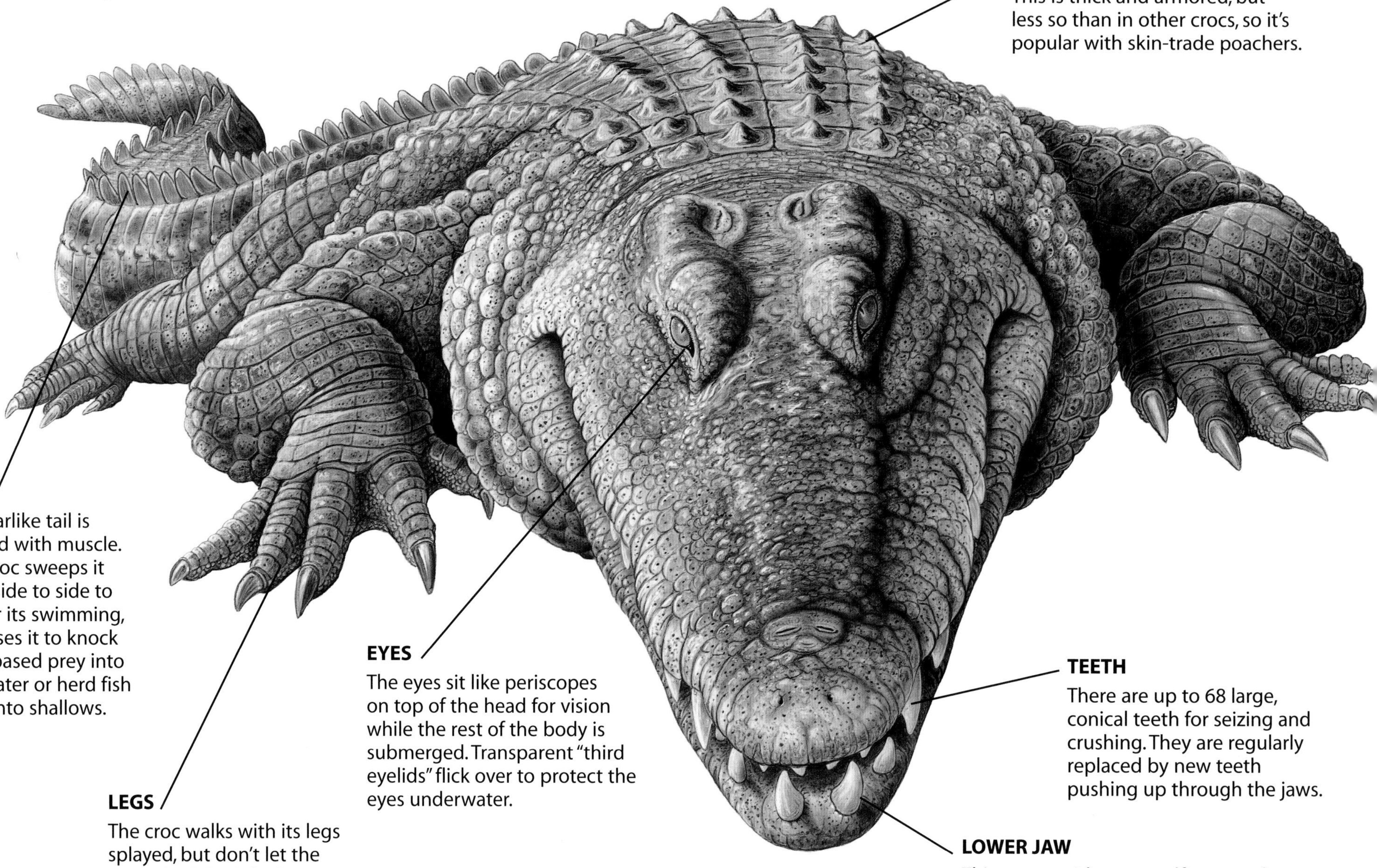

**HIDE**

This is thick and armored, but less so than in other crocs, so it's popular with skin-trade poachers.

**TAIL**

The oarlike tail is packed with muscle. The croc sweeps it from side to side to power its swimming, and uses it to knock land-based prey into the water or herd fish prey into shallows.

**EYES**

The eyes sit like periscopes on top of the head for vision while the rest of the body is submerged. Transparent "third eyelids" flick over to protect the eyes underwater.

**LEGS**

The croc walks with its legs splayed, but don't let the "squashed" look fool you: it can run fast.

**TEETH**

There are up to 68 large, conical teeth for seizing and crushing. They are regularly replaced by new teeth pushing up through the jaws.

**LOWER JAW**

This opens wide to engulf prey and to keep the head cool in hot weather.

With a tough hide and teeth like a meat-eating dinosaur, this savage killer uses strength and speed to prevail over prey. For the wildebeest migrating over the African savannah each year, each river in their path is a valley of death. In the shallows lurks the Nile crocodile, hidden from view until the moment when it lunges explosively for the kill.

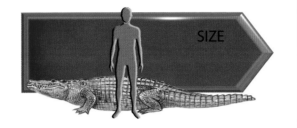

SIZE

1 The croc waits submerged until a wildebeest draws close. Then, whipping its tail furiously, it bursts out and grabs the victim.

2 When it has drowned the mammal, the croc wedges it under a riverbed log and leaves it for a few days. The soggy, softened carcass will be easier to rip into bite-size chunks.

## KEY DATA

| | | |
|---|---|---|
| LENGTH | Up to 19ft (6m), average 11ft (3.5m) | |
| WEIGHT | Up to 3 tons (1 tonne) | The Nile crocodile occupies a big chunk of Africa, from the River Senegal, Lake Chad, and Lake Nasser in the north, south as far as the River Cunene bordering Namibia and Angola, the Okavango Swamps of Botswana, and the northern Transvaal and Natal in South Africa, with a sparse population in Madagascar. |
| EGGS | 16–80 in a clutch | |
| PREY | Antelope, zebra, wildebeest, warthogs, buffalo, fish, birds, carrion —and humans | |
| ATTACK | Lunges, bites, drags prey down to drown it, rolls carcass to tear off chunks of flesh | |
| LIFESPAN | 70–100 years or more | |

## Did You Know?

● Big male crocs fight fiercely in the breeding season. The victor may end up devouring the loser.

● Up to 90 percent of Nile crocodiles die in their first year, as storks, monitor lizards, hyenas, and baboons take the eggs and infants.

● The crocodile has the most acidic stomach of any vertebrate (backboned animal), enabling it to digest bones, horns, and hoofs.

● On Madagascar, village elders used to give crocodiles the task of "judging" criminals, who would be forced to cross their waters. Some wrongdoers were spared—others paid the ultimate penalty.

# SALTWATER CROCODILE

**Latin name:** *Crocodylus porosus*

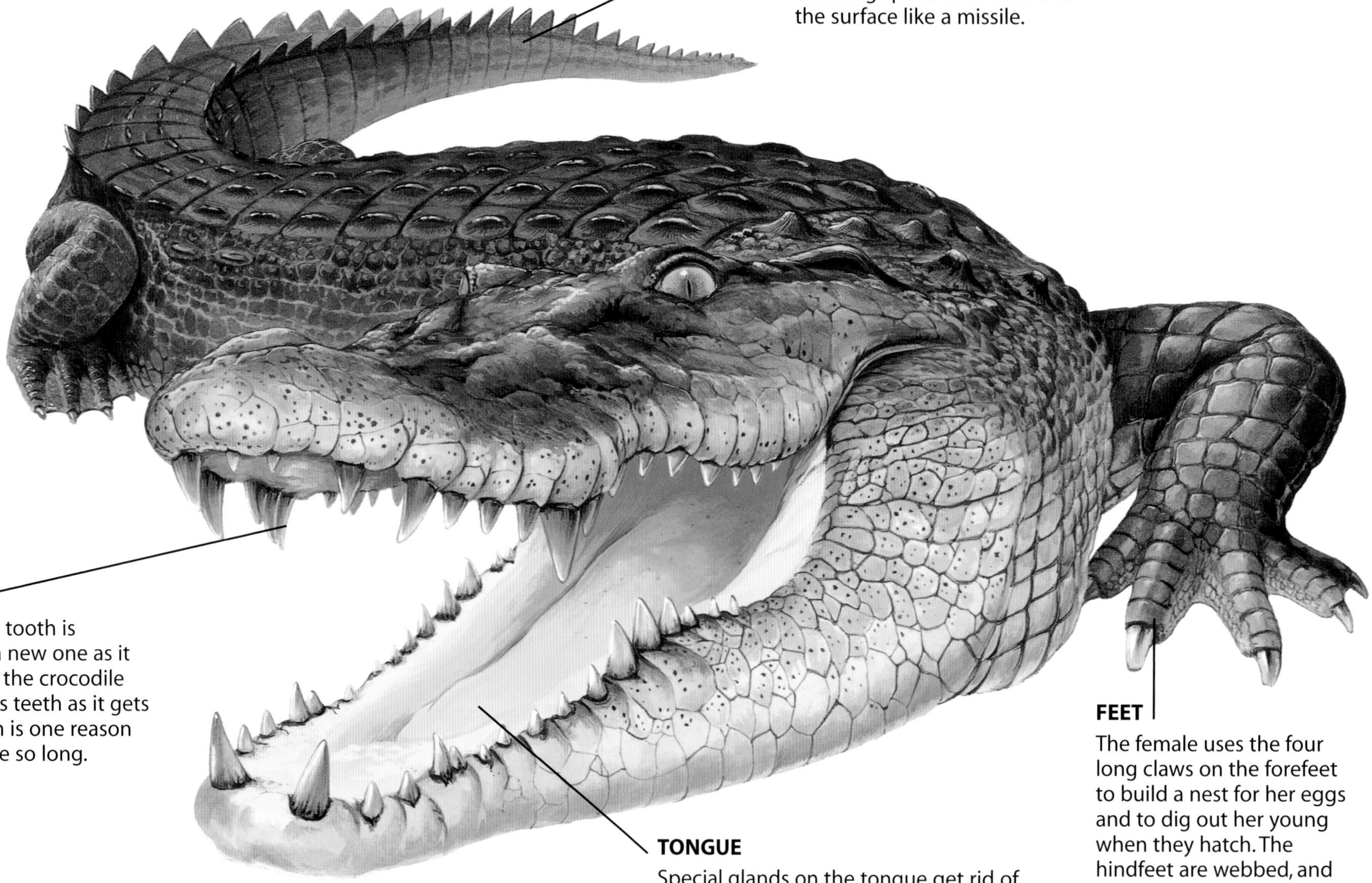

**TAIL**

Using powerful sweeps of its long tail, the crocodile can swim at alarming speed and burst from the surface like a missile.

**TEETH**

Each pointed tooth is replaced by a new one as it wears out, so the crocodile never loses its teeth as it gets older—which is one reason why it can live so long.

**TONGUE**

Special glands on the tongue get rid of excess salt in the body, so the crocodile can spend long periods in salty sea water.

**FEET**

The female uses the four long claws on the forefeet to build a nest for her eggs and to dig out her young when they hatch. The hindfeet are webbed, and help the crocodile balance and steer in the water.

This low-slung, leathery monster is the world's biggest living reptile. It is also one of the most dangerous and can easily bring down a fully grown buffalo. A true maneater, it is believed to kill and devour hundreds of people every year. Any intruder on its lair, be it animal or human, is fair game. For such a heavy beast it can explode into action with terrifying speed to grab a victim and wrestle it down to a watery grave.

SIZE

**1** A water buffalo visits a cool river in rural Malaysia to slake its thirst. It neither sees nor hears the crocodile that glides, low in the water, to within striking distance. Suddenly, the reptilian killer hurls its mighty body from the water and slams its jaws shut around the buffalo's neck.

**2** The crocodile hauls the buffalo out into midwater, its jaws holding the helpless, bellowing mammal in a vice-like grip. With a single flip of its broad tail, the crocodile drags the buffalo's head below water to drown the victim.

**3** The crocodile cannot chew, and must reduce the size of its meal by violently shaking the carcass to pieces. Sometimes it sinks its spiked teeth into the body and whirls around, ripping away great chunks of hide, flesh and bone.

## KEY DATA

| | |
|---|---|
| LENGTH | Average 15ft (4.5m), monsters of 23ft (7m) have been known |
| WEIGHT | Average 1102lb (500kg); up to 2204lb (1000kg) or more |
| TEETH | 64–68 sharp spikes |
| DIET | Fish, birds, pigs, deer, buffalo, monkeys, and people; also carrion |
| METHOD OF ATTACK | Ambush and drowning |
| LIFESPAN | Up to 100 years |

The saltwater crocodile lives in rivers, estuaries, and coastal waters in tropical parts of the Indo-Pacific: from India, through Sumatra, Borneo, the Philippines, and New Guinea, to northern Australia and Fiji.

## Did You Know?

● Some stories tell of saltwater crocodiles 30ft (10m) long. The crocodile continues growing all its life, so such tall tales could well be true.

● A crocodile often swallows stones to grind up the food in its stomach. Similar stones have been found with dinosaur fossils.

● On one night in 1945, saltwater crocodiles were reported to have killed more than 500 Japanese soldiers trying to escape from a swampy island near Burma.

● So terrifying is the saltwater crocodile that it is often shot on sight. It is becoming rare, and is now protected in some countries.

# GHARIAL

**Latin name:** *Gavialis gangeticus*

**SNOUT**

A mature male has a swelling on his snout, possibly for use in mating displays.

**HEAD**

Unlike most crocodiles, the gharial's head is quite distinct from its long, narrow jaws.

**TAIL**

The long tail drives the gharial through the water like a fish.

**LEGS**

The short legs are too weak to support the gharial's weight on land.

**TEETH**

The gharial's slender, pointed teeth are regularly replaced throughout the extremely long life of the crocodile.

Armed with long, powerful jaws and over 100 viciously sharp teeth, this colossal crocodile from Asia can do serious damage to anyone who gets in its way. A gharial loves big catfish and gobbles one up as soon as it swims into range. Unfortunately, If someone fishing hooks a catfish on a line and its violent struggles attract a gharial, the beast won't hesitate to launch a nightmare attack.

SIZE

**1** After spending hours trying to hook a catfish, a boy feels a tug on his line and begins to pull in his prize. Suddenly, in an explosion of spray, a gharial appears and grabs the fish.

## KEY DATA

| | | |
|---|---|---|
| LENGTH | Up to 23ft (7m) | |
| WEIGHT | Up to 551lb (250kg) | |
| PREY | Mainly fish | |
| WEAPONS | Powerful jaws lined with rows of sharp teeth | |
| LIFESPAN | Possibly up to 100 years | |

The gharial lives in the rivers of Pakistan, Nepal, northern India, Bhutan, Bangladesh, and Burma (Myanmar), but is now scarce in most countries. Its favored habitats are the calmer stretches of fast-moving rivers and estuaries.

**2** With a jerk of its head, the beast snaps the line like a thread. The fish clamped between its jaws is too big to swallow whole, so the reptile thrashes its prey from side to side to break the meal into bite-size chunks. Meanwhile, the boy races to safety, grateful to escape with his life.

## Did You Know?

● The gharial was once widespread throughout northern India and central Asia, but has been wiped out in many areas by human activity.

● The gharial is now rare and endangered in many regions, but in India its numbers are slowly growing thanks to captive breeding and conservation programmes.

● A female lays an average of 40 eggs, but a clutch of 97 was once found. Many gharials die young though, and only one in 100 survives to breeding age.

● The "pot-like" swelling on the male's snout surrounds the nostrils, and so may work as a resonator to amplify the loud whistles and hisses that the crocodile uses to attract a female during the breeding season. The female responds with similar calls, but they are much softer and quieter, perhaps because she lacks the male's amplifying equipment.

# ALLIGATOR SNAPPING TURTLE

**Latin name:** *Macroclemys temminckii*

**HEAD**

The grotesque head is made more hideous by a covering of tendrils and spikes.

**JAWS**

The "snapper" can open its long, sharp-edged jaws into an enormous gape to engulf prey or threaten an attacker.

**CLAWS**

The turtle uses these to shred large prey into bite-size pieces.

**LOWER SHELL**

The lower shell, or plastron, is made up of horny plates fused together.

This hideous reptile is undisputed ruler of its watery realm. With its pincer jaws and ripping claws, it has little to fear from bigger beasts and regards smaller creatures as lunch. At night the alligator "snapper" prowls the waterways hunting for food. During the day, it has a deadly ploy to trap its prey: it lurks in weeds and mud and dangles a worm-like part on its tongue to lure victims to their doom.

SIZE

## KEY DATA

| | | |
|---|---|---|
| LENGTH | Up to 30in (80cm), plus a tail of the same length | |
| WEIGHT | Up to 176lb (80kg) | The alligator snapping turtle lives in waters that drain into the Gulf of Mexico in southeastern USA. It is found in all river systems from the Swanee River in Florida to eastern Texas, and from as far north as Kansas, Illinois and Indiana down to the Gulf. The snapper likes deep, slow-running rivers, canals, lakes, swamps, and bayous. |
| DIET | Fish, mollusks, snakes, frogs, reptiles, mammals, birds, carrion, and some plants | |
| LIFESPAN | Up to 70 years in captivity | |

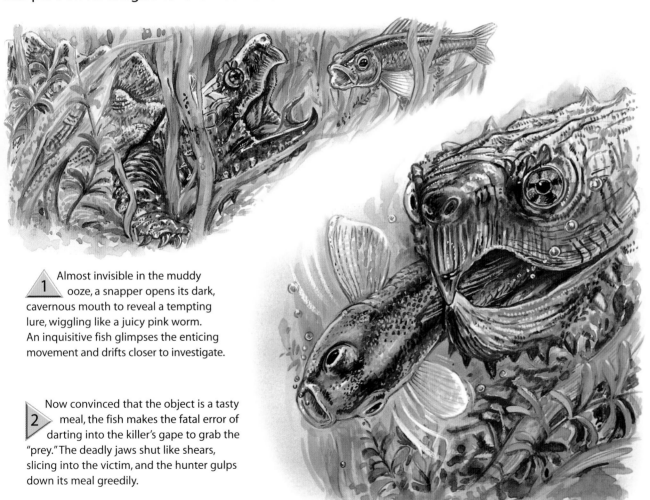

**1** Almost invisible in the muddy ooze, a snapper opens its dark, cavernous mouth to reveal a tempting lure, wiggling like a juicy pink worm. An inquisitive fish glimpses the enticing movement and drifts closer to investigate.

**2** Now convinced that the object is a tasty meal, the fish makes the fatal error of darting into the killer's gape to grab the "prey." The deadly jaws shut like shears, slicing into the victim, and the hunter gulps down its meal greedily.

## Did You Know?

● Humans pose a double threat to the alligator snapping turtle. It is hunted for meat, and much of its marshland habitat is now being drained for farmland. As a result, the turtle is on the World Wildlife Federation's Top Ten endangered list.

● Lying motionless on the muddy bottom, the alligator snapping turtle stays submerged for 40–50 minutes before it must surface for air.

● An alligator snapping turtle bites by reflex and its jaws maintain a vice-like grip even after its head has been cut from its body.

● The male snapping turtle never leaves its watery home willingly; the female only goes on dry land to lay her eggs, close to the water's edge.

● The sex of turtle hatchlings is ruled by temperature; warm eggs at the top of a buried clutch produce females, while the cooler eggs lower down produce males.

# STINKPOT TURTLE

**Latin name:** *Sternotherus species*

**HEAD**
The large head houses the viciously sharp and powerful jaws, which are used both for defense and for crushing up hard-shelled prey.

**CARAPACE**
The tough, steeply domed carapace provides strong protection from enemies and is camouflaged by a covering of algae growing on the top.

**FEET**
The feet have webbing, for extra paddling power, and sharp, gripping claws, which enable the turtle to climb trees.

**NECK**
The long neck enables the turtle to reach behind the carapace to bite its foes.

Small and pugnacious, the stinkpot turtle is a highly aggressive handful with a big bite and a bad temper. Worse, it has a secret weapon: a foul-smelling fluid to make the hungriest predator feel sick. Stinkpot turtles sometimes leave the water and scale the trunks of slanting trees to doze on overhanging branches. If they want to make a quick exit they simply drop into the water—without a thought for anyone passing underneath.

SIZE

## KEY DATA

| | |
|---|---|
| LENGTH | 3–6in (8–15cm) |
| DIET | Worms, snails, crayfish, freshwater clams and mussels, insects, frogs, fish, carrion, vegetation |
| DEFENSES | Snapping beak, foul smell |
| LIFESPAN | Up to 30 years in the wild |

The stinkpot, or common musk turtle, flourishes through spring and summer in the waterways of eastern North America. It prefers shallow, slow-moving, muddy water, with a soft bottom where it can forage through weed and silt. In winter, it buries itself in the mud and hibernates for five or six months.

1 Two men are paddling through a bayou. They pass under a sloping trunk just as three stinkpot turtles are climbing above their heads.

Startled by the men's sudden appearance, a turtle drops off the tree and lands, with an audible "clonk" on one man's head. 2

3 As the victim rubs the egg-size bump on his head, his friend lifts the turtle from the bottom of the boat. Just as he is about to throw the animal overboard, it releases a spray of stinking musk that leaves them both retching.

## Did You Know?

● Stinkpot turtles that manage to avoid predators and reach adulthood can often look forward to a ripe old age. The turtle's average lifespan in the wild, 20–30 years, is remarkable for such a small reptile but it is even longer-lived in captivity—a stinkpot that was kept in a Philadelphia zoo survived to the age of 54 years.

● Turtles and tortoises are not the only animals that fall out of the sky. There are regular reports of fish and even frogs raining down on people often living far from any waterway. This phenomena is caused by small whirlwinds, called waterspouts, that suck up water from the sea, rivers, lakes, and ponds, along with the aquatic creatures living there, and deposit them on perplexed humans.

● In the southern part of the stinkpot's range, some females lay several clutches of eggs in one season, although others may delay the development of fertilized eggs in their bodies until the following year.

# Amphibians

*Amphibians are cold-blooded masters of survival. Splitting their lives between water and land, they have successfully adapted to many different environments.*

The ornate horned frog has a huge mouth and will eat just about anything—including birds and other frogs. The Malaysian horned toad has extra folds of skin that help it blend in with leaves, so it can ambush its prey. Some amphibians have amazing defenses to avoid becoming another animal's next meal. The brilliantly colored poison-dart frog oozes poison from its skin, and predators quickly discover that a crested newt is covered in a foul-tasting goo. The African bullfrog inflates to twice its size to scare off enemies. Some amphibians are simply bizarre. The axolotl has both gills and lungs, and it never changes from infant to adult. The paradoxical frog actually gets smaller as it grows into an adult, shrinking to a third of its younger size. Many amphibians have special features that help them get around. The pipa toad has flipper-like webbed feet that propel it through water, and other amphibians have sticky toes for clinging to tree branches. In the strange world of amphibians, you can see the ingenuity of nature at work in many amazing ways.

# AXOLOTL

**Latin name:** *Ambystoma mexicanum*

**EYES**

In the animal's infant form, these are small and lidless.

**GILLS**

Blood flowing through the gills shows clearly in an albino axolotl. The gills are frilly to absorb as much oxygen from the water as possible.

**LATERAL LINE**

A line of pressure sensors runs along each flank. These lateral lines enable the axolotl to detect vibrations made by predators and prey in the water.

**SKIN**

The scaleless, smooth, thin skin absorbs oxygen from the water.

**FEET**

The toes are partially webbed so the feet can act as paddles.

Found in only one lake, high in the mountains of Mexico, this odd amphibian apparently stays in an undeveloped infant form for the whole of its natural life, without changing into an adult. No one knows if the axolotl ever turns into an adult in the wild, but it can be induced to do so in the laboratory. The process takes several weeks, and is irreversible. Once it grows up, an axolotl can never turn back into its infant form.

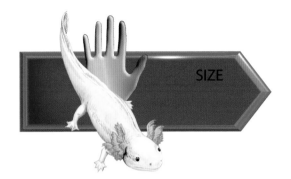

SIZE

Most axolotls bred in captivity are albino —they lack skin pigmentation, so are pinkish-white—but some are a natural muddy gray or green. When an axolotl becomes an adult, it loses its feathery gills and tail fin, its eyes bulge and grow lids, and its skin thickens.

An infant axolotl has lungs, but gulps air only when there is not enough oxygen in the water. An adult axolotl really needs its lungs, and breathes through its nostrils.

With its improved eyesight, an adult axolotl can catch land insects such as crickets, as well as worms and snails.

## KEY DATA

| | | |
|---|---|---|
| LENGTH | Up to 12in (30cm) | Found only in Lake Xochimilco, high in the mountains of the Sierra Madre, southeast of Mexico City. Once common in lakes in the Mexican mountains, some of these, such as Lake Chalco, dried up. In other cases, the axolotl was wiped out by trout introduced for food, or was overhunted. |
| WEIGHT | Up to 10oz (300g) | |
| PREY | Aquatic insects, worms, snails and fish; in adult form, land insects too | |
| LIFESPAN | Unknown in the wild; up to 25 years in captivity | |

## Did You Know?

● The word axolotl comes from the language of the Aztecs, who lived in Mexico before Europeans invaded America. It means "water monster."

● The axolotl's home lake is now threatened by pollution, and by shrinkage as water is drawn off for use in Mexico City. But the axolotl is bred in large numbers in captivity, as it is a popular pet and is widely used in scientific research. So the species is in no danger of becoming extinct.

● In the wild, the axolotl lays about 400 eggs a year. In captivity, though, it often spawns repeatedly: one female in captivity laid more than 3500 eggs in a single year.

● In captivity, axolotls often eat each other in the first few months after they hatch. Some grow quicker than others, and the big ones tend to eat the small ones. They snap at anything that moves, and frequently bite off each other's toes and feet—though these soon grow back again.

# GIANT SALAMANDER

**Latin name:** *Andrias davidianus, A. japonicus*

**HEAD**

This is broad and flat, with prominent warts. Large nostrils detect the slightest scent of prey.

**TEETH**

The mouth is broad with rows of tiny sharp teeth for gripping slippery prey. If the creature traps a victim in one side of its mouth, it can exert extra pressure on that side.

**LEGS**

These are stubby and splayed, for paddling and walking underwater.

**COLOR**

The skin varies from pinkish-brown to near-black and is almost always mottled, for camouflage.

**SKIN**

The skin is slack and slimy, and smooth except for the head.

**TAIL**

Long, flat, and muscular, the tail powers the salamander through the water to catch large, fast-swimming prey.

**FOLDS**

Loose flaps of skin, rich in blood vessels, run along both sides of the body. They increase the salamander's surface area, allowing it to absorb more oxygen from the water.

Wrinkly, warty skin, beady eyes, and gaping mouths make the giant salamanders of China and Japan truly grotesque. Death stalks the riverbed when night falls and the giant salamander stirs from its hideout. By day, this bulky beast is easy for prey to spot in the sunlit crystal water. But in the dark, it can move about unseen like a shadowy enemy submarine.

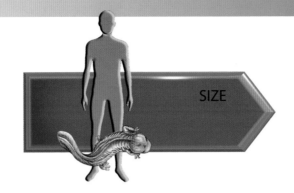
SIZE

Under a rocky overhang, a giant salamander waits in ambush. The creature's flat body and wrinkled, mottled skin help it blend into the gloom. Eventually a fish swims close by, unaware that its every move is being sensed by a monstrous enemy. With a slow, careful flexing of its body, the salamander slips out and walks stealthily across the riverbed, sneaking up on the fish from behind. Then, in a flash, it unleashes a devastating strike. All the animal's apparent sloth disappears as, in a split second, it launches forward, opens its huge mouth and engulfs the fish in its jaws.

## KEY DATA

| | |
|---|---|
| LENGTH | 3–4ft (1.1–1.2m) on average, but some grow to 5ft (1.5m) or more; the largest on record was 6ft (1.8m) long |
| WEIGHT | 22–143lb (10–65kg) |
| PREY | Fish, frogs, worms, shrimps, crayfish, crabs, snakes, turtles, rats, snails, insects, and other salamanders |
| LIFESPAN | Unknown in wild, thought to be the longest-living amphibians |

*Andrias davidianus* lives in clear, cold mountain tributaries of China's Yangtze, Yellow, and Pearl rivers. *Andrias japonicus* occurs in Japan, in mountain streams in central and southern Honshu (mainland Japan) and northern Kyushu island.

### Did You Know?

● The slime of the Japanese giant salamander is said to smell like sansho, a pepper used in Japanese cooking.

● Practitioners of traditional Chinese medicine sometimes prescribe giant salamander eggs to pregnant women, to help them produce healthy children.

● When the first giant salamander fossil was found in Germany in 1725, people initially thought it was the remains of a human victim of the Biblical Flood of Noah's Ark fame.

● When caught, the Chinese giant salamander is said to make a noise like a crying baby—its Chinese name, Wa-wa yu, means "baby fish."

# CANE TOAD

**Latin name:** *Bufo marinus*

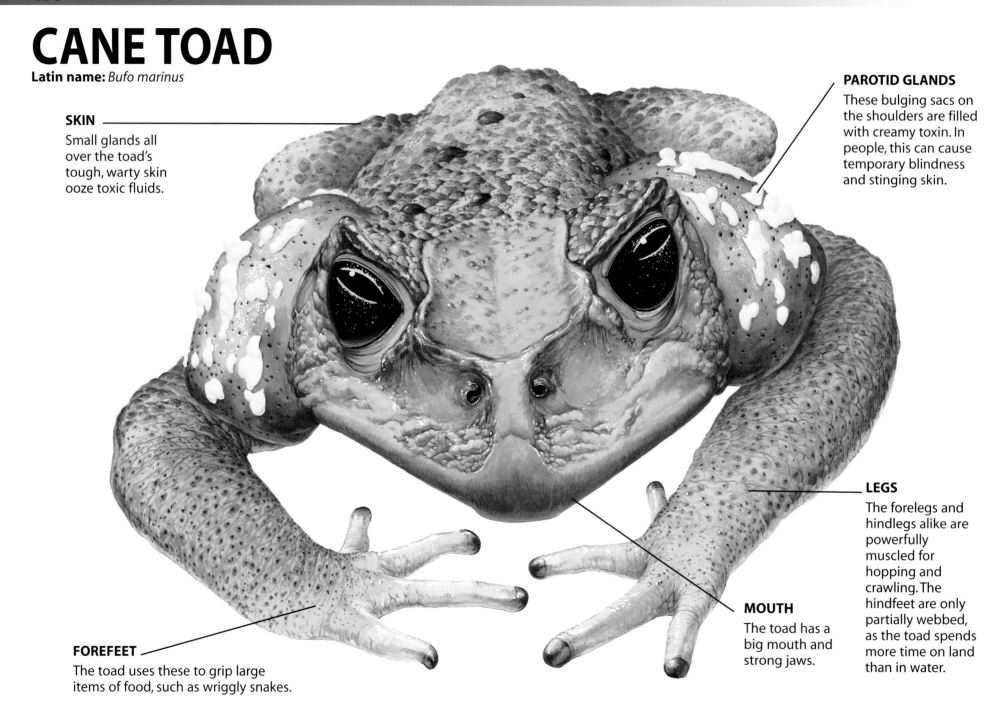

**SKIN**

Small glands all over the toad's tough, warty skin ooze toxic fluids.

**PAROTID GLANDS**

These bulging sacs on the shoulders are filled with creamy toxin. In people, this can cause temporary blindness and stinging skin.

**LEGS**

The forelegs and hindlegs alike are powerfully muscled for hopping and crawling. The hindfeet are only partially webbed, as the toad spends more time on land than in water.

**MOUTH**

The toad has a big mouth and strong jaws.

**FOREFEET**

The toad uses these to grip large items of food, such as wriggly snakes.

The bloated cane toad eats almost anything and is deadly poisonous to pretty much anything that tries to eat it. No wonder, then, populations reach plague proportions. A cane toad looks an easy meal if you've never seen one before. Outside its native range, though, few animals yet possess the adaptations needed to prey successfully on this poisonous toad—as many find out to their cost.

**1** Not a pretty sight itself, a hungry Gould's monitor in Australia approaches an unconcerned cane toad, which puffs itself up with air to make itself look even bigger than it is. But to the giant lizard, the fat toad is there for the taking.

**2** The monitor clamps its jaws around the toad. They can crush bone, but the lizard is instantly repulsed by the foul taste of the toad, which sprays toxin from its shoulder glands for good measure.

**3** Within seconds, the poison in the lizard's mouth is disrupting the monitor's nervous system. The lizard's heartbeat and breathing increase rapidly and become erratic. Soon, it is struggling to breathe and is thrashing around in panic. Minutes later it is dead. Unharmed and unperturbed, the toad hops away to find its own breakfast.

## SIZE

## KEY DATA

| | |
|---|---|
| LENGTH | Up to 9–10in (24cm) |
| WEIGHT | Up to 5lb (2.3kg) |
| DIET | Insects, other invertebrates, frogs, toads (including its own kind), mice, nestlings, snakes, lizards |
| LIFESPAN | 15–20 years |

The cane toad is native to South and Central America and the southwestern USA. It has been introduced to Florida, Pacific islands, the Caribbean, Taiwan, Japan, the Philippines, New Guinea, and eastern Australia.

## Did You Know?

● Also known as the marine toad, the cane toad cannot actually live in the sea—only in brackish water.

● The cane toad's tough skin is sometimes used to make bags and purses. This commercial use of the toad may help control its numbers.

● The greed of the cane toad is legendary. One cane toad once tried to swallow a similar-sized toad whole. It was so reluctant to loosen its grip that both toads eventually died.

● In Australia, where the cane toad has no natural predators or parasites to keep its numbers down, it occurs at a density ten times greater than that in South America.

● The vampire bat is not only immune to the cane toad's poison, it bites directly into the poison glands.

● In times of drought, the cane toad often lays its eggs in swimming pools in suburban gardens.

# ORNATE HORNED FROG

**Latin name:** *Ceratophrys ornata*

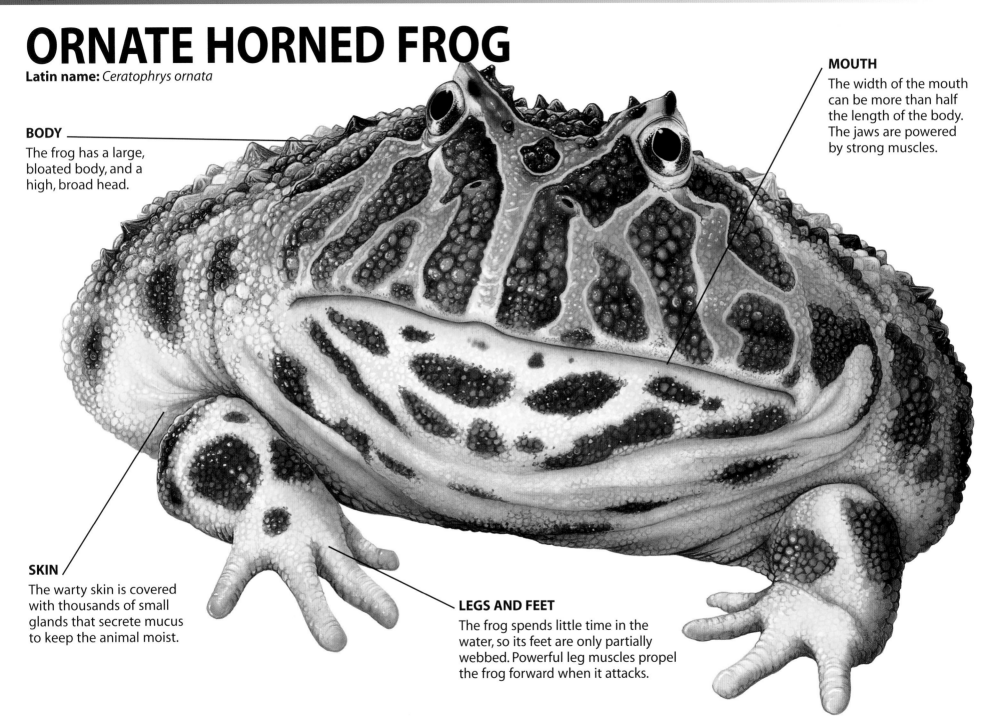

**BODY**

The frog has a large, bloated body, and a high, broad head.

**MOUTH**

The width of the mouth can be more than half the length of the body. The jaws are powered by strong muscles.

**SKIN**

The warty skin is covered with thousands of small glands that secrete mucus to keep the animal moist.

**LEGS AND FEET**

The frog spends little time in the water, so its feet are only partially webbed. Powerful leg muscles propel the frog forward when it attacks.

Almost all mouth, the ornate horned frog eats first and asks questions later. It isn't interested in what its prey tastes like—its only concern is whether it can fit its victims into its greedy mouth. The ornate horned frog's need to stuff its face means that it even hunts birds—a surprise considering the frog's bulk. The flabby predator waits patiently until an unwary victim flutters within range.

SIZE

| KEY DATA | |
|---|---|
| **LENGTH** | About 6in (15cm) |
| **WEIGHT** | Up to 1lb 2oz (500g) |
| **DIET** | Insects, birds, frogs, reptiles, and small mammals |
| **WEAPONS** | All-engulfing mouth |
| **LIFESPAN** | 6 years |

The ornate horned frog—sometimes known as the Argentine horned frog—is found in southern Brazil, Uruguay, Paraguay, and northeastern Argentina. It lives mainly on the damp, muddy floors of rainforests. It is also found on pampas prairies. In the dry season, it is forced to hibernate in burrows to avoid drying out.

**1** Motionless, silent, but keenly alert, an ornate horned frog waits for its next meal to come along. Unaware of the danger, a flycatcher forages close by.

**2** When the flycatcher hops within range, the frog strikes like lightning, propelling itself forward with its legs and grabbing the bird in its vice-like jaws.

**3** The frog settles back down to enjoy its meal—or at least most of it. The bird is so large that its legs poke out of the frog's mouth!

## Did You Know?

● In some parts of South America, it is said that grazing horses often die after being bitten on the lip by a horned frog. This seems unlikely as the frog does not have a venomous bite. However, it is possible that deaths occur when a gaping wound left by the frog's bite turns septic.

● Young ornate horned frogs have been seen using their hind toes as lures to catch prey. The frog lifts its rear feet up over its back and then waggles its toes. This movement encourages animals to come closer to investigate and the frog then simply gobbles them up.

● Approximately 80 percent of a frog's weight is made up of water.

● The ornate horned frog is so voracious that it even gobbles up the young of its own species!

● This frog is often called "the mouth with legs" because its gaping mouth takes up so much of its body.

# POISON-DART FROG

**Latin name:** *Dendrobatidae family*

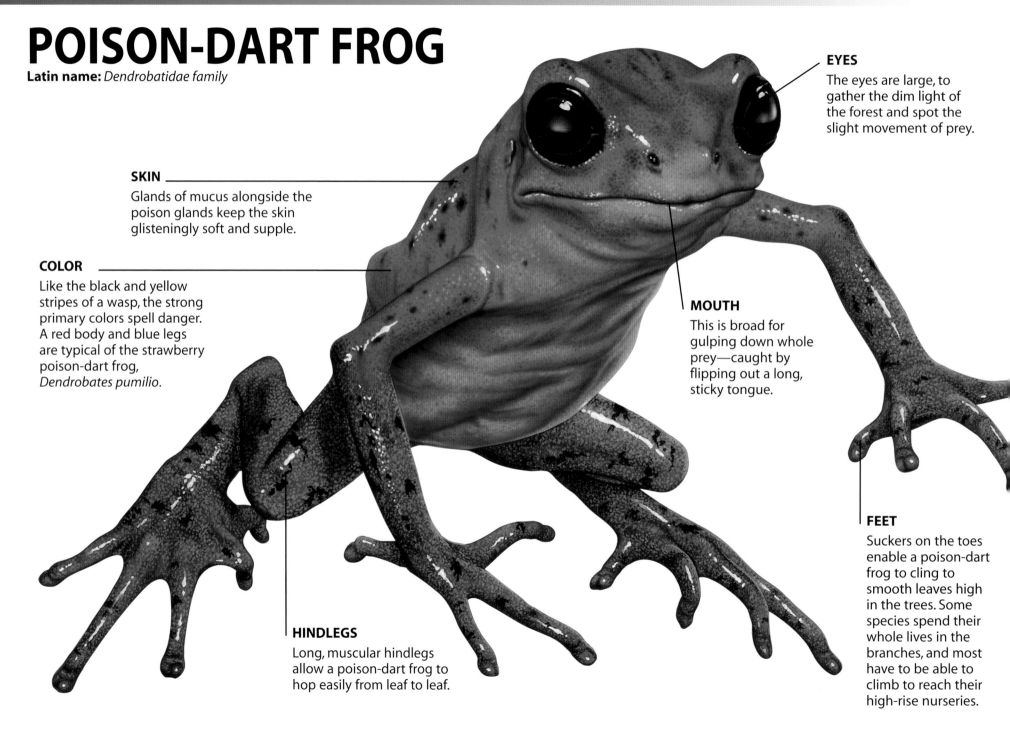

**EYES**
The eyes are large, to gather the dim light of the forest and spot the slight movement of prey.

**SKIN**
Glands of mucus alongside the poison glands keep the skin glisteningly soft and supple.

**COLOR**
Like the black and yellow stripes of a wasp, the strong primary colors spell danger. A red body and blue legs are typical of the strawberry poison-dart frog, *Dendrobates pumilio*.

**MOUTH**
This is broad for gulping down whole prey—caught by flipping out a long, sticky tongue.

**FEET**
Suckers on the toes enable a poison-dart frog to cling to smooth leaves high in the trees. Some species spend their whole lives in the branches, and most have to be able to climb to reach their high-rise nurseries.

**HINDLEGS**
Long, muscular hindlegs allow a poison-dart frog to hop easily from leaf to leaf.

The vivid colors of a poison-dart frog are a warning to predators to keep away, for its moist skin oozes some of the most potent toxins in the natural world. The Choco indians of Colombia hunt some species of poison-dart frog for the thing that should protect them: their poison. Sometimes they roast the frogs alive until their skin bubbles with toxins.

ACTUAL SIZE

1 A Choco Indian catches a frog by pinning it to the ground with a stick, then traps it in the split end of a cane and props it over the flames of a roaring fire.

2 As the luckless frog heats up, the skin on its back starts to weep poison. The toxic white liquid boils and steams, becoming thick and sticky like glue—and increasingly concentrated.

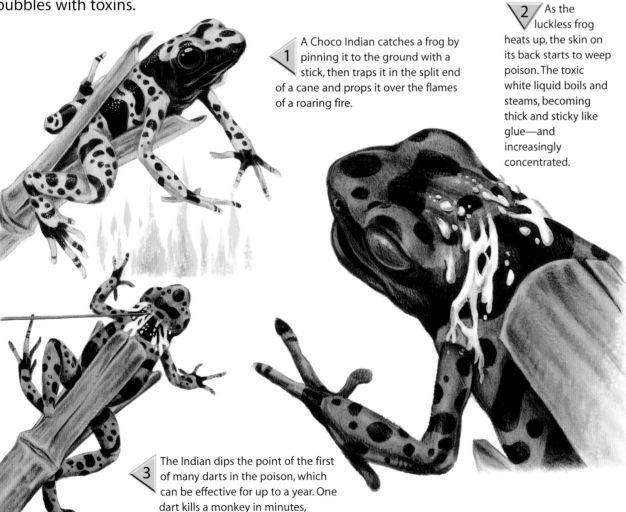

3 The Indian dips the point of the first of many darts in the poison, which can be effective for up to a year. One dart kills a monkey in minutes, bringing it crashing to the ground.

## KEY DATA

| | |
|---|---|
| LENGTH | ¾in–2in (1.5–5cm), depending on species |
| PREY | Mainly ants, flies, spiders, beetles, and millipedes |
| POISON | A mix of toxins, produced by glands in the skin, that causes heart failure if it enters the bloodstream |
| BREEDING | In most species, 2 to 10 big eggs, each nurtured to ensure its development |
| LIFESPAN | Probably 3–5 years for most species |

All poison-dart frogs live in the humid tropical rainforests of Central and South America. No one knows how many species there are. New ones are found every year, while some are seen only once. Also, frogs of the same species can vary enormously in color, making identification difficult.

## Did You Know?

● The sparkling fire-bellied snake, *Leimadophis epinephelus* is unique in that it eats poison-dart frogs with relish. Experts are baffled by its immunity to their toxins

● Male poison-dart frogs defend territories with calls and dancing displays, and wrestle with any trespassing rivals. After a fight, the winner celebrates by calling up a mate with his rasping song.

# MANTELLA FROG

**Latin name:** *Family Mantellidae*

**COLOR**
Unique color combinations identify each mantella species, as well as warning predators of the toxic risks.

**SKIN**
Numerous glands pepper the mantella's skin: some secreting moisture to stop the frog from drying out, and others producing powerful defensive toxins.

**TOES**
Mantellas are land dwellers, so there is little need for webbing between their toes. But one species, the climbing mantella, has toe pads that help it climb up trees.

**FORELEGS**
A male mantella has special pads on the inner side of its forelegs, which help it hang on to the female from behind during mating: a grip known as the amplexus embrace.

**THROAT**
The skin of the throat swells and stretches as call notes are articulated, and each species uses a specific call for each specific situation.

**EYES**
Although the mantella frog hunts by day, it's often gloomy in the forest, so large round eyes help it gather every glimmer of light as it goes in pursuit of its insect prey.

It may be tiny, but meddle with this colorful frog at your peril, for its skin is laced with toxic fluid that irritates and even kills. These juicy little frogs might seem like ideal snacks for larger predators, but their jewel-bright coloring provides a vivid warning of their toxic powers. So woe betide any snake or bird rash enough to try and make a meal of one.

ACTUAL SIZE

## KEY DATA

| | |
|---|---|
| LENGTH | ¾in-1¼in (1.5–3cm) |
| WEIGHT | Less than 1/16th of an ounce (about 2g or less) |
| EGGS | 12–100 per clutch |
| PREY | Ants, termites, and other tiny invertebrates |
| LIFESPAN | Unknown |

The tiny mantella frogs are found only on Madagascar, an island 186 miles (300km) east of continental Africa, and 994 miles (1600km) long. The mantellas are rainforest dwellers, dependent on regular rains to enable their tadpoles to hatch and survive. The different species occupy various rainforest habitats, from the coast up to mid-alpine altitudes.

**1** It's daytime, and a golden mantella is out hunting for insects. But as it hops on to a mossy clump, a hungry snake comes slithering silently up behind.

**2** Sneaking closer, the snake opens its jaws wide and engulfs the mantella with a sudden snap. As the little frog disappears headfirst into the creature's mouth, its fate seems certain.

**3** But inside the snake's mouth, the mantella rapidly secretes toxic mucus from its skin. The burning and foul taste are too much for the snake to tolerate, and it quickly spits the frog out again, unharmed. It won't make the same mistake again.

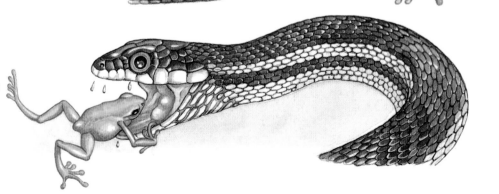

## Did You Know?

● The females of some species of mantella care for their tadpoles after they have hatched by providing them with meals of unfertilized eggs.

● Although the golden mantella (*Mantella aurantiaca*) is the most common species in Madagascar, it is confined to the nature reserve of Périnet in the eastern rainforest belt.

● In 1989, dealers exported more than 11,000 golden mantellas to supply the growing market in the pet trade. It was only recently that this mantella frog was listed as an endangered species, not to be traded.

● Only two of Madagascar's 170 classified frog species are not native to the island. One of these is the introduced Asian bullfrog, and the other a mainland African species.

# BUDGETT'S FROG

**Latin name:** *Lepidobatrachus laevis*

**SKIN**

The skin is covered by a thin layer of mucus to reduce moisture loss and make it difficult for predators to get a grip.

**EYES**

The frog's bulging eyes give good vision day and night. Like the nostrils, they are perched high up on the frog's head, so the animal can watch out for its prey while lying partly concealed by the water.

**THUMBS**

The male has patches of rough skin called nuptial pads on his thumbs to help him hold a female during mating.

**LEGS AND FEET**

The frog burrows backward with its hindlegs, shoveling mud aside using spade-like horny growths (tubercles) on its feet.

**MOUTH**

The lower jaw has two large, tooth-like projections that are capable of giving you a painful bite.

Meet the mouth on legs! This greedy South American frog hides itself away for months on end, building up its appetite—then goes out to gobble up every mouth-sized creature that crosses its path. Constantly hungry, the voracious Budgett's frog doesn't always know when it has had enough. It may even make the fatal mistake of trying to devour another fully grown Budgett's frog that it finds on a hunting trip…

SIZE

1 ▷ Searching hungrily for food, two Budgett's frogs unexpectedly come face to face. Squaring up to each other, their mouths gaping, the two amphibians begin a desperate battle to the death.

2 ▷ There's a frantic struggle as each frog tries to scoff the other. Size wins the day, and the larger frog begins to gulp down its opponent. But the loser is just too big to swallow. With one frog wedged firmly in the other's throat, both animals meet an undignified end.

## KEY DATA

| | |
|---|---|
| LENGTH | Female up to 5½ in (14cm), male about 4in (10cm) |
| PREY | Anything it can fit in its mouth: mainly insects, worms, small snakes, small mammals, and other frogs |
| LIFESPAN | About 10 years in the wild; more in captivity |

Budgett's frog is found on the arid Gran Chaco plains of northern Argentina and western Paraguay, where it lives in small ponds and shallow pools. The ponds often evaporate in winter, but the frog manages to survive by burying itself in mud. The frog is becoming increasingly popular as a pet in many countries and is easy to breed, so its numbers in captivity are rising.

## Did You Know?

● Budgett's frog gets its name from the explorer J.S. Budgett, who described it to science in 1899.

● When being bred in captivity, the adult frogs must be removed immediately after mating, or they try to eat each other.

● Budgett's frog tadpoles are all cannibals—ready and eager to dine on their young brothers and sisters.

● Frogs swallow their prey whole rather than biting off chunks. So a frog's meal is limited by the size of its mouth—the bigger the mouth, the larger the prey it can tackle.

● Budgett's frog is dwarfed by the Goliath frog (*Conraura goliath*) from West Africa, which grows to 16in (40cm). In South America, another greedy amphibian is the ornate horned toad (*Ceratophrys ornata*). This brightly colored beast is also bigger than Budgett's frog—although not as mammoth as the Goliath frog.

# HORNED TOAD

**Latin name:** *Megophrys montana*

**"HORNS"**
The three flexible "horns" are really fleshy folds of skin, one above each eye and another sticking out from the snout. These pointy projections help break up the animal's outline.

**BACK FOLDS**
Two folds of skin on the back look like the midribs of leaves, adding to the toad's disguise.

**EYES**
The eyes see well in the dark. Glands keep them moist, and transparent membranes protect them from dust.

**TOES**
The toad's toes are barely webbed, making its feet suitable for a life spent mainly on land.

**VOCAL SAC**
A large, expandable vocal sac and voice box enable the male to make a loud, mechanical-sounding call, attracting females to come and mate with him.

Lurking on the rainforest floor, this devilish-looking creature is cunningly camouflaged. Concealed among rotting leaf litter, it waits to launch a surprise attack on an unsuspecting victim. The Malaysian horned toad has a voracious appetite, tackling creatures as big as mice and lizards. The smaller male toad may sometimes fall prey to the female: given the chance, she gobbles him up in one mouthful.

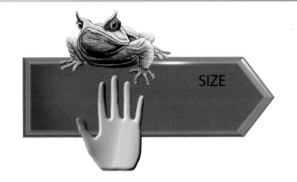

SIZE

1 On a moonlit night, a big female toad crouches in the leaf litter of the forest floor, invisible to predators and prey. Her keen ears pick up the faint sound of an approaching animal. Will it be a predator, or a potential meal?

2 Luckily for the female, the visitor is a male horned toad, only half her size. As he passes, she leaps forward and clamps her sharp teeth on to his hindleg. The unlucky male wriggles desperately, but in vain: there is no escaping her grip.

3 As the male thrashes about in her huge mouth, she slowly starts to swallow him whole. She may draw her eyes back into her head in the process, helping her to force the big mouthful down her throat.

## KEY DATA

| | | |
|---|---|---|
| LENGTH | Female 6¼in (16cm); male 3½ in (9cm) | |
| COLOUR | Various shades of brown, fawn, and gray; undersides of body and eyehorns darker than the back | Lives in rainforest in parts of southeastern Asia, from Thailand and the Malay Peninsula, across Indonesia, to Borneo and the Philippines. The *race nasuta* has the longest "horns" and is found only on the island of Borneo. |
| DIET | Large insects, slugs, worms, other frogs and toads, lizards, and small mammals | |

## Did You Know?

● When a horned toad is threatened by a predator, it inflates its body by sucking in great gulps of air and raises its hindquarters. These actions make the toad seem much bigger than it really is and are an attempt to scare away the enemy. Sometimes the toad adds to the display by opening its mouth wide and giving loud calls; it may even leap at the threatening animal.

● The horned toad's disguise is so good that visitors can rarely spot it when it rests motionless on the leaf-strewn forest floor, even when a guide points out the location. Male toads are more often caught and exported as pets, as trappers can locate them by their calls.

● The Latin name for the genus of Asian horned toads, *Megophrys*, means "big eyebrows."

● Sometimes the horned toad is referred to as the Asian horned frog or nose-horned frog.

# PIPA TOAD

**Latin name:** *Pipa species*

## COLORING

The toad has a dull-green or brown back, to blend in with the silty, leaf-strewn bottoms of waterways.

## PITS

A female can still swim freely with a batch of toadlets embedded in her swollen back. After they leave, their nursery holes soon vanish.

## FINGERS

These are slim and flexible, with tiny spines to hold fast on to slippery, lively prey. At the tip of each long finger is a star-shaped cluster of sensitive filaments, which act like tiny antennae.

## MOUTH

The mouth is broad and opens wide to swallow large prey. The toad may have to wait many hours between meals, so the bigger the mouthful it can tackle, the better.

## NOSTRILS

Two tiny nostrils protrude from the toad's snout like periscopes, allowing the animal to breathe safely at the surface without exposing its whole body to predators.

## FEET

Large, webbed, and flexible, these work like a diver's flippers.

## BODY

Even a female carrying young has a fairly flat body, allowing her to hide among leaves, so keeping her brood safe from predatory fish.

## ARMS

The toad's slender arms are surprisingly powerful. They work together to catch prey with split-second speed.

With its tiny eyes and flat body, the pipa toad seems ill-suited to be a hunter. Yet it is endlessly patient, grabbing any creature that swims within reach before cramming it into its wide-open mouth. Craftily camouflaged as a leaf, the pipa toad lies motionless for hour after hour, waiting in ambush. Eyes are next to useless in the muddy waters of the jungle, so the pipa toad has developed extra-long fingers to "feel" for prey.

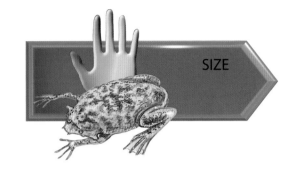

SIZE

## KEY DATA

| | | |
|---|---|---|
| LENGTH | 1½in–7in (4–18cm), depending on species | Pipa toads live in tropical South America east of the Andes, on the Caribbean island of Trinidad and in parts of Central America. They are found in leaf-choked, silty waterways, ranging from ponds, streams, and swamps to mighty rivers such as the Orinoco and Amazon. |
| DIET | Fish, fish eggs, tadpoles, and small aquatic invertebrates and their larvae, including beetles and shrimps: also scavenges carrion | |
| LIFESPAN | 4–6 years | |

**1** Hiding under rotting leaves on a streambed, a pipa toad goes unnoticed by a little fish swimming close by—but the toad's delicate, outstretched fingertips sense the creature's every movement.

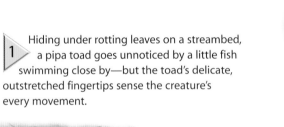

**2** The toad lunges, grabbing the fish in both arms. The fish is slimy and flaps frantically to break free, but the toad's flexible fingers grip it securely.

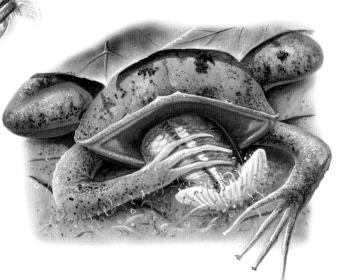

**3** Quickly and without ceremony, the toad stuffs the still-struggling fish headfirst into its mouth—this way round, the fish's spiny fins won't jam in the toad's throat lining. Then, gradually, the predator swallows its fresh meal whole with a series of great gulps. After dining, the sated toad slips back into cover.

## Did You Know?

● Early naturalists thought baby pipa toads grew directly from the skin of their mother's back.

● The pipa toad lacks vocal cords, but can make noises by clicking the tiny bones in its larynx or airway. Male pipas do this repeatedly in the breeding season, to attract females.

● Fossils found in Israel show that close relatives of the pipa toad lived alongside dinosaurs 145 million or more years ago.

● The best-known pipa toad, *Pipa pipa*, is also called the Surinam toad. It is often kept in aquariums and is a popular pet in some countries.

● Although the pipa toad has adopted an underwater lifestyle, it still breathes air, surfacing every half hour or so to take a gulp.

● When food is plentiful, the pipa toad always pigs out, to build up an energy store for when it is scarce.

# PARADOXICAL FROG

**Latin name:** *Pseudis paradoxa*

**FINS**
Long fins lining the upper and lower tail surfaces help the tadpole wriggle at speed through the water.

**TAIL**
The huge tail is fully absorbed by the time the animal has turned into a frog.

**HANDS**
All members of this frog's family have extra-long toes and fingers. The hands lack webbing, and are very good at handling objects.

**HINDLEGS**
When the tadpole is ready to change into a frog, these are the first limbs to appear. Webbing between all five toes helps the frog paddle about.

**BODY**
The egg-shaped body of the tadpole contains all the organs needed for breathing and feeding.

The paradoxical frog of South America seems to live life in reverse. Bizarrely, this amazing amphibian shrinks as it gets older until, fully shrunk, the adult is dwarfed three times over by its own monstrous tadpoles. For the most part, breeding in paradoxical frogs is typically froggy. A female spawns in the water, with a male fertilizing her eggs. Each fertile egg develops into a tadpole—but from here, the story takes a wild turn.

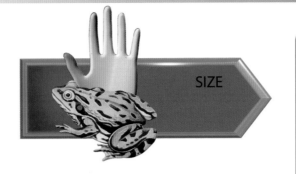

SIZE

## KEY DATA

| | |
|---|---|
| LENGTH | Tadpole 10in (25cm); frog 2¾in (7cm) |
| HABITS | Solitary, water-dwelling |
| BREEDING | Lays eggs in floating foam |
| DIET | Tadpole eats plants; frog eats insects |
| LIFESPAN | Unknown in the wild |

The paradoxical frog is widespread in humid rainforests and damp woods throughout the lowlands of tropical South America, from Trinidad south to northern Argentina. Many populations are isolated, and have evolved into distinct local subspecies.

**2** When the tadpole hatches it is tiny, but it soon starts eating and growing. The bigger it gets, the more the tadpole eats, until it is almost four times the size of an adult.

**1** A frog pair mates in a suitable pond or stream. Clinging to the female frog as she lays her eggs, the male smothers them with sperm to ensure they are fertilized. The eggs float on the surface in a raft of foam while they develop.

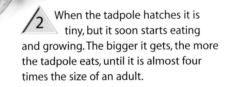

**3** To turn into an adult frog the tadpole has to grow strong hopping legs, a different type of mouth and a completely new digestive system. It absorbs all the energy stored in its tail, which shrivels away to nothing.

## Did You Know?

● Any tadpole may keep on growing, without being transformed into a frog, if there is no trace of iodine in the water. The reason is that, without iodine, the tadpole's thyroid gland cannot produce thyroxin—the growth hormone responsible for the transformation.

● In some parts of South America the local people go "fishing" for the giant tadpoles, and take them to market to sell for food.

● The naturalist Gerald Durrell was astonished by his first encounter with paradoxical tadpoles, during a trip he made to South America in 1950. He found an expressive way of retelling the scene—it was like finding ants the size of terriers!

● Some amphibian experts have kept paradoxical frogs in captivity, housing them in an aquarium and feeding them on live crickets. They report that the frog's noisy croak sounds like the grunt of a pig.

# AFRICAN BULLFROG

**Latin name:** *Pyxicephalus adspersus*

**BODY**
To deter enemies, the frog can inflate its ball-like body to nearly twice its usual size.

**FEET**
Each foot has a sharp bony bump on the outside that the frog uses to dig into the dry earth.

**SKIN**
The skin is kept moist by special mucus glands lying just under the surface.

**HANDS**
The frog uses its hands to grab prey to stuff in its mouth.

**MOUTH**
The mouth opens wide to enable the bullfrog to seize and swallow prey almost as big as itself.

This wrinkly giant hates strangers and does everything it can to make this clear to them. The bad-tempered bullfrog charges toward unwelcome visitors with its mouth open wide, grunts, bites, and even swells up like a balloon. Baking heat and drought mean death to many animals, but the African bullfrog has a foolproof way to survive the dry season. It burrows deep into the ground, seals itself in a moisture-proof cocoon, and simply waits for rain.

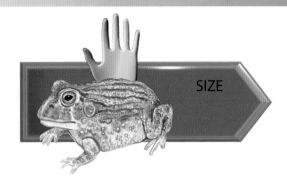

SIZE

## KEY DATA

| | |
|---|---|
| Length | 3–8in (8–20cm) |
| Prey | Insects, spiders, small snakes, rodents, and frogs |
| Defenses | Inflates body |
| Weapons | Tooth-like projections |
| Lifespan | 30–40 years |

Lives in central, eastern and southern Africa. In the rainy season, found above ground on savannahs and bushlands, often sitting in a puddle, it hides under the ground during droughts. It isn't endangered, but is becoming scarce where it is taken to be eaten as a delicacy or sold as a pet.

1 Digging furiously with its hindlegs, an African bullfrog gradually sinks into the dusty earth of the dry savannah. It keeps digging until it is deep enough to be insulated from the intense heat of the sun.

## Did You Know?

● An African bullfrog was once found in the snake enclosure at Pretoria Zoo in South Africa, having eaten 16 baby cobras. It was halfway through another when it was discovered.

● A breeding female bullfrog lays up to 4000 eggs in great masses of frogspawn. The eggs are eagerly sought by predators, however, so few survive to develop into adults.

● The African bullfrog usually hunts by night to avoid being dried out by the fierce African sun.

● When it breaks out of its waterproof cocoon at the beginning of the rainy season, the bullfrog recycles the covering by eating it.

● The African bullfrog is often kept as a pet and fed on crickets, worms, small fish, lizards and even mice. It can't be placed with others of its species as the ever-hungry amphibian will happily gobble up its neighbors if it gets the chance.

2 The frog forms a cocoon around itself from layers of shed skin bound with mucus. Safe from drying out, the frog may stay inside its cosy den for several months, until the rainy season starts.

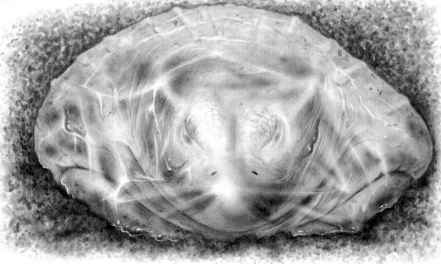

# CRESTED NEWT

**Latin name:** *Triturus cristatus*

**CREST**

A sexually mature male develops a large crest along his back to attract females. Once the breeding season is over, the crest is reabsorbed into the animal's body, to reappear the following spring.

**SKIN**

The moist, warty skin is coated in mucus to prevent the animal drying out on land.

**BELLY**

The belly's bright coloring acts as a warning to would-be predators that the crested newt tastes foul.

**TAIL**

This is used mainly for swimming, but in the spring the male's tail sports silver stripes to make him look more desirable to females.

**EYES**

The large, sensitive eyes help the newt locate smaller victims to feed on and spot enemies in good time to avoid them.

**TOES**

The newt uses its long, slender, dextrous toes to grip victims and to wrap its eggs in leaves to hide them from predators.

**MOUTH**

The large mouth opens wide to enable the newt to swallow its meals whole.

L ooking like a miniature dragon, this hunter feasts on almost any animal that it can fit in its mouth. But if a predator tries to make a meal of the crested newt it's in for a nasty surprise. Foul-tasting fluid oozes out of its skin and forces enemies trying to eat it to spit it out. An adult crested newt is a greedy hunter, feasting on worms, water snails, insect larvae, frogspawn, and tadpoles. If such victims are in short supply, the predator is willing to wolf down smaller members of its own kind.

SIZE

## KEY DATA

| | |
|---|---|
| LENGTH | Up to 8in (20cm) |
| PREY | Frogspawn, tadpoles, other newts, and land and water invertebrates including slugs, worms, snails,, insects and their larvae |
| LIFESPAN | Up to 27 years in captivity; up to 7 years in the wild |

The crested newt is found throughout much of northern and central Europe but not Spain, Portugal, southwestern France, parts of Greece, or the Mediterranean islands. It is also absent from Ireland. Its range extends east to the Ural mountains, and to northern Iran in Asia.

1 A large male crested newt is lurking unnoticed among tangled water weeds at the bottom of a pond, when a smaller crested newt swims slowly by.

2 The larger animal grabs his small relative firmly in his jaws and shakes it vigorously until the desperate quarry stops struggling.

3 Stunned and battered, the smaller amphibian puts up little resistance. The victor swallows the tasty prey whole, head-first. The hunter takes his time gulping down his prize – after all, there's no point in hurrying a good meal…

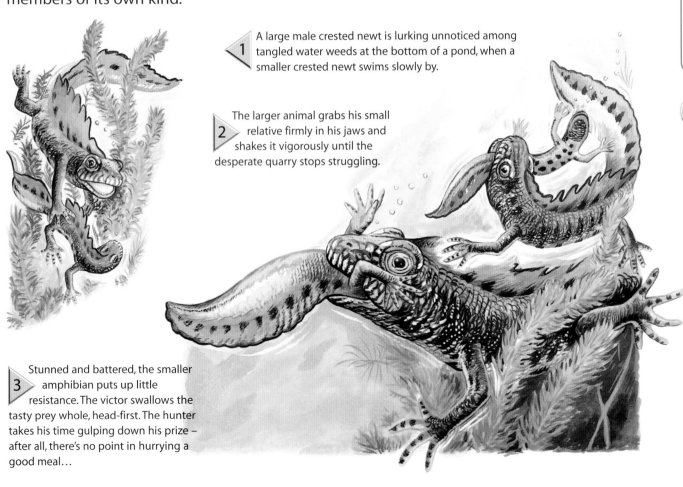

## Did You Know?

● Like most amphibians, the crested newt can regrow amputated body parts such as the tail, legs and even parts of the head. In fact, a young newt can regrow a totally new limb in less than six months.

● Crested and other newts continue to grow throughout life, even after reaching sexual maturity, so they have to slough (shed) their skin periodically. The newts eat their sloughed-off skin to recycle the nutrients it contains.

● Earthworms that fall into ponds are considered tasty enough to be worth fighting for; it's not unusual for two crested newts to start eating the same worm from either end—with trouble in store when they eventually meet in the middle!

● Life for crested newts is highly precarious—only the lucky survive: 50 percent of adults and 80 percent of juveniles are killed every year.

# GLOSSARY

**AMPHIBIANS**
Vertebrate animals that live in the water during their early life (breathing through gills), but usually live on land as adults (and breathe with lungs). They include frogs, toads, newts, salamanders, etc.

**CAMOUFLAGE**
Natural adaptations of color, shape or size that enable animals to blend with their surroundings.

**CARAPACE**
The top piece of a turtle's shell. Plastron is the name given to the bottom piece.

**CARNIVORE**
A meat-eating creature that usually has sharp teeth and powerful jaws.

**CARRION**
The dead flesh of an animal.

**CLASS**
In classification, a class is a group of related or similar organisms. A class contains one or more orders. A group of similar classes forms a phylum.

**CONTINENT**
One of the great landmasses on Earth—Africa, North American, South America, Antartica, Asia, Australasia, and Europe.

**CRUSTACEANS**
An Arthropod with a toughened outer shell covering their body and typically jaws and gills. Most are aquatic.

**DEWLAP**
A flap of skin that hangs beneath the lower jaw of some amphibians, reptiles, birds, and mammals.

**GENUS**
In classification, a genus is a group of related or similar organisms. A genus contains one or more species. A group of similar genera (the plural of genus) forms a family. In the scientific name of an organism, the first name is its genus (for example, people are *Homo sapiens*—our genus is *Homo*).

**GILLS**
Most animals that live in water use gills to breathe: water passes over the gills, usually at either side of the head, and from the water oxygen can be extracted.

**GULLET**
The throat.

**HABITAT**
The environment where an animal usually lives.

**HERPETOLOGY**
The branch of zoology concerned with studying amphibians and reptiles.

**INSECT**
Invertebrates with three parts to their body (head; thorax; abdomen) and two antennae.

**INVERTEBRATE**
Animals that don't have a backbone.

**MAMMAL**
Warm-blooded animals with hair that nourish their young with milk.

**MARSUPIAL**
Mammals that are born incompletely developed and so when young are usually carried or suckled in a pouch on their mother's belly.

**MOLLUSK**
Animals such as squid, octopuses, and snails, which have shells made of one or two pieces, inside which is a soft, unsegmented body.

**ORDER**
In classification, an order is a group of related or similar organisms. An order contains one or more families. A group of similar orders forms a class.

**PLASTRON**
The lower part of a turtle's shell. The top part is called a carapace. The carapace and plastron are bony structures that usually join one another along each side of the body, creating a rigid skeletal box.

**POISONOUS**
Having a deadly substance, such as venom, that causes illness or death.

**PREHENSILE TAIL**
A tail that an animal has adapted to be able to grasp, hold or turn objects.

**PREY**
An animal is prey when another animal hunts and kills it for food.

**REPTILE**
Class of cold-blooded, air breathing animals. They have strong, scaly outer skin and lay eggs.

**SERUM**
Chemical combination usually by injection as a cure for an animal's bite or sting.

**SPECIES**
In classification, a species is a group of closely related organisms that can reproduce. A group of similar species forms a genus. In the scientific name of an organism, the second name is its species (for example, people are *Homo sapiens*—our species is *sapiens*).

**STEREOSCOPIC VISION**
Three-dimensional vision produced from having two different viewpoints: such as eyes widely spaced apart or on opposing sides of the head.

**TOXIN**
A poison produced by an animal.

**VENOM**
A poisonous fluid made by snakes and other animals which is usually transmitted by a bite or a sting.

**VERTEBRATE**
Animals that have a backbone.

# INDEX

## A – C

| | |
|---|---|
| *Acathophis* (death adder) | 10, 10-11 |
| adder | |
| death | 10, 10-11 |
| European | 94, 94-95 |
| puff | 16, 16-17 |
| African bullfrog | 186, 186-87 |
| African egg-eating snake | 40, 40-41, 51 |
| African horned viper | 27 |
| African twig snake | 88, 88-89 |
| *Agkistrodon piscivorus* (cottonmouth snake) | |
| | 12, 12-13 |
| alligator, American | 148, 148-49 |
| *Alligator mississippiensis* (American alligator) | |
| | 148, 148-49 |
| alligator snapping turtle | 160, 160-61 |
| *Amblyrhynchus cristatus* | 98, 98-99 |
| *Ambystoma mexicanum* (axolotl) | 166, 166-67 |
| American alligator | 148, 148-49 |
| American cobra *see* coral snake | |
| amphibians | 164-65 |
| axolotl | 166, 166-67 |
| crested newt | 188, 188-89 |
| *see also* frog; salamander; toad | |
| anaconda | 54, 54-55 |
| *Andrias davidianus* (giant salamander) | 168, 168-69 |
| anole, green | 100, 100-101 |
| *Anolis carolinensis* (green anole) | 100, 100-101 |
| Asian cobra | 45, 64, 64-65 |
| Asian horned frog *see* toad, horned | |
| Asian pit viper | 90, 90-91 |
| Asian python | 82, 82-83 |
| Asian saw-scaled viper | 27 |
| asp viper | 92, 92-93 |
| *Atheris* (bush viper) | 14, 14-15 |
| axolotl | 166, 166-67 |
| | |
| banded krait | 45 |
| basilisk lizard | 102, 102-3 |
| *Basilliscus* (basilisk lizard) | 102, 102-3 |
| beaded lizard, Mexican | 116, 116-17 |
| bearded dragon | 126, 126-27 |
| *Bitis arietans* (puff adder) | 16, 16-17 |
| *Bitis nasicornis* (rhinoceros viper) | 18, 18-19 |
| black mamba | 44, 44-45 |
| blackneck cobra | 66, 66-67 |
| boa | |

| | |
|---|---|
| emerald tree | 36, 36-37 |
| New Guinea | 11 |
| rainbow | 52, 52-53 |
| boa constrictor | 20, 20-21 |
| *Boiga dendrophila* (mangrove snake) | 22, 22-23, 35 |
| boomslang | 46, 46-47 |
| *Bothrops asper* (fer-de-lance) | 24, 24-25 |
| *Bothrops insularis* (fer-de-lance) | 24, 24-25 |
| *Bothrops nummifer* (jumping viper) | 26, 26-27 |
| *Bothrops schlegelii* (eyelash viper) | 28, 28-29 |
| *Brookesia* (ground chameleon) | 104, 104-5 |
| brown snake | 80, 80-81 |
| Budgett's frog | 178, 178-79 |
| *Bufo marinus* (cane toad) | 170, 170-71 |
| bullfrog, African | 186, 186-87 |
| bushmaster | 58, 58-59 |
| bush viper | 14, 14-15 |
| | |
| *Candoia aspera* | 11 |
| candy-stick snake *see* coral snake | |
| cane toad | 170, 170-71 |
| carpet python | 62, 62-63 |
| *Cerastes cerastes* (desert horned viper) | 30, 30-31 |
| *Cerastes vipera* | 31 |
| *Ceratophrys ornata* (ornate horned frog) | |
| | 172, 172-73, 179 |
| *Chamaeleo jacksonii* (Jackson's chameleon) | 106-7 |
| *Chamaeleo pardalis* (panther chameleon) | 108, 108-9 |
| chameleon | |
| dead-leaf | 105 |
| ground | 104, 104-5 |
| Jackson's | 106, 106-7 |
| panther | 108, 108-9 |
| *Chelus fimbriatus* (matamata) | 150, 150-51 |
| *Chelydra serpentina* (snapping turtle) | 152, 152-53 |
| *Chlamydosaurus kingii* (frilled lizard) | 110, 110-11 |
| *Chondropython viridis* (green tree python) | 32, 32-33 |
| *Chrysopelea ornata* (golden tree snake) | 34, 34-35 |
| chuckwalla | 128, 128-29 |
| cobra | |
| American *see* coral snake | |
| Asian | 45, 64, 64-65 |
| blackneck | 66, 66-67 |
| king | 70, 70-71 |
| *Conraura goliath* (Goliath frog) | 179 |
| *Corallus canina* (emerald tree boa) | 36, 36-37 |
| coral snake | 60, 60-61 |
| *Cordylus* (sungazer lizard) | 112, 112-13 |
| cottonmouth snake | 12, 12-13 |
| crested newt | 188, 188-89 |
| crocodile | |
| gharial | 158, 158-59 |
| Nile | 154, 154-55 |
| saltwater | 156, 156-57 |
| *Crocodylus niloticus* (Nile crocodile) | 154, 154-55 |

| | |
|---|---|
| *Crocodylus porosus* (saltwater crocodile) | 156, 156-57 |
| *Crotalus atrax* (rattlesnake) | 38, 38-39 |

## D – F

| | |
|---|---|
| *Dasypeltis* (African egg-eating snake) | 40, 40-41, 51 |
| dead-leaf chameleon | 105 |
| death adder | 10, 10-11 |
| *Dendroaspis angusticeps* (green mamba) | 42, 42-43 |
| *Dendroaspis polylepis* (black mamba) | 44, 44-45 |
| *Dendroaspis viridis* (green mamba) | 42, 42-43 |
| *Dendrobatidae* (poison-dart frogs) | 174, 174-75 |
| desert horned viper | 30, 30-31 |
| *Dispholidus typus* | 46, 46-47 |
| *Draco volans* (flying lizard) | 114, 114-15 |
| dragon | |
| bearded | 126, 126-27 |
| Komodo | 140, 140-41 |
| *Echis carinatus* (saw-scaled viper) | 41, 50, 50-51, 81 |
| egg-eating snake, African | 40, 40-41, 51 |
| emerald tree boa | 36, 36-37 |
| *Epicrates cenchria* (rainbow viper) | 52, 52-53 |
| escorpion | 117 |
| *Eunectes* (anaconda) | 54, 54-55 |
| European adder | 94, 94-95 |
| eyelash viper | 28, 28-29 |
| | |
| fer-de-lance | 24, 24-25 |
| fierce snake | 72, 72-73 |
| flying lizard | 114, 114-15 |
| frilled lizard | 110, 110-11 |
| frog | |
| African bullfrog | 186, 186-87 |
| Asian horned *see* toad, horned | |
| Budgett's | 178, 178-79 |
| Goliath | 179 |
| mantella | 176, 176-77 |
| nose horned *see* toad, horned | |
| ornate horned (Argentine horned frog) | |
| | 172, 172-73, 179 |
| paradoxical | 184, 184-85 |
| poison-dart | 174, 174-75 |

## G – J

| | |
|---|---|
| *Gavialis gangeticus* (gharial) | 158, 158-59 |
| gecko, leaf-tailed | 134, 134-35 |
| gharial | 158, 158-59 |
| gigantic lace lizard | 138, 138-39 |
| Gila monster | 118, 118-19 |
| golden lancehead | 25 |
| golden tree snake | 27, 34, 34-35 |
| Goliath frog | 179 |
| green anole | 100, 100-101 |

| | |
|---|---|
| green iguana | 120, 120-21 |
| green mamba | 42, 42-43 |
| green tree python | 32, 32-33 |
| ground chameleon | 104, 104-5 |
| | |
| harlequin snake *see* coral snake | |
| *Heloderma horridum* (Mexican beaded lizard) | |
| | 116, 116-17 |
| *Heloderma suspectum* (Gila monster) | 118, 118-19 |
| *Hemachatus haemachatus* (ringhals) | 54, 54-55 |
| horned lizard, regal | 124, 124-25 |
| horned toad | 180, 180-81 |
| | |
| iguana | |
| green | 120, 120-21 |
| marine | 98, 98-99 |
| *Iguana iguana* (green iguana) | 120, 120-21 |
| inland taipan *see* fierce snake | |
| | |
| Jackson's chameleon | 106, 106-7 |
| Jesus Christ lizard *see* basilisk lizard | |
| jumping viper | 26, 26-27 |

## K – O

| | |
|---|---|
| king cobra | 70, 70-71 |
| Komodo dragon | 140, 140-41 |
| krait, banded | 45 |
| | |
| lace lizard | 139 |
| gigantic | 138, 138-39 |
| *Lachesis muta* (bushmaster) | 58, 58-59 |
| lancehead, golden | 25 |
| leaf-tailed gecko | 134, 134-35 |
| *Leimadophis epinephelus* | |
| (sparkling fire-bellied snake) | 175 |
| *Lepidobatrachus laevis* (Budgett's frog) | 178, 178-79 |
| Levant viper | 31 |
| lizard | 96-97 |
| basilisk | 102, 102-3 |
| bearded dragon | 126, 126-27 |
| chuckwalla | 128, 128-29 |
| flying | 114, 114-15 |
| frilled | 110, 110-11 |
| gigantic lace | 138, 138-39 |
| Gila monster | 118, 118-19 |
| green anole | 100, 100-101 |
| green iguana | 120, 120-21 |
| ground chameleon | 104, 104-5 |
| Jackson's chameleon | 106, 106-7 |
| Komodo dragon | 140, 140-41 |
| leaf-tailed gecko | 134, 134-35 |
| marine iguana | 98, 98-99 |
| Mexican beaded | 116, 116-17 |
| Nile monitor | 142, 142-43 |

panther chameleon — *108*, 108-9
regal horned — *124*, 124-25
Salvador's monitor — *144*, 144-45
savannah monitor — *136*, 136-37
shingleback skink — *132*, 132-33
sungazer — *112*, 112-13
thorny devil — *122*, 122-23
tuatara — *130*, 130-31
long-nosed snake — *48*, 48-49

*Macroclemys temminckii* (alligator snapping turtle) — *160*, 160-61
mamba
    black — *44*, 44-45
    green — *42*, 42-43
mangrove snake — *22*, 22-23, 35
mantella frog — *176*, 176-77
*Mantellidae* (mantella frogs) — *176*, 176-77
marine iguana — *98*, 98-99
massasauga — *86*, 86-87
matamata — *150*, 150-51
*Megophrys montana* (horned toad) — *180*, 180-81
Mexican beaded lizard — *116*, 116-17
*Micrurus* (coral snake) — *60*, 60-61
*Moloch horridus* (thorny devil) — *122*, 122-23
monitor
    Nile — *142*, 142-43
    Salvador's — *144*, 144-45
    savannah — *136*, 136-37
*Morelia spilota variegata*
    (carpet python) — *62*, 62-63
mulga — *76*, 76-77

*Naja naja* (Asian cobra) — *64*, 64-65
*Naja nigricollis* (blackneck cobra) — *66*, 66-67
New Guinea boa — 11
newt, crested — *188*, 188-89
Nile crocodile — *154*, 154-55
Nile monitor — *142*, 142-43
nose horned frog *see* toad, horned
*Notechis scutatus* (tiger snake) — *68*, 68-69

*Ophiophagus hannah* (king cobra) — *70*, 70-71
ornate horned (Argentine horned) frog — *172*, 172-73, 179
*Oxyuranus microlepidotus* (fierce snake) — *72*, 72-73
*Oxyuranus scutellatus* (taipan) — *73*, *74*, 74-75

## P – S

panther chameleon — *108*, 108-9
paradoxical frog — *184*, 184-85
*Phrynosoma solare* (regal horned lizard) — *124*, 124-25
pineapple snake *see* bushmaster
*Pipa* (pipa toad) — *182*, 182-83

pipa toad — *182*, 182-83
*Pogona* (bearded dragon) — *126*, 126-27
poison-dart frog — *174*, 174-75
*Pseudechis porphyriacus* (red-bellied black snake) — *78*, 78-79
*Pseudis paradoxa* (paradoxical frog) — *184*, 184-85
*Pseudonaja* (brown snake) — *80*, 80-81
puff adder — *16*, 16-17
python
    Asian — *82*, 82-83
    carpet — *62*, 62-63
    green tree — *32*, 32-33
    reticulated — *84*, 84-85
*Python molurus* (Asian python) — *82*, 82-83
*Python reticulatus* (reticulated python) — *84*, 84-85
*Pyxicephalus adspersus* (African bullfrog) — 186-87

rainbow boa — *52*, 52-53
rattlesnake — *38*, 38-39
red-bellied black snake — *78*, 78-79
regal horned lizard — *124*, 124-25
reptiles *see* alligator; crocodile; lizard; snake; turtle
reticulated python — *84*, 84-85
rhinoceros viper — *18*, 18-19
*Rhinocheilus* (long-nosed snake) — *48*, 48-49
ringhals — *54*, 54-55
river jack *see* viper, rhinoceros

salamander, giant — *168*, 168-69
saltwater crocodile — *156*, 156-57
Salvador's monitor — *144*, 144-45
*Sauromalus* (chuckwalla) — *128*, 128-29
savannah monitor — *136*, 136-37
saw-scaled viper — *41*, *50*, 50-51, 81
shingleback skink — *132*, 132-33
*Sistrurus catenatus* (massassauga) — *86*, 86-87
skink, shingleback — *132*, 132-33
small-scaled snake *see* fierce snake
snake — 8-9
    African egg-eating — 40, 40-41, 51
    African twig — *88*, 88-89
    anaconda — *54*, 54-55
    Asian cobra — 45, *64*, 64-65
    Asian pit viper — *90*, 90-91
    Asian python — *82*, 82-83
    asp viper — *92*, 92-93
    black mamba — *44*, 44-45
    blackneck cobra — *66*, 66-67
    boa constrictor — *20*, 20-21
    boomslang — *46*, 46-47
    brown — *80*, 80-81
    bushmaster — *58*, 58-59
    bush viper — *14*, 14-15
    carpet python — *62*, 62-63
    coral — *60*, 60-61

cottonmouth — *12*, 12-13
death adder — *10*, 10-11
desert horned viper — *30*, 30-31
emerald tree boa — *36*, 36-37
European adder — *94*, 94-95
eyelash viper — *28*, 28-29
fer-de-lance — *24*, 24-25
fierce — *72*, 72-73
golden tree — 27, *34*, 34-35
green mamba — *42*, 42-43
green tree python — *32*, 32-33
jumping viper — *26*, 26-27
king cobra — *70*, 70-71
long-nosed — *48*, 48-49
mangrove — *22*, 22-23, 35
massassauga — *86*, 86-87
mulga — *76*, 76-77
puff adder — *16*, 16-17
rainbow boa — *52*, 52-53
rattlesnake — *38*, 38-39
red-bellied black — *78*, 78-79
reticulated python — *84*, 84-85
rhinoceros viper — *18*, 18-19
ringhals — *54*, 54-55
saw-scaled viper — 41, *50*, 50-51, 81
taipan — *73*, *74*, 74-75
tiger — *68*, 68-69
snapping turtle — *152*, 152-53
sparkling fire-bellied snake — 175
*Sphenodon guntheri* (tuatara) — *130*, 130-31
*Sphenodon punctatus* (tuatara) — *130*, 130-31
*Sternotherus* (stinkpot turtle) — *162*, 162-63
stinkpot turtle — *162*, 162-63
sungazer lizard — *112*, 112-13
Surimam toad *see* toad, pipa

## T – Z

taipan — *73*, *74*, 74-75
    inland *see* fierce snake
*Thelotornis capensis* (African twig snake) — *88*, 88-89
*Thelotornis kirtlandii* (African twig snake) — *88*, 88-89
thorny devil — *122*, 122-23
tiger pit viper — 91
tiger snake — *68*, 68-69
*Tiliqua rugosa* (shingleback skink) — *132*, 132-33
toad
    cane — *170*, 170-71
    horned — *180*, 180-81
    pipa — *182*, 182-83
    Surimam *see* toad, pipa
tree snake, golden — 27, *34*, 34-35
*Trimeresurus* (Asian pit viper) — *90*, 90-91
*Triturus cristatus* (crested newt) — *188*, 188-89
tuatara — *130*, 130-31

turtle
    alligator snapping — *160*, 160-61
    matamata — *150*, 150-51
    snapping — *152*, 152-53
    stinkpot — *162*, 162-63
twig snake, African — *88*, 88-89

*Uroplatus* (leaf-tailed gecko) — *134*, 134-35

*Varanus exanthematicus* (savannah monitor) — *136*, 136-37
*Varanus giganteus* (gigantic lace lizard) — *138*, 138-39
*Varanus komodoensis* (Komodo dragon) — *140*, 140-41
*Varanus niloticus* (Nile monitor) — *142*, 142-43
*Varanus salvadori* (Salvador's monitor) — *144*, 144-45
viper
    African horned — 27
    Asian pit — *90*, 90-91
    Asian saw-scaled — 27
    asp — *92*, 92-93
    bush — *14*, 14-15
    desert horned — *30*, 30-31
    eyelash — *28*, 28-29
    jumping — *26*, 26-27
    Levant — 31
    rhinoceros — *18*, 18-19
    saw-scaled — 41, *50*, 50-51, 81
    tiger pit — 91
*Vipera aspis* (asp viper) — *92*, 92-93
*Vipera berus* (European adder) — *94*, 94-95
*Vipera lebetina mauritanica* (Levant viper) — 31

water moccasin *see* cottonmouth snake

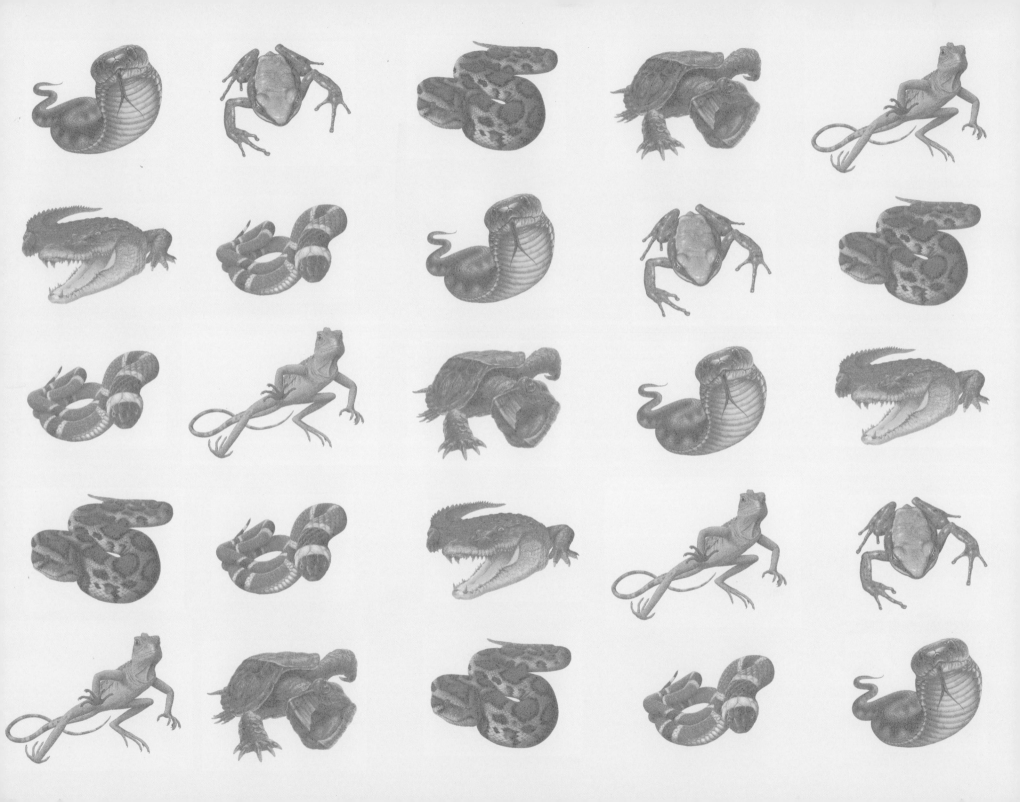